THE SIMON & SCHUSTER GUIDE TO
THE WINES OF
GERMANY

IAN JAMIESON

A Fireside Book
Published by Simon & Schuster Inc.
Simon & Schuster Building, Rockefeller Center,
1230 Avenue of the Americas, New York, NY 10020

Edited and designed by Mitchell Beazley International Ltd
Michelin House, 81 Fulham Road, London SW3 6RB

First published 1984 as *The Mitchell Beazley Pocket Guide to German Wines* by
Ian Jamieson. This edition, revised, updated and expanded, published 1992

Executive Editor: Anne Ryland
Art Director: Tim Foster
Art Editor: Paul Tilby
Production: Sarah Schuman
Maps: Eugene Fleury

Typeset in Bembo by Servis Filmsetting Ltd, Manchester, England
Colour reproduction by Scantrans Pte Ltd, Singapore
Produced by Mandarin Offset, Hong Kong
Printed and bound in Hong Kong

10 9 8 7 6 5 4 3 2 1

Library of Congress Cataloging-in-Publication Data
Jamieson, Ian.
     The Simon and Schuster guide to the wines of Germany / Ian Jamieson.
         p.   cm.
     "A Fireside book."
     "A Mitchell Beazley book."
     ISBN 0-671-79709-3
     1. Wine and wine making–Germany.   I. Title.
     TP559.G3J36   1993
     641.2'2' 0943–dc 20   92-19088
                                                                CIP

THE SIMON & SCHUSTER GUIDE TO
THE WINES OF
GERMANY

IAN JAMIESON

A Fireside Book

Published by Simon & Schuster Inc.

New York   London   Toronto   Sydney   Tokyo   Singapore

Abbreviations

hl/ha	hectolitres per hectare
w	white wine
r	red wine
(in parentheses)	relatively unimportant
Hess Berg	Hessische Bergstrasse
Mrh	Mittelrhein
M-S-R	Mosel-Saar-Ruwer
Rhg	Rheingau
Rhh	Rheinhessen
Rhpf	Rheinpfalz
S	Sachsen
S U	Saale-Unstrut
Würt	Württemberg
DTW	Deutscher Tafelwein
QbA	Qualitätswein eines bestimmten Anbaugebietes
QmP	Qualitätswein mit Prädikat
VDP	Verband Deutscher Prädikatsweingüter

See page 9 for more information

Contents

Foreword

German wines, and all the sensuous subtleties of pleasure they offer, are rather like a story-book castle whose key is hidden in a tortuous labyrinth guarded by ravaging heraldic beasts. The generality of wine drinkers take the *Autobahn* labelled Liebfraumilch, Niersteiner or some such safe and familiar name. They skirt the problem, and never find the reward. Our hero, though, steadies his gaze at the menacing Gothic script, braves the barbed entanglements of nomenclature, and carries off the chalice of golden nectar. In other words, if German labels scare you, you will never discover how glorious German wine can be.

This book is the code-cracker. It can put the chalice in your hands. I won't pretend that all obscurities will dissolve as you turn the first page. But Ian Jamieson is a practical man whose knowledge of Germany and its wine has been sharpened on the steel of commerce. He knows the ways of grower and merchant. He knows the laws. And he knows and cares where the real treasures lie.

Ian has often been my guide through the more arcane complexities of his favourite subject. To me it has fascinations, and offers rewards, that are a match for any category of wine. Let Jamieson lead you to them.

Hugh Johnson

Introduction

'If you can't work with claret, I suppose Hock is the next best thing.' Thirty-five years ago, as was his custom, Allan Sichel helped a young man to enter the wine trade. Eight months in the Dickensian atmosphere of his cellar had not diminished my enthusiasm. In Switzerland I had learnt that the taste and smell of a wine was decided mainly by the soil, vine variety and climate, and that all three combined to produce a drink that could be both predictable and full of surprises. How a vintage put its stamp on good Bordeaux was a lifetime study for Mr Sichel, and in German wine he recognized the individuality that was so strong a characteristic of the wines of the Médoc.

In the 1990s, the search for solutions has gained momentum and the secrecy with which German wine producers used to surround their trade has now all but vanished. Many of the younger German winemakers train at the same internationally frequented viticultural schools, and having worked in vineyards on the other side of the world, they now attend the same seminars where they meet their former colleagues. German producers know what is happening in Australia (and vice versa) and, as Germany is the largest importer of wines in the world, they can easily refresh their memories by a visit to the local wine merchant. If there is a theoretical risk that some wines could lose their individuality through a standard, modern approach to winemaking, the climate in the northern German regions will make sure it does not disappear for long. The most important changes taking place in German wine are discussed on pages 28–30.

The choice of geographical names under which German wine is sold was much reduced by the 1971 Wine Law, but the styles of wine offered have increased greatly since then. The export markets of the world still prefer *lieblich* or medium-sweet wines, and there are many parts of the German vineyard which virtually never export any wine, unless anonymously in a commercial blend. The near-absence in Britain and the USA of estate-bottled wine from the Süd Pfalz or from the Bereich Zell is not explained by its quality. The hard-pressed traditional wine trade in these importing countries feels it cannot afford to take a chance, and so it tends to avoid new styles of wine and concentrates on 'followers' to that which it was able to sell in the past. Given the conservatism or the lack of knowledge of wine in the restaurant trade, this policy is understandable, but when German wines are selected by name and not by quality, some of the best will stay at home. In Britain (the largest market for German wine – *see* page 27), in spite of the enterprise of some of the supermarket wine buyers, the range of German wine is still very small, and so the recommendation to the wine lover is to buy at source. Information about visiting the vineyards is given on pages 35–36.

This guide makes few judgements. It is an observer rather than a participant. As I wrote in its predecessor, *The Pocket Guide to German Wines*, 'German wine is more than capable of speaking for itself, provided one can understand its language'. This new, updated and enlarged version is here to help.

How to Use this Book

The guide is divided into three sections: introductory chapters, an A–Z section, and a map section. The introductory chapters cover the background and structure of German wine, and ideally should be read first as scene-setters. In order to look up an area, an estate, a vineyard, or a wine term, turn to the A–Z section which begins on page 41. The maps, starting on page 319, show the basic geography of the German wine regions and list some of the producers in these regions. For a guide to the important growers of, say, Rheingau wines, turn to the map on pages 322–323. The names can then be looked up in the A–Z section.

The top line of the geographical entries – regions, rivers, towns, villages, vineyard sites and so forth – gives the following information, where applicable, in abbreviated form:

- The wine region in which the entry is located. The 13 wine regions (and their abbreviations) are:

Ahr	Nahe
Baden	Rheingau (Rhg)
Franken	Rheinhessen (Rhh)
Hessische Bergstrasse	Rheinpfalz (Rhpf)
(Hess Berg)	Sachsen (S)
Mittelrhein (Mrh)	Saale-Unstrut (S U)
Mosel-Saar-Ruwer (M-S-R)	Württemberg (Würt)

  A map of all the wine regions is on pages 14–15.

- The type of wine produced: w for white, r for red, (w) or (r) in parentheses if the quantity produced is unimportant when related to the total production of the location. In some instances red wine production is sufficient to be noted against the village name but is too small to be mentioned in connection with a larger geographical unit. (For example, the Mosel village Pommern warrants an (r) but the Mosel-Saar-Ruwer region does not.)

Cross-references, noted with ★, throughout the A–Z section help to expand the information given in individual entries. However, the wine regions (such as Ahr, Baden), grape varieties (such as Riesling) and German terms (such as *trocken*, *Sekt*) are automatically included in the A–Z and are not normally cross-referred. German adjectives used to describe wine are listed in appropriate alphabetical order and explained in the A–Z section.

The area of an estate in hectares is that which is planted with vines, not all of which may be old enough to be in production.

The use of the available single-site (*Einzellage*) names to describe wines is declining on some estates. Thus, a note that a grower has a holding in an *Einzellage* does not guarantee that he will sell wine under the *Einzellage* name.

For an explanation of the frequent mention of vineyards being planted on steep slopes, reference should be made to the entry in the A–Z section under *Steillagen*.

Approximate production figures are expressed in cases. These are average figures based on the years 1988, 1989 and 1990. (The size of the vintage can vary greatly from year to year.) A 'case', for the purposes of this guide, is taken as 12 × 750ml (0·75 litre) bottles, or nine litres. (In the wine trade, the term 'case' is obsolete as few people nowadays buy a 'case' of one wine.) All liquid measurements are given in litres, the standard measurement for German wine (one litre equals 2·1134 US pints). Alcohol is expressed as percentage by volume.

German Wine Law

Wine production in Germany is as meticulously structured as the wording on a German wine label. This is the result of Germany's own wine laws and those of the European Common Market.

In 1970 the EC produced regulations for the organization of wine within its borders. These came into immediate effect and took precedence over national laws, so that Germany was obliged to revise its own wine laws forthwith. In 1971 the fifth German Wine Law came into force, replacing the previous law of 1930. Since then there have been a great many amendments, including a major revision in 1982 that established *Landwein* as a new category of *deutscher Tafelwein*, made *Eiswein* into a *Prädikat* (quality distinction) of its own and altered several other details of the earlier law.

Probably the best-known results of all this legislation – and the most significant to the consumer – are the division of wine into different quality categories and the organization of wine regions (*see following pages*).

The Quality Categories

Wine in the EC is separated into quality wine and table wine. In German terms this means *Qualitätswein* (QmP, the top quality, and QbA, a middle level); *Tafelwein* (*deutscher Tafelwein*, or DTW, comes entirely from German vineyards, while plain *Tafelwein* originates partially or totally in other EC countries); and *Landwein*, a superior *deutscher Tafelwein*, from one of 19 specified districts.

The chart shows the relationship of the 13 quality-wine regions to the table-wine and *Landwein* districts. Unlike France, where the grading of quality wines is largely geographical, in Germany exactly the same vineyards that produce quality wine can also produce table wine and *Landwein*. The source remains the same; only the category of wine changes. Although they are legally

Quality wine (QbA, QmP)		Table wine (DTW)		Landwein
Specified region (bestimmte Anbaugebiet)	District (Bereich)	District (Weinbaugebiet)	Sub-district (Untergebiet)	District (Gebiet)
Ahr	Walporzheim/Ahrtal	Rhein-Mosel	Rhein	Ahrtaler Landwein
Hessische Bergstrasse	Starkenburg Umstadt			Starkenburger Landwein
Mittelrhein	Loreley Siebengebirge			Rheinburgen-Landwein
Nahe	Kreuznach Schloss Böckelheim			Nahegauer Landwein
Rheingau	Johannisberg			Altrheingauer Landwein
Rheinhessen	Bingen Nierstein Wonnegau			Rheinischer Landwein
Rheinpfalz	Südliche Weinstrasse Mittelhaardt/ Deutsche Weinstrasse			Pfälzer Landwein
Mosel-Saar-Ruwer	Zell/Mosel Bernkastel		Mosel	Landwein der Mosel
	Obermosel Saar-Ruwer Moseltor		Saar	Landwein der Ruwer Landwein der Saar

established, the *Landwein* names for Franken are not used.

Do not expect to meet all the *Bereich*, district and sub-district names on wine labels – some of them exist more for administrative purposes than for the benefit of the consumer trying to unravel the intricacies of German laws and labelling (*see* Learning from the Label, pages 18–19).

We speak of 'quality' categories but perhaps style categories would be a better description. The creation of premium ranges of wines, so popular with cooperative cellars in Baden and Württemberg; the development of new types and concepts in dry winemaking on many estates in the northern regions; and the high standards set by the Charta (see A–Z section) association in the Rheingau, have made the old system of quality categories less relevant. Perhaps the standards by which the quality of German wine is officially judged should now be re-examined.

Quality wine (QbA, QmP)		Table wine (DTW)		Landwein
Specified region (bestimmte Anbaugebiet)	District (Bereich)	District (Weinbaugebiet)	Sub-district (Untergebiet)	District (Gebiet)
Franken	Steigerwald Maindreieck Mainviereck	Bayern	Main	Fränkischer Landwein
			Donau	Regensburger Landwein
	Bayerischer Bodensee		Lindau	Bayer. Bodensee-Landwein
Württemberg	Remstal–Stuttgart Württembergisches Unterland Kocher–Jagst–Tauber Oberer Neckar Württembergischer Bodensee	Neckar		Schwäbischer Landwein
Baden	Bodensee Markgräflerland Kaiserstuhl Tuniberg Breisgau Ortenau	Oberrhein	Römertor	Südbadischer Landwein
	Badische Bergstrasse/ Kraichgau Badische Frankenland		Burgengau	Unterbadischer Landwein Taubertäler Landwein
Sachsen	Elbetal Elstertal			Sächsischer Landwein
Saale-Unstrut	Seeburg Schloss Neuenburg			Anhaltiner Landwein

The Wine Regions

Germany lies at the northern edge of that part of Europe in which grapes will ripen. The climate is cool in comparison with that of other European wine-producing countries – a fact recognized by the EC which divides member states, for administrative purposes, into wine-producing zones that correspond very approximately to the different climatic conditions. All the German vine-growing regions, with the exception of Baden in the south, are placed in Zone A (with the UK and Luxembourg). Baden shares the warmer

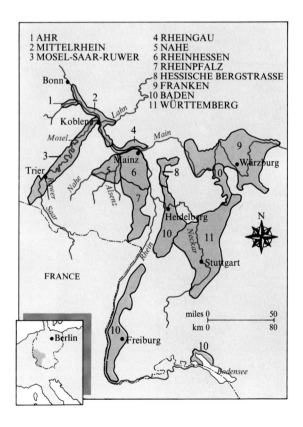

1 AHR
2 MITTELRHEIN
3 MOSEL-SAAR-RUWER
4 RHEINGAU
5 NAHE
6 RHEINHESSEN
7 RHEINPFALZ
8 HESSISCHE BERGSTRASSE
9 FRANKEN
10 BADEN
11 WÜRTTEMBERG

Zone B with Alsace, Lorraine, Champagne, Jura, Savoie and the Loire valley.

There are 13 specified regions for quality-wine production (*Anbaugebiete*) in Germany. They are described in the A–Z section and are shown in more detail in the maps that begin on page 319.

In the most northerly regions – the Ahr, Mittelrhein, Mosel-Saar-Ruwer, Saale-Unstrut and Sachsen – usually only those sites facing south-southeast to southwest can usefully bear vines, with the very best vineyards facing from south to south-southwest. An additional rule of thumb is that the average temperature will drop some 0·5°C for every 100 metres above sea level. As a result, while

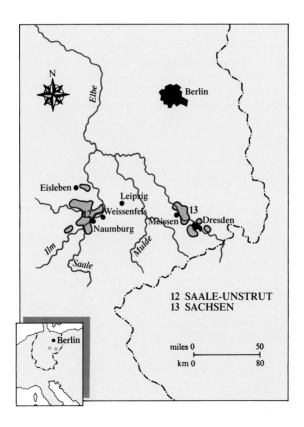

300 metres above sea level is regarded as the maximum height for vineyards on the Mosel near Koblenz, in the warmer south of Baden, near the Bodensee, vines are grown successfully at 530 metres above sea level.

Each of the wine regions is organized into districts (*Bereiche*), collections of sites (*Grosslagen*) and individual sites (*Einzellagen*). This is where the style of wine begins to be more narrowly defined.

A *Bereich* is a combination of collective or individual sites. It is usually the largest wine-producing unit within a region and sometimes allows a well-known name – Bernkastel in the Mittelmosel, for example – to be applied to wine from anywhere within the *Bereich* boundaries. Wine marketed solely under a *Bereich* name is unlikely to be more than a pleasant everyday blend, and this will be reflected in its price.

A *Grosslage* is a grouping of sites centred on one or more villages or towns (*Gemeinden*). In the Bereich Bernkastel, for example, the *Grosslage* Badstube covers six (since 1986) *Einzellagen* at Bernkastel. Generally *Grosslagen* include a number of wine villages within their boundaries, all of which will lie within the same region. A *Grosslage*, or an *Einzellage* name, must always be accompanied by that of a village or community; for example, Bernkasteler Badstube, not just Badstube, must appear on the label.

These *Grosslagen* enable the bottler or wine merchant to offer large quantities of wine of similar quality and style under one name familiar to the consumer. Use of a *Grosslage* name does not mean that the wine will automatically be inferior, but the best-quality wines in any grower's or bottler's range will normally be offered under the *Einzellage* name. Some well-respected producers are moving away from the use of *Gross-* or *Einzellage* names as they believe that the most important influence on quality, their own name, should be given greater and unrivalled prominence.

An *Einzellage* is an individual site, the smallest vine-growing unit recognized by the law. There are currently some 2,600 *Einzellagen*, varying in size from 0·2 up to about 250 hectares. They are officially registered and in most cases their boundaries are precisely defined. Only quality (QbA and QmP) wines may carry an *Einzellage* name – not table wine (DTW) or *Landwein*.

The unifying factor within an *Einzellage* should be the flavour and style of wine it can produce. Some sites, because of their inherent qualities combined with the winemaking ability of the growers concerned, have a reputation for producing top-quality wine (for example, Bernkasteler Doctor). In larger sites, where many growers have holdings, the quality will be more variable.

It is impossible to tell from the information on a label whether a wine comes from one of 2,600 or so *Einzellagen*, or from the roughly 150 *Grosslagen*. The grower's name is almost always a better indication of the likely quality of a wine than that of the site name.

Between 1964 and 1988 the German vineyard increased by nearly a half. Because of overproduction in regions bordering the Mediterranean, plantings of new vineyards in other parts of the EC are restricted. In Germany, where such legislation is taken seriously, the present approximate area under vine of 100,000 hectares is not likely to expand, although the eastern German vineyards will have added another 700 hectares or so to the total.

Evolution of the Vineyards
Area under vine in hectares by wine region

Region	1964	1970	1988
Ahr	444	446	428
Baden	7,631	10,014	15,000
Franken	2,203	2,720	5,523
Hess. Bergstrasse	189	261	389
Mittelrhein	870	857	751
Mosel-Saar-Ruwer	9,835	10,962	12,859
Nahe	3,516	3,955	4,579
Rheingau	2,680	2,821	2,904
Rheinhessen	16,444	19,826	24,871
Rheinpfalz	17,066	18,676	22,625
Württemberg	5,844	6,834	9,791
Total	66,722	77,372	99,720*

* Includes trial vineyards for new crossings, etc.
Source: from figures published by the Deutscher Weinbauverband
Details of the area under vine from 1989 onwards are expected in 1992.

Learning from the Label

All bottled wines sold to the consumer in the European Common Market must be labelled and all labels must, by law, carry certain specified information.

Most German wines have a main (body) label and a neck label that shows the vintage, if applicable. Some estate bottlers abandon the neck label and include the vintage on the main label. (The famous Rautenstrauch estate on the Ruwer, however, takes the opposite course and uses only a neck label.)

As well as being a legal requirement, labels are considered to be a most important part of the marketing and selling of wine. The use of back labels carrying extra information is increasing and can be very helpful to the consumer. When a wine has won an official award (DLG, for example – *see* Deutsche Landwirtschaft Gesellschaft in the A–Z section), it is usually indicated on the bottle by a strip or circular label.

Labelling regulations are unavoidably complicated for they must provide for all the possibilities of nomenclature and description legally open to wine.

Most German quality-wine labels used in the last 20 years bear the type of information (where applicable) shown on the illustration that follows. That which is obligatory (specified region of origin, liquid content of the bottle, etc) must be easily read. The size of the lettering used for the specified region is important, for to it must be related that of the *Prädikat* (*Kabinett*, *Spätlese*, etc), where there is one, and the name of the village or town in which the wine was bottled. For a 750 ml bottle, the liquid content and alcoholic strength must be indicated in characters at least 3 mm high. The obligatory mention of the phrase 'Qualitätswein mit Prädikat' is tautologous as the *Prädikat* itself already shows the wine's official quality category.

1	**MOSEL-SAAR-RUWER**	
2	Bernkasteler Bratenhöfchen	3
4	1990er	
5	**RIESLING KABINETT**	6
7	Qualitätswein mit Prädikat	
8	Halbtrocken	
9	AP Nr 1 23 456 789 91	
10	Erzeugerabfüllung	
11	J M SCHMIDT	
12	9% Bernkastel-Kues	13
14	750 ml e Produce of Germany	15

1 Specified region (*Anbaugebiet*)
2 Village (*Gemeinde*)
3 Individual site (*Einzellage*)
4 Vintage. The 'er' is an adjectival ending. *See* Recent Vintages, pages 31–34.
5 Grape variety. If a wine is not made from a traditional vine
   variety, its name is often omitted from the label, although this will vary from
   one region to another.
6 Quality distinction. *See* Qualitätswein mit Prädikat in the A–Z section.
7 Quality category. *See also* Qualitätswein eines bestimmten Anbaugebietes in the
   A–Z section.
8 Medium-dry, as defined by German law.
9 Control number (Amtliche Prüfungsnummer). The first figure is the number of
   the control centre where the wine was tested. The next two figures are the
   number of the location in which the wine was bottled. The third set of figures is
   the registered number of the bottler. The fourth set is the sequential number in
   the year of application from the bottler, unique to this bottling. The last two
   figures are the year of application for the AP number. This configuration is not
   uniform throughout Germany.
10 Producer-bottled
11 The name of the bottler
12 The alcoholic strength by volume
13 The address of the bottler
14 The liquid content, which might also be shown as 0·75 l. The 'e' indicates that
    the volume of wine in the bottle is within the parameters set by EC regulations.
15 Country of origin

Vine Varieties

Of the area under vine, 85 percent is planted with varieties that produce white wine – although in some cases (the Ruländer, for example) the grape may be 'blue', but the wine it produces remains white. At the last official survey for which results are available, in 1979–80 14 percent of the vines in Germany were 20 years old or more, 36 percent were ten to 20 years old, 41 percent three to ten years old and nine percent were under three years old. (Vines do not become really productive until they are three years old.) The high proportion of vines under ten years old was partly the result of the reconstruction and subsequent replanting of the vineyards (*see* Flurbereinigung in the A–Z section) over the past 45 years to make vine growing more efficient.

To ripen grapes in Germany is often a triumph of science, planning and dedication over less than ideal conditions. At these latitudes, local environmental factors take on an importance unknown in places with a more equable climate, and the choice of which variety to plant is crucial. German wine-growing regulations offer a long list of varieties from which to choose – varieties that vary considerably in their needs, and yield widely differing types and amounts of wine.

In making a decision, growers must consider the climate, the site and the soil of their vineyards, and the present and future state of the wine market. The climate is, at best, predictably uncertain: unseasonable rain, hail and frost are constant hazards at different times of the year. Each grower must decide whether to aim for quality or quantity, but sometimes the vineyard site will dictate the decision – a high yield cannot be expected from Riesling on a 45° slope, and only the return that comes from quality-wine production can justify viticulture at such a bizarre angle. Most vines adapt to a wide variety of soils but some have individual preferences. Silvaner, for example, dislikes a dry soil on a sloping site that Riesling will happily tolerate.

The chart opposite shows the extent to which the distribution of the main vine varieties altered between 1981 and 1988. It is followed by a list of other vine varieties, which are also described in the A–Z section of the book.

White varieties in hectares				% of ALL varieties in 1988	% change 1981– 1988
	1981	1985	1988		
Bacchus	3,174	3,573	3,573	3·6	+13
Elbling, Weisser	1,115	1,178	1,177	1·2	+6
Faberrebe	2,115	2,280	2,176	2·2	+3
Gutedel, Weisser	1,195	1,258	1,295	1·3	+8
Huxelrebe	1,606	1,758	1,684	1·7	+5
Kerner	5,784	6,960	7,409	7·4	+28
Ortega	1,170	1,208	1,266	1·3	+8
Riesling, Weisser	18,821	19,615	20,716	20·8	+10
Scheurebe	4,083	4,385	4,159	4·2	+2
Weissburgunder	872	926	1,009	1·0	+16
Morio-Muskat	2,975	2,641	2,242	2·3	−25
Müller-Thurgau	24,810	25,292	23,881	23·9	−4
Optima	514	499	471	0·5	−8
Ruländer	3,379	3,123	2,811	2·8	−17
Silvaner, Grüner	9,184	8,050	7,562	7·6	−18
Traminer, Roter (Gewürztraminer)	937	889	832	0·8	−11
Other whites	2,859	2,961	2,793	2·8	−2
Total white	84,593	86,596	85,056	85·4	+1
Red varieties in hectares					
Dornfelder	208	620	926	0·9	+345
Limberger, Blauer	413	542	611	0·6	+48
Müllerrebe	1,101	1,473	1,685	1·7	+53
Portugieser, Blauer	3,012	3,183	3,508	3·5	+16
Spätburgunder, Blauer	3,753	4,486	5,003	5·0	+33
Trollinger, Blauer	1,983	2,196	2,154	2·2	+9
Other reds	546	619	692	0·7	+27
Total red	11,016	13,119	14,579	14·6	+32
Total red & white	95,609	99,715	99,635		+4

Source: Deutscher Weinbauverband/Statistisches Bundesamt

Other vine varieties of which more than 30 hectares are planted

For white wine

Auxerrois	Kanzler	Rieslaner
Ehrenfelser	Muskateller, Gelber	Schönburger
Findling	Nobling	Siegerrebe
Freisamer	Regner	Würzer
Gutedel, Roter	Reichensteiner	

For red wine

Domina	Frühburgunder,	Heroldrebe
Dunkelfelder	Blauer	Samtrot
	Helfensteiner	

Because of the restrictions on planting new vineyards in the EC, the expansion of the area occupied by a vine variety in Germany must almost automatically be at the expense of another. Thus while more Riesling, Weissburgunder and Gutedel are grown now than in the mid-1980s, Morio-Muskat, Müller-Thurgau, Silvaner and Ruländer are on the decline. It is said that the clonal selection of Silvaner has aimed at developing more productive vines, and the sometimes not very inspiring quality and indifferent reputation of its wine may be the result. Be that as it may, the area planted in Silvaner has declined steadily over the years in Germany as it has elsewhere in Europe. The spread of Kerner is probably the result of its performance in the vineyard rather than the attraction of its wine. Now that it may form a major part of a Liebfraumilch blend, the demand from merchants for Kerner wine in bulk will ensure its place in the German vineyard – assuming sales of cheap wine abroad continue at their present level.

An excellent producer at Laubenheim on the Nahe told me he thought he had planted Bacchus in a moment of 'mental derangement', but I have tasted Bacchus from a low yield grown by a producer in Franken in full command of his faculties, that was well above the usual level of quality.

The profile of the Burgunder (Pinot) family is higher than it has been for years and it surely cannot be long before the area planted in Ruländer (Graburgunder) stops shrinking. Weissburgunder is being grown all over Germany and, at *Spätlese* level, it has been successful as far north as the Saar valley and the vineyards of eastern Germany. Chardonnay, which needs a good Riesling site, rich in limestone, has also been planted in a number of vineyards over the past few years.

Spätburgunder is currently on the crest of a wave of popularity and the quality of many of its wines is very much to the international taste (well structured and moderately tannic). In general, the Ortenau and Kaisterstuhl districts of Baden offer the best value for money for Spätburgunder wines. The Rheinpfalz also has its good red winemakers, who are building the reputation not just of Spätburgunder but of Dornfelder as well. Here, the relationship between the two wines is similar to that of Pinot Noir and Gamay in Burgundy.

In spite of the legitimate interest in the new red and white Burgunder wines, Riesling remains the brightest star of the German white wine galaxy. In regions north of Baden-Württemberg the clean, fresh style of its wines is unique, as the three vintages running up to 1990 have reminded us.

German Wine Market

Since the start of the 1980s the area in Germany under vine has increased by about four percent while the number of those growing grapes has steadily declined. The Federal State Statistical Office (Statistisches Bundesamt) will not publish the results of its 1989/90 census before 1992 but the picture that will then appear is already clear in outline, if not in detail. Families who have tended their vines for many years as a part-time occupation have decided that their hard work is inadequately rewarded and, consequently, vineyards have been leased or sold. In Rheinland-Pfalz, which produces some two-thirds of Germany's wine, almost half of those with less than 0·5 hectares under vine gave up growing grapes in the 1980s. As a result of the poor economic state of viticulture, which of course can vary from one district to another, land prices are low. In these circumstances, Japanese involvement with the well-known estates of Schloss Vollrads (Rheingau) and Weingut Reichsrat von Buhl (Rheinpfalz) in the 1980s showed a confidence in the future of German vine growing that was welcome.

Growers exercise their right to complain, but prices for wine sold in bulk in the northern regions in 1990 and the first half of 1991 were above the level of 1989. At the other end of the scale the more expensive German red wines have recently broken the price barrier of 30 DM per bottle and one or two have even exceeded 40 DM. When a wine sells at 40 DM others can more easily ask for 18 DM.

How Germany divides the ownership of its vineyards compared to other members of the EC is shown in the table opposite.

The first line of figures shows the number of grape-growing establishments in 1,000s, and the second line (*in italics*) the amount of land under vine and in production in 1,000s of hectares. Both are related to the sizes of holding shown in the first column.

Five hectares is about the minimum size of vineyard upon which a family can survive in Germany without another source of income. In 1987, 90 percent of her growers, with 59 percent of the area under vine, owned less than this amount. Relatively few produce and bottle wine. Many sell in bulk to merchants, of which there is a concentration on the Mosel. The result is that nearly half of the production of Germany's largest wine region (the Rheinhessen) is

Grape growers in the EC in 1987

Area in hectares	Germany	France	Italy	Greece	Spain	Portugal	Luxem-bourg	Total in 1,000s
0–0·5	16·7	118·5	688·3	176·5	94·8	227·1	0·3	1,322·1
	4·9	*29·4*	*146·9*	*33·8*	*19·2*	*41·4*	*0·1*	*275·7*
0·5–1	12·1	38·6	228·3	37·4	45·9	59·0	0·1	421·4
	8·6	*25·8*	*141·2*	*24·1*	*28·6*	*38·7*	*0·1*	*267·1*
1–2	9·7	25·9	161·8	27·4	65·5	39·9	0·1	330·3
	13·7	*35·8*	*197·4*	*35·9*	*83·2*	*52·0*	*0·2*	*418·2*
2–5	9·5	35·4	99·2	15·3	70·5	23·3	0·2	253·5
	29·8	*113·2*	*279·7*	*41·7*	*212·8*	*66·5*	*0·8*	*744·5*
5–10	3·9	27·3	19·7	0·9	33·4	4·7	—	90·0
	26·2	*194·1*	*125·9*	*4·9*	*229·6*	*31·2*	*0·2*	*612·2*
10–20	0·7	19·6	6·8	—	19·5	1·7	—	48·4
	9·1	*269·7*	*87·8*	*0·3*	*261·7*	*22·6*	—	*651·1*
20–30	0·1	5·5	1·5	—	5·1	0·5	—	12·6
	1·6	*129·4*	*35·1*	—	*119·1*	*10·6*	—	*295·9*
30 and over	0·1	3·9	1·2	—	4·7	0·4	—	10·3
	3·0	*189·3*	*63·4*	—	*269·4*	*36·0*	—	*561·0*
Total	52·8	274·7	1,206·8	257·5	339·4	356·6	0·7	2,488·5
	96·9	*986·7*	*1,077·4*	*140·7*	*1,223·6*	*299·0*	*1·4*	*3,825·7*
Share in %	2·1	11·0	48·5	10·3	13·6	14·3	—	
	2·5	*25·8*	*28·2*	*3·7*	*32·0*	*7·8*	—	
Average holding per grower in hectares	1·8	3·6	0·9	0·5	3·6	0·8	2·0	

Source: figures supplied by the Deutscher Raiffeisenverband eV

bottled well away from the area in which the grapes were grown. The notion, abandoned by the EC in 1990 after two years' discussion, that quality wine (some 95 percent of German wines) should be bottled in the region of origin would have required an inconceivable redistribution of Germany's bottling plants.

Germany has proportionally the lowest number of growers in the EC who belong to cooperative cellars, but conditions of vine growing vary so much between the northern, southern, and now eastern regions of the country that caution is needed when writing of German cooperatives as a whole. Their largest catchment area is in Baden, Württemberg and the Rheinpfalz. Obliged as they are to take into account the contradictory views of their members, the big central cooperative cellars sometimes seem from the outside to be almost ungovernable when it comes to forming a strategy for the market. In spite of this, good ideas and new 'products' have emerged in the early 1990s from the largest wine cooperative in Europe, the Badischer Winzerkeller. Baden can also claim to have the most dynamic village cooperatives. Their stocks are large enough to allow new 'lines' to be marketed seriously, and as their members own nearly all the vineyards in their villages they have access to the best available grapes. The 1991 report of the German cooperatives published by the Deutscher Raiffeisenverband incorrectly states that only the larger establishments are in a position to develop an export market. This would be true if the movement were dedicated exclusively to producing cheap wines to fill the supermarket shelves of the world, but many of its members have other aims. A small cooperative can find customers outside Germany just as well as a private estate of similar size, and some are starting to prove the point.

Cheap German wine sells easily abroad, notably in Britain, but a few private estates such as the Domdechant Werner'sches Weingut (Rheingau), Thanisch-Knabben and von Hövel (Mosel-Saar-Ruwer), Gustav Adolf Schmitt (Rheinhessen) and Michael Schäfer (Nahe) have been successful in exporting 40 percent or more of their wine of a much higher quality. Until now 95 percent of the cooperatives' sales have been in Germany, with 69 percent to grocery chains and supermarkets. Practically all producers sell directly to the consumer. Many believe that the finer restaurants provide the best possible showground for their wines.

German Wine Exports

Country	1985 Quantity in hl	1987 Quantity in hl	1990 Quantity in hl	% change 1985–1990
Great Britain	1,360,970	1,461,974	1,494,436	+ 9·8
Japan	60,387	82,321	71,078	+ 17·7
Belgium & Luxem	35,898	35,298	48,234	+ 34·4
Norway	29,365	32,190	56,900	+ 93·8
Finland	9,823	12,851	38,260	+ 289·5
Total	1,496,443	1,624,634	1,708,908	+ 14·2
USA	506,291	256,936	155,917	− 69·2
Netherlands	256,413	220,555	213,037	− 16·9
Canada	153,482	81,218	78,710	− 48·7
Denmark	114,519	110,654	94,812	− 17·2
Sweden	84,822	62,728	75,177	− 11·4
Total	1,115,527	732,091	617,653	− 44·6
Other countries	115,058	104,029	260,917	+ 126·8
Grand total	2,727,028	2,460,754	2,587,478	− 5·1

Source: Deutsches Weininstitut/Deutscher Weinbauverband

The market abroad takes a quarter of Germany's vintage and of this amount Great Britain accounts for more than half. As statistics consistently show, the bulk of exported German wine is cheap and it has been claimed that the success of Liebfraumilch and Niersteiner Gutes Domtal at low prices has prevented Germany's better wines from receiving proper recognition. If this is true, the signs in 1991 that sales of cheap German wine in Britain and elsewhere abroad are declining will be welcomed by lovers of the country's many good-quality wines.

Changes in German Wine

The changes in the style of German wine, which started in the 1970s, continue. The Green Party may have lacked the cohesion to become a successful political force judged by normal standards, but their ecologically aware thinking has taken over the wine-producing world. Nearly all growers mentioned in this guide now say that they are either using, or aiming to use, the absolute minimum of chemicals in their vineyards. One fervent convert to 'biological viticulture' was so enthused as to claim to be no longer poisoning his customers. However, if the hype surrounding the new 'working with nature' approach sometimes seems to be blown up into a tiresome sales argument, that should not be allowed to diminish the value of the changes that have been made in vine growing in the past ten years.

Yields are reduced more severely than before and grape bunches are cut away in summer so that the remainder produce a more concentrated juice. Where possible and sensible, traditional vine varieties (Riesling and the Burgunder [Pinot] family) are replacing the new crossings. Often the latter had been planted in inferior sites and allowed to overcrop to feed the market for commodity wine. Perhaps in the 1990s it will be discovered that they are capable of much better wine than has been supposed, although they are unlikely to be able to claim a spot in the best vineyards, where the Germans have laid out their towels permanently for Riesling and Spätburgunder. Trials of fungus-resistant interspecific crossings (*see* Rebsorte in the A–Z section) are being carried out on a scale limited by the EC.

The excellent '88, '89 and '90 vintages stimulated an interest in fine wines of *Auslese* quality and upwards and this very special, image-building sector of the market is one in which many producers, including the excellent cooperative cellar at Thüngers-heim, would like to excel. The emphasis here must be on the phrase 'fine wines', as the cheap *Auslesen* produced from new crossings in the Rheinhessen to the long-term profit of nobody would be better banned from the market.

The interest in drinking wine with food continues to encourage the consumption of dry white and red wine. Much German

Spätburgunder has more structure and tannin than its predecessors. The following chart shows that the amount of dry wine that received a quality control number (AP Nr – *see* Amtliche Prüfung in the A–Z section) between 1985 and 1990 increased by 77 percent.

Dry quality wine awarded an AP number

Region	1985 Hectolitres	% of all Quality wine	1990 Hectolitres	% of all Quality wine	% change 1985–1990
Ahr	6,529	20	11,506	29	+ 76
Baden	326,000	31	565,280	44	+ 73
Franken	149,744	36	296,071	52	+ 98
Hess Berg	8,185	27	12,417	42	+ 52
Mrh	5,164	22	8,444	28	+ 64
M-S-R	68,199	6	123,020	11	+ 80
Nahe	35,625	13	65,049	18	+ 83
Rhg	44,840	28	81,011	38	+ 81
Rhh	118,481	7	243,392	11	+105
Rhpf	331,478	18	488,811	24	+ 47
Würt	140,570	15	288,650	25	+105
Total	1,234,815		2,183,651		+ 77

Source: Die Weinwirtschaft/Deutsches Weininstitut

Many winemakers are experimenting with maturing their wines in young casks (*barriques*), from Allier, Limousin, Vosges, and from German (Swabian, Hunsrück, Baden, Odenwald and Spessart) oak. A few, such as Weingut 'Schwarzer Adler', use the new wood for fermentation as well as maturation.

On estates such as Richtershof and Bert Simon in the Mosel-Saar-Ruwer, or Breuer, Knyphausen and Wegeler-Deinhard in the Rheingau, wines are being offered without the use of the name of the individual vineyard from which they come. This particular change will take time if customers are not to be lost in the process, but it is likely to continue and spread.

In Württemberg and Baden, cooperative cellars have introduced superior ranges of wine whose quality depends on a particularly small yield and a crop from older vines. The presentation, that is to say the bottles and the labels, used for some of these new wines is most striking and helps to suggest an expensive 'product'. Marketing has arrived.

Finally, almost all the estates in this guide now offer a *Sekt* from their own base wine. Some make it themselves and others employ a contract *Sekt* manufacturer to do the work for them. Because of the relatively small amounts involved the secondary fermentation usually takes place in the bottle in which the wine is to be sold. The *per capita* consumption of sparkling wine in Germany in 1990 amounted to 5·1 litres, according to the IFO-Institut. *Sekt* is drunk often and not just on high days and holidays.

In eastern Germany, wages are about half of the equivalent level in the old West Germany, but this is likely to change within five years. What the effect will then be on wine consumption is not known, but at the moment the still and sparkling wine sold in eastern Germany is almost all of the cheapest sort.

Recent Vintages

Three top-quality vintages in a row are very unusual in Germany, but '88, '89 and '90 managed the hat trick. Looking at records it seems we may have to go back as far as the 18th century until we come upon a similar success. In fact, the vintages from 1746 to 1750 were even more remarkable for all five were described as *vorzüglich* or excellent. A really good vintage will often be the result of an early flowering, allowing the grapes as long as possible to ripen, followed by adequate rain in summer to prevent the inhibiting effect of drought on the formation of sugar. In a warm and sunny autumn noble rot (*Edelfäule*) may well appear.

More usually, by harvest time, while some grapes are very ripe others are still distinctly sour. Except in great years, such as 1971 and 1976, it is only when the pressing has started and the must weight and acidity have been measured that the real value of the harvest can be accurately assessed.

The quality of cheap German wine maintains a steady level, almost regardless of vintage, as blending smooths away the bumps. Most everyday wine is made to be drunk within two years of the harvest, so there is little point in storing it longer.

On the other hand, Riesling QbA and the better, usually producer-bottled QmP wines improve with age (*see* Bottle-age in the A–Z section).

Because of the predictability of much QbA wine, vintage assessments refer more to the QmPs – *Kabinett, Spätlese, Auslese* and, in great years, *Beerenauslese* and *Trockenbeerenauslese* (*Eiswein* can be produced in indifferent vintages). A poor year for a grower is one that produces little or no *Spätlese* wine. In a good vintage the sugar and acid contents are high, but this is a theme with many variations. As sales of the finest and most expensive wines are not very fast, producers will normally welcome a vintage with much wine of potential *Kabinett* and *Spätlese* quality. Lighter *Spätlesen* can be downgraded to *Kabinett* level, and those *Kabinett* wines that have only just made the grade may well be sold as QbA. From wines of this sort the growers make a living, but they need a balanced range of stock to support their lists, and as far as nature permits, wines will be produced with this aim in view.

The ratings in the chart that follow seem to reflect best the results in the northern regions.

Year	Yield		Rating	Quality category*		
	Total	hl/ha		DTW	QbA	QmP
1980	4,634,960	51·8	moderate	3·0	65·0	32·0
1981	7,159,176	80·4	good	1·0	55·0	44·0
1982	15,402,949	173·0	moderate	8·0	69·0	23·0
1983	13,040,937	144·3	good	2·0	51·0	47·0
1984	7,993,489	86·7	moderate to low	13·0	80·0	7·0
1985	5,402,394	58·1	good	0·1	40·3	59·6
1986	10,062,456	108·1	moderate	4·4	78·5	17·1
1987	8,942,386	95·9	moderate	1·9	77·1	21·0
1988	9,314,610	99·6	good	0·2	46·4	53·4
1989	13,226,232	140·8	good to very good	0·6	51·5	47·9
1990	8,514,000	89·8	very good	0·2	39·3	60·5

*Potential quality category based on must weight
Source: from figures published by the Statistisches Bundesamt

In almost every vintage it is possible for the effect of a good microclimate to produce wines of above average quality, but it is only in the really great years that fine wine is made throughout Germany. Often the wines of any one year will have a particular style or flavour that makes them easily identifiable. This common vintage characteristic can spread across northern Europe but the differences fade with bottle-age. It is not obligatory for a wine of one year to bear a vintage, but if it does, 85 percent of the grapes used for the wine must have been grown in the year stated.

The qualities that can be expected from the various grades of Riesling wine in poor, average and great years are set out below. Of course, within any region there can be many exceptions to the general standard of the harvest, brought about by site, micro-climate and the winemaking. In mediocre years many interesting and enjoyable German wines can still be produced, as their attraction does not depend on a high alcohol content.

Eiswein can be made in small amounts in most years when it is sufficiently cold, usually from mid-November onwards.

Poor Year

QbA Riesling	Good, sound wine
Kabinett	Light, agreeable. Lacks real quality
Spätlese	None, except for small quantities of non-Riesling wines
Auslese	None

Average Year

QbA Riesling	Good, balanced wine
Kabinett	Light, stylish, typical of vine variety and site
Spätlese	Sound, reflecting regional character well but limited in quantity
Auslese	Rare except from non-Riesling

Great Year

QbA Riesling	Many good wines, but fuller than usual
Kabinett	Good quality, but some can miss the character of those in an average year
Spätlese	Splendid wines of great depth of flavour
Auslese	Superb, unique wines
Beerenauslese and Trockenbeerenauslese	Rarities. Only possible in significant quantities in great years

The production of must for the large '89 vintage can be compared with the average for the 1980s in the following chart.

Region	Main vine	Yield in hl/ha '89			Total average yield
		red	white	total	'80–'89
Ahr	40% Spätburgunder 23% Portugieser 13% Riesling	122	101	115	80
Baden	36% Müller-Thurgau 23% Spätburgunder	108	124	120	85
Franken	47% Müller-Thurgau 20% Silvaner	121	157	155	90
Hess Berg	55% Riesling 17% Müller-Thurgau	107	116	116	82
Mrh	75% Riesling	–	114	114	84
M-S-R	55% Riesling 22% Müller-Thurgau	–	168	168	120
Nahe	26% Müller-Thurgau 23% Riesling 12% Silvaner	146	118	118	92
Rhg	82% Riesling 7% Spätburgunder	105	115	114	81
Rhh	23% Müller-Thurgau 13% Silvaner	145	138	138	102
Rhpf	22% Müller-Thurgau 17% Riesling	142	136	137	118
Würt	25% Riesling 22% Trollinger 15% Müllerrebe	189	144	167	109
Germany		149	139	141	104

Source: Deutscher Weinbauverband/Statistisches Bundesamt

Visiting the Vineyards

The ideal way to discover German wines is, of course, to visit the wine regions. Indeed, the only way to enjoy many German wines is in the setting of the vineyards that produce them, because relatively few are exported.

By happy circumstance the vineyards encompass some of the most picturesque countryside in Germany, even without the attraction of the wines to be tasted in the restaurants and wine bars. 'Wine roads' (*Weinstrassen*) are marked by appropriate signs with such symbols as a bunch of grapes or a wine glass. For the more energetic there are also well-marked footpaths (*Weinlehrpfade*) in many of the vineyards, punctuated at timely intervals by rest stops where the local wines can be sampled.

Visiting wine cellars is not quite as simple as it is in France, and the equivalent sign to '*Visitez nos caves*' is absent. Nevertheless, most estates and cooperative cellars are happy to welcome interested visitors during business hours – usually between 9am and 5pm on weekdays – although they do expect advance warning, either by letter or by telephone. Some cellars set a firm maximum and minimum to the number of persons they will receive in any one party. If a tasting is provided free of charge, it is courteous to buy a few bottles when leaving. The Germans are, by nature, very hospitable, but the visitor to a small estate should remember that although tasting in a producer's cellar is one of the most enjoyable aspects of visiting a wine-producing region, it may be occupying a large part of the estate owner's working day and the welcome should not be overstayed.

Almost all producers sell their wines directly to the consumer and have a *Weinstube* or tasting room set aside for this purpose. While customers sit around tables or at a bar the wines are served to them. Facilities for spitting are willingly provided if requested. General comment on the wines is made after each has been introduced by the cellar master (*Kellermeister*) or by the estate owner (*Weingutsbesitzer*). Such tastings quickly become a social occasion, although the wines still receive proper attention. Their relatively low alcohol content makes it possible to taste many wines in this way and remain clear-headed. (In the course of his duties the professional taster will willingly tackle 70 or more German white wines in one session. For wines with a higher alcohol content this would hardly be possible.) Tastings at a cooperative cellar are more impersonal but there is always a competent person on hand to answer questions. Unfortunately there are few establishments where it is possible to taste wines from a range of growers in a particular village or district. The success of wine bars of this style in Austria suggests they could do equally well in the touristic parts of the German vineyard.

Each region has a number of wine festivals of varying sizes, especially in the months of August and September – in the Mosel-Saar-Ruwer alone there are some 72 local festivals in August. There are also a number of wine museums, among the best known being that housed in the Historisches Museum der Pfalz in Speyer, which traces vine growing in Germany back to its origins, and the important Deutsches Weinbaumuseum in Oppenheim. Small local wine museums also have much to tell about the history of winemaking in Germany.

More information can be obtained from the regional wine information offices (*see* Useful Addresses, page 40) or from the central wine information office, the Deutsches Weininstitut, Gutenbergplatz 3–5, Postfach 1705, W-6500 Mainz, telephone 06131 28 29 0.

German Pronunciation

The German language is often more daunting in appearance than in practice, thanks largely to the German fondness for combining into one eye-numbing word what might be an entire sentence in English (a *Gebietswinzergenossenschaft*, for example, is simply the cooperative cellar of a district). Fortunately, in spoken German every word is clearly articulated and never runs into the following word, as happens in French officially and in English colloquially, so at least it is usually possible to distinguish where words begin and end.

The main variations in pronunciation between German and English arise from the following differences:

'j'	as in Juffer	pronounced as in English 'y'
'v'	as in Vollrads	pronounced as in English 'f'
'w'	as in Winkel	pronounced as in English 'v'
'z'	as in Zwierlein	pronounced as in English 'ts'
'ch'	as in Enkirch	pronounced as in 'loch' by a Scot (ie not 'lock')
'd'	as in Boppard, at the end of a word, is pronounced as a 't'; elsewhere as in English	
'eu'	as in Neumagen	is pronounced 'oi' as in 'rejoice'
'g'	as in muffig, following an 'i' at the end of a word, is soft, almost like 'ch'; elsewhere as in English	
'Sch'	as in Schönhell	pronounced as the English 'sh'
'sp'	as in Spiegelberg	pronounced as the English 'shp'
'st'	as in Stuttgart	pronounced as the English 'sht'
's'	as in Siegerrebe	pronounced as the English 'z' before a vowel

In addition, the pronunciation of German vowels is altered by an Umlaut:

'ä'	as in Spätlese	'Spät' rhymes, more or less, with the English 'ate'
'ö'	as in Östrich	'Ö' rhymes with the English 'fur'
'ü'	as in Mühlheim	no equivalent English sound; similar to the French 'u' as in '*tu*'

The general rule on 'ei' and 'ie' is:

'ei'	as in Wein	pronounced as 'i' as in 'vine'
'ie'	as in Riesling	pronounced as 'ee' as in 'geese'

Consonants are always pronounced, and so is the 'e' at the end of a word: for example in *Auslese* the 'Aus' is pronounced as the English 'house' without the 'h', 'lese' is pronounced as in 'laser'.

Food and Wine in Germany

The producers listed in this guide were asked to indicate their case sales to private customers, and to hotels and restaurants, as a percentage of their total turnover. This resulted in average figures for each of the larger regions which were as follows:

	Private customers %	Hotels and restaurants %
Rheingau	26	27
Franken	49	23
Baden	42	20
Württemberg	40	18
Mosel-Saar-Ruwer	37	17
Rheinhessen	46	13
Nahe	58	13
Rheinpfalz	59	11

NB Where a producer did not sell directly to the consumer, or to the hotel and restaurant trade, his reply was ignored for the purposes of the above computation.

Supplying wine to a restaurant can be an expensive business and cannot always be justified in strict financial terms. Nevertheless, many marketing-orientated producers believe that by appearing on a good restaurant list, their wines gain publicity and an improved image. In particular, members of organizations such as Charta (*see* A–Z section) in the Rheingau see their wines as an ideal accompaniment to food, and the smart restaurant table as the natural place for the wine to be served.

The number of high-quality restaurants in Germany has much increased in the last decade, as the Michelin Guide confirms, but the choice of wine served by the glass in more ordinary restaurants in the northern German wine regions remains poor. The reasons for

this are somewhat complicated and concerned with the structure and distribution of the trade in cheaper German wine, which is dominated by large and indifferent merchants (*Kellereien*).

In principle, the further south and east you travel in Germany the better the food in basic restaurants seems to become.

Some, with the best intentions, make a proper meal of it when they discuss the marriage of wine and food, but there is absolutely no problem unique to German wine that makes its consumption with food difficult. One benefit of all the exalted talk about harmony of flavours has been the wider appreciation that *lieblich* or medium-sweet Riesling can be happily served at the dining table. But the range of good German wine is now so wide that it can satisfy the wishes of even the most fastidious 'foodie' throughout the meal on almost all occasions.

Useful Addresses

More information about visiting the wine regions, including details of wine festivals, wine museums etc, may be obtained from the Wine Information Office in each region:

Ahr
Das Bäder-, Wein- und Wanderland
Rhein, Ahr, Eifel eV
Postfach 1340
Wilhelmstrasse 24
W-5483 Bad-Neuenahr-Ahrweiler
Germany
Tel: 02641 5015

Baden
Weinwerbezentrale
Badischer Winzergenossenschaften
Kesslerstrasse 5
W-7500 Karlsruhe
Germany
Tel: 0721 557028

Franken
Frankenwein-Frankenland eV
Juliusspital-Weingut
Postfach 5848
W-8700 Würzburg 1
Germany
Tel: 0931 12093

Hessische Bergstrasse
Weinbauverband Bergstrasse
Königsbergerstrasse 4
W-6148 Heppenheim
Germany
Tel: 06252 2101

Mittelrhein
Mittelrhein – Burgen und Wein eV
Am Hafen 2
W-5401 St Goar
Germany
Tel: 06741 7644

Mosel-Saar-Ruwer
Weinwerbung Mosel-Saar-Ruwer eV
Gartenfeldstrasse 12a
W-5500 Trier
Germany
Tel: 0651 76621/45967

Nahe
Weinland Nahe eV –
Gebietsweinwerbung
Brückes 63
W-6550 Bad Kreuznach
Germany
Tel: 0671 27563

Rheingau
Der Rheingau – der Weinbau
Johannisberg
Im alten Rathaus
W-6222 Geisenheim
Germany
Tel: 06722 8117

Rheinhessen
Rheinhessen eV
An der Brunnenstube 33–35
W-6500 Mainz
Germany
Tel: 06131 681058

Rheinpfalz
Rheinpfalz – Weinpfalz
Chemnitzerstrasse 3
Postfach 101002
W-6730 Neustadt an der Weinstrasse
Germany
Tel: 06321 130 93–96

Württemberg
Weinwerbung Württembergischer
Weingärtnergenossenschaften
Heilbronnerstrasse 41
W-7000 Stuttgart 1
Germany
Tel: 0711 20 40 26 25

Wine Information Offices have not yet been established in Saale-Unstrut or Sachsen.

A–Z of German Wine

Abberen
To separate the grapes from the stems.

Abfüllung
Bottling. Top-quality (QmP) wine is usually bottled as soon as it is
microbiologically and chemically stable, between March and June
following the vintage. Cheaper wines are more often stored in bulk
and bottled to meet an order. Much German wine retains residual
sugar, so a necessary part of the bottling operation is the removal of
all yeast and undesirable micro-organisms. To achieve this 'wine
sterility', almost all German wine is bottled by the cold sterile
method, in which the bottling machinery and other equipment is
sterilized with steam. The remainder is either warm-bottled (the
wine is heated before bottling to between 45° and 60°C) and/or
bottled with the addition of the sterilizing agent sorbic acid.

Abril, Weingut Baden
Estate of 6·5 hectares with holdings mainly at Bischoffingen and at
Schelingen, planted 31 percent Ruländer (Grauburgunder), 27
percent Spätburgunder and 16 percent Müller-Thurgau, Chardon-
nay and others. Trials will soon be started with Cabernet
Sauvignon and Merlot. Some Grauburgunder, Spätburgunder and
Gewürztraminer are aged in *barrique*. Annual production is 4,200
cases: 70 percent is *trocken*; 85 percent is sold to private customers.
Address: Talstrasse 9, W-7818 Vogtsburg-Bischoffingen
Tel: 07662 255

Abtswind Franken w
Small community near the Steigerwald with an over-large range of
vine varieties, some small estates and vineyard holdings owned by
the *Würzburg Staatlicher Hofkeller. *Grosslage*: Schild.

Achkarren Baden w r
A good village for tourists and lovers of wines with body and good
structure from the usual range of Bereich *Kaiserstuhl varieties.
Grosslage: *Vulkanfelsen.

Achkarren eG, Winzergenossenschaft Baden

Cooperative in the heart of the warmest district in Germany, the Bereich *Kaiserstuhl, supplied by 170 hectares immediately adjoining the cellars, planted 40 percent Ruländer (Grauburgunder), 20 percent Spätburgunder, 20 percent Weissburgunder and others. Full, powerful wines and a premium range based on vines more than 20 years old. Also a lighter wine offered *en primeur* – in November following the vintage. Annual production is 150,000 cases, 50 percent of it *trocken*.

Address: Schlossbergstrasse 2, W-7818 Vogtsburg-Achkarren
Tel: 07662 6092

Acidity

See Säure

Adelmann, Weingut Graf Würt VDP

Fifteen-hectare high-profile estate northeast of Stuttgart, very much a leader in the region. The vineyards at Kleinbottwar are planted with the range of traditional Württemberg vine varieties including a small and perhaps unique parcel of Urban – some of the vines are 80 years old. The aim is for well-structured whites and tannic reds, which leads to the use of *barriques*. Annual production is 10,400 cases, of which five percent is exported.

Address: Burg Schaubeck, W-7141 Steinheim 2
Tel: 07148 6665

Adelseck, Weingut Carl Nahe

Seven-hectare estate with holdings at *Münster-Sarmsheim (including *Dautenpflänzer, *Pittersberg) and *Laubenheim, planted 50 percent Riesling. Yields are restricted and the wines win many prizes in the *DLG competitions.

Address: Saarstrasse 41, W-6538 Münster-Sarmsheim
Tel: 06721 43001

Affaltrach, Schlosskellerei Würt

Estate dating from the 13th century, owned since 1928 by the family of Dr Reinhold Baumann. Ten hectares in Affaltrach and Sülzbach planted with a range of traditional red and white vine varieties, producing about 4,000 cases only per year. The wines are mostly dry, although a Müller-Thurgau *Trockenbeerenauslese* was produced in 1988. Sales are mainly to the restaurant trade. The estate also takes in grapes from 120 hectares for an *Erzeugergemeinschaft* and is a successful *Sekt* producer.

Address: W-7104 Obersulm 1, Krs Heilbronn

Tel: 07130 557

Affental, Affentaler Spätburgunder Rotwein

Certain villages immediately south of Baden–Baden have the right to produce a red wine, Affentaler Spätburgunder Rotwein, either as QbA or QmP. It is sold in a normal slim German wine bottle, embossed with a monkey clinging to its sides (Affental, which translates as 'monkey valley', is a corruption of Ave Maria Tal).

AG

Aktiengesellschaft. Limited company, as in Günther Reh AG (*see* Reh, Franz).

Ahr r (w)

Second-smallest of the wine regions with 428 hectares of vineyards on both sides of the river Ahr, which flows into the Rhein just south of Bonn. In spite of its northerly position, 72 percent is planted with red-wine varieties, mainly Spätburgunder and Portugieser, which at this latitude produce wines that incline to the pale and light. They are often bottled with residual sugar, excepting those of Weingut *Meyer-Näkel. The white wines from Riesling and Müller-Thurgau are attractive but cannot compare in quality to the finest from regions further south. The best Rieslings, from slaty soil, recall the wines of the nearby Mittelrhein, with their somewhat earthy, occasionally steely flavour. For many, vine growing in the Ahr valley is a part-time occupation and 84 percent of the crop is made into wine by cooperative cellars.

Ahr wine does not attempt to compete with the best that can be found on the international market and therefore the place to meet it is in the valley itself. The region is exceedingly pretty and the steep vineyards are easily accessible through the 'Rotweinwanderweg', a well-signposted footpath some 30 kilometres in length, which can be joined at many different points. The valley is a great attraction for tourists, especially those from Köln and the Ruhr district. Its narrow roads are often crowded with visitors but there are many places to stop and eat and to enjoy the local wines. The capital is ★Bad Neuenahr.

Albig Rhh w
Village with a long tradition of vine growing, surrounded by 415 hectares of hilly vineyards, perhaps planted with an over-large range of vine varieties, but the village's reputation for wine is improving. *Grosslage*: Petersberg.

Alcohol
Alcohol level is not so significant as a quality factor in wines from the northern German regions as it is in those from elsewhere. Its importance lies mainly in its relationship to the acidity, and to the sugar and extract contents. Some producers, however, aim for a high natural alcohol content in certain wines, such as dry *Auslesen* from Weiss- or Grauburgunder, and today's good-quality wines are often more alcoholic than their predecessors in the 1960s. *See also* Anreicherung and Trockenbeerenauslese.

Alf M-S-R w
One of the better-known small wine villages in the Bereich ★Zell, on the Lower Mosel near ★Cochem. The steep vineyards are planted mainly with Riesling. *Grosslage*: Grafschaft.

Allendorf, Weingut Fritz Rhg Charta
Noted Winkel estate owned by a family established in the Rheingau since 1292, with 25 hectares in ★Assmannshausen, ★Rüdesheim, ★Johannisberg, ★Geisenheim, ★Winkel, ★Oestrich, ★Hallgarten, ★Eltville and elsewhere. Vines are 80 percent Riesling, 13 percent Spätburgunder. The largest holding is in the Winkeler ★Jesuitengarten, of which Allendorf owns a quarter. The estate makes the full range of regional wines, matured in wood.
Address: Georgshof, Kirchstrasse 69, W-6227 Oestrich-Winkel
Tel: 06723 5021

Alsenz Nahe w
Secluded wine village on a Nahe tributary of the same name. *Grosslage*: Paradiesgarten.

Alsheim Rhh w

Attractive village between ★Worms and ★Oppenheim, making distinguished Riesling wines. ★Frühmesse in the *Grosslage* ★Rheinblick, which is restricted to the sloping sites, is well known but ★Fischerpfad is the best Riesling *Einzellage*. Alsheim's flatter land is in the larger *Grosslage* ★Krötenbrunnen.

Altärchen M-S-R w

Large *Einzellage* of some 245 hectares lying on both sides of the Mosel at ★Trittenheim. Sixty percent is on steep slopes facing south, southeast and west, producing good-quality wines from Riesling and Müller-Thurgau. *Grosslage*: ★Michelsberg. Growers: Bischöfliche Weingüter, Friedrich-Wilhelm-Gymnasium, Grans-Fassian, Krebs-Matheus-Lehnert, Milz, Reh (Josefinengrund).

Alte Badstube am Doktorberg M-S-R w

High-quality Riesling *Einzellage* at ★Bernkastel, created in 1986 by the redefinition of the boundaries of the Bernkasteler Doctor site. *Grosslage*: ★Badstube. Owners: Heidemanns-Bergweiler, Lauerburg, Pauly-Bergweiler, Wegeler-Deinhard.

Altenahr Ahr r (w)

Small town on the river Ahr, near the upstream end of the vinegrowing region. It almost sinks under the weight of the well-behaved tourists who arrive in coachloads from the Ruhr district. Some 54 hectares of vineyard are planted with Riesling, Spätburgunder, Müller-Thurgau and others, producing typical Ahr wines that are drunk almost exclusively in the region. *Grosslage*: Klosterberg.

Altenbamberg Nahe w

Secluded village on the river Alsenz where excellent wine is made from Riesling grown on porphyritic soil. *Grosslage*: ★Burgweg.

Altenberg M-S-R w

Altenberg is a frequently used site name – there are at least 20 scattered across Germany. The *Einzellage* Altenberg at ★Kanzem is a steep site typical of the best in the Saar, producing wines of quality and charm, mainly from Riesling. *Grosslage*: ★Scharzberg.

Growers: Bischöfliche Weingüter, Kanzemer Berg, Vereinigte Hospitien.

Altenkirch, Weingut Friedrich Rhg Charta

Family-owned estate dating from 1826 with 14 hectares of vineyards, mainly on steep sites at *Lorch but also in *Rüdesheim (*Berg Rottland). Vines are 82 percent Riesling, eight percent Spätburgunder. The present energetic owner, Peter Breuer, is proud of the fruity acidity of his wines from steep sites, matured in the 300-metre-long cellars that lie deep beneath his vineyards.
Address: Binger Weg 2, W-6223 Lorch
Tel: 06726 374

Alzey Rhh w (r)

Town first mentioned in AD 223, set in rolling country deep in the Rheinhessen. Very much a centre for the local wine trade, it is best known for its Landesanstalt für Rebenzüchtung – the viticultural institute whose first director, in 1909, was Georg Scheu, who bred the Scheurebe and other well-known vines. The town also has its own wine estate, the Weingut der Stadt Alzey (*see next entry*). It is the home of the wine-exporting house *Sichel. *Grosslagen*: Petersberg, Sybillenstein.

Alzey, Weingut der Stadt Rhh

Estate of 13 hectares owned by the town of *Alzey, established in 1916. Many vine varieties are in commercial production. The aim is to make balanced, positive, wines. Annual production is 8,300 cases (40 percent *trocken*), sold mainly to private customers.
Address: Schlossgasse 14, W-6508 Alzey
Tel: 06731 8238

Amalienhof, Weingut Würt VDP

Estate of 27 hectares, founded in 1954. Sole owners of 21·8-hectare Beilsteiner Steinberg *Einzellage*, with further holdings at *Heilbronn, *Flein and Talheim. Vines are 34 percent Riesling, 21 percent Trollinger, 13 percent Spätburgunder, plus others. Good reputation in Württemberg for its Riesling wine.
Address: Lukas-Cranach-Weg 5, W-7100 Heilbronn
Tel: 07131 51735

Amtliche Prüfung

Official testing. Quality German wines (approximately 95 percent of the annual harvest) of all categories must submit to an official 'blind' tasting and chemical analysis. If successful, a wine will be granted an Amtliche Prüfungsnummer (AP number) which must be displayed on the label; 93–97 percent of applications are successful. This countrywide system of quality control, operating through ten centres, is unique to Germany. It ensures that wines with apparent faults at the time of examination do not reach the market, but says little about the quality of a wine.

Anbaugebiet, bestimmtes

A designated wine region, of which there are 13 in Germany (shown on the maps on pages 14 and 15). It is the largest geographical unit for quality wine and the *Anbaugebiet* name must always appear on the label of a quality (QbA or QmP) wine. The differences between the wines of the various regions are clear, although they naturally tend to be less pronounced in the vineyards at the boundaries of adjoining regions.

Anheuser, Weingut Ökonomierat August E Nahe VDP

Estate of some 50 hectares founded in 1869 by the Anheuser family, to whom the exporting house Anheuser & Fehrs also belongs. Sites include ★Brückes, ★Krötenpfuhl and ★Narrenkappe at ★Bad Kreuznach. About 75 percent of the vines are Riesling, the rest are mainly Müller-Thurgau, Silvaner, Ruländer and Scheurebe. Good-quality wines, typical of the region.
Address: Brückes 53, W-6550 Bad Kreuznach
Tel: 0671 2077

Anheuser, Weingut Paul Nahe VDP

Estate established in 1888 by the vine-growing Anheuser family, also responsible for the American brewery Anheuser-Busch, covering 55 hectares. Vines are 70 percent Riesling in leading sites at ★Altenbamberg, ★Bad Kreuznach, ★Niederhausen, ★Norheim, ★Roxheim, ★Schlossböckelheim and elsewhere. No *Grosslage* names are used. Cool fermentation and maturation in oak casks produces the full range of Nahe flavours. Half the wines are *trocken*. The style is crisp, fresh and *spritzig*.

Address: Strombergerstrasse 15–19, W-6550 Bad Kreuznach
Tel: 0671 28748

Anheuser & Fehrs, Weinkellereien Nahe

Wine merchants established in 1869, under the same family
ownership as Weingut Ökonomierat August E Anheuser, selling
quality wines on the home and export markets.
Address: Brückes 41, W-6550 Bad Kreuznach
Tel: 0671 2077

Annaberg Rhpf w

Once-famous little five-hectare *Einzellage* planted with Riesling,
Scheurebe, Weissburgunder, Silvaner and Ruländer. Until 1971 the
wine was sold simply under the site name Annaberg but now the
label must include the village name *Kallstadt. *Grosslage*:
*Feuerberg.

Anreicherung

Enrichment. The addition of sugar in various forms (saccharose,
concentrated grape juice) to increase the actual alcohol content and
thus produce a balanced wine has been practised for some 200 years
in many countries. In Germany only QbA and *deutscher Tafelwein*,
including *Landwein*, may be enriched. This means that wines of
Kabinett quality and upwards will never have sugar added, as their
superior quality depends on freshness and elegance, not on
enhanced alcohol content. *See also* Alcohol.

Ansprechend

Attractive. A somewhat imprecise but useful term for describing a
wine, often used as in *ansprechende Süsse* ('attractive sweetness') or
ansprechende Säure ('attractive acidity').

AP Nr

Abbreviation of Amtliche Prüfungsnummer, found on wine labels.
See Amtliche Prüfung.

Apfelsäure

Malic acid. With tartaric acid (*Weinsäure*) it forms approximately
90 percent of the acidity in German grape must (it is also found in

many other fruits). The process of malolactic fermentation, in which malic acid is converted into lactic acid and carbon dioxide, does not normally occur in the relatively acidic German white wines. If the malic acid content of a wine is excessive it may legally be chemically reduced. *See* Deacidification.

Apfelwein
Wine made from apple juice by a process that is very similar to grape-wine vinification. Additions of sugar and water are normal. A popular drink in Germany.

Apotheke M-S-R w
Einzellage lying on both sides of the Mosel at ★Trittenheim, producing top-quality, elegant Rieslings. *Grosslage*: ★Michelsberg. Growers: Bischöfliche Weingüter, Friedrich-Wilhelm-Gymnasium, Grans–Fassian, Kesselstatt, Krebs-Matheus-Lehnert, Milz, Reh (Josefinengrund).

Aromatisch
Aromatic. Term used to describe wines with a pronounced bouquet, especially the wines of the Rheinhessen and Rheinpfalz, from vine varieties such as Morio-Muskat, Traminer and Scheurebe. The strength of the aroma will be affected by the style of the vintage, the soil, vinification and length of maturation in bottle.

Aromatisierte Weine
Wines to which herbs, spices or other flavourings have been added (such as vermouth).

Aschrott'sche Erben, Geheimrat Rhg VDP
Estate dating from 1823 with 18·5 hectares of holdings in the best ★Hochheim sites, including ★Domdechaney, ★Hölle and ★Kirchenstück. The vines are 97 percent Riesling and the naturally cool cellars (ten to 12°C throughout the year) produce fresh-tasting wines, typical of Hochheim. Annual production is 13,300 cases; half is *trocken*.
Address: Kirchstrasse 38, W-6203 Hochheim
Tel: 06146 2207

Assmannshausen Rhg r (w)
Small town some four kilometres downstream from ★Rüdesheim, where the river turns north and the Wagnerian Rhein gorge begins. It is best known for its fine old 'Zur ★Krone' hotel and restaurant, and its expensive Spätburgunder. The best, from estates such as Weingut August ★Kesseler, is stylish and tannic but less full-bodied than a wine of similar quality from Baden. *Grosslage*: ★Steil.

Auctions
See Versteigerung

Auflangen Rhh w
Grosslage of 159 hectares covering some of the best south-facing sites on the ★Rheinterrasse above ★Nierstein, including ★Ölberg and ★Orbel. Distinguished wines from Riesling and Silvaner, rounded but not flabby, with powerful flavour in good years.

Auggen Baden w (r)
Large village at the foot of its vineyards, on the Rhein plain in the Bereich ★Markgräflerland. Good, solid wines from Gutedel in particular, and from Müller-Thurgau, Gewürztraminer and Ruländer. *Grosslage*: Burg Neuenfels.

Auggen eG, Winzergenossenschaft Baden
Cooperative supplied by 221 hectares in the local Schäf and Letten *Einzellagen*, planted 60 percent Gutedel, 15 percent Müller-Thurgau, and others. Environmentally friendly viticulture is regarded as very important. Attractive, true-to-type wines, of which 70 percent is *trocken*. Annual production is equivalent to 208,300 cases.
Address: An der B3, W-7841 Auggen
Tel: 07631 4045

Aus dem Lesegut
On a label this indicates that the wine has been made from grapes grown by the person stated (such as Aus dem Lesegut Herrn Schmidts). Not a term that is used very often. *See also* Harvest.

Ausdrucksvoll
Characterful. Suggests that the positive qualities of a wine are strongly pronounced. It might be applied to a well-developed Riesling wine from the Rheingau or Rheinpfalz.

Ausdünnen
Removal of grapes after flowering to reduce yield, thus producing a more concentrated must – an increasingly common practice among good grape-growers and winemakers.

Ausgeglichen
Well balanced. Describes a wine in which the constituent parts, particularly alcohol, acids and residual sugar, are in harmony. Sometimes achieved only after several years' bottle-age.

Auslese
Legally established term used in Germany to describe quality (QmP) wine made from selected – but not necessarily late-picked – grapes whose must weight reached certain minimum levels (for example, for Rheingauer Riesling *Auslese* the minimum level is 95° Oechsle, or 13 percent of potential alcohol). Riesling *Auslese* wines from the Rhein regions are made in great years from grapes with an increased sugar content caused by noble rot (*Edelfäule*). Such wines will also taste sweeter (through an enhanced fructose and glycerin

content) and will be darker in colour than wines of lower quality. *Auslese* wines from most of the new vine varieties cannot compare in quality with a Riesling *Auslese*. Dry *Auslesen* are no longer unusual, with those from the Burgunder family being among the most successful.

Ausschankwein
German equivalent of the French *vin ouvert* ('open wine'), usually bottled into litres and served in a large, 200ml (250ml in southern Germany) glass in cafés and wine bars. In most cafés the *Ausschankwein* is ordinary but many estates offer their better quality (QmP) wine by the glass in their own wine bar.

Auxerrois
Vine variety producing a low yield of white grapes with a must weight some 10° Oechsle higher than that of Müller-Thurgau. The wine is relatively soft, full-bodied and neutral in flavour. Planted in 69 hectares, 75 percent in Baden.

Ayl M-S-R w
Rural village in the Saar devoted to viticulture, where great wines are made in the best years. The finest wines usually come from the *Einzellage* ★Herrenberger and the best parts of the ★Kupp. *Grosslage*: ★Scharzberg.

Bacchus
White grape variety, a crossing of (Silvaner × Riesling) × Müller-Thurgau, planted in 3,573 hectares, of which 55 percent is in the Rheinhessen. If the yield is restricted, the quality is much improved, and the wine recalls Sauvignon Blanc. It has a slight Muskat bouquet and is normally at its best when young and fresh. It blends well with wines of pronounced acidity, to which it brings body and flavour. Many of the best Bacchus wines come from Franken, where plantings of the vine are increasing.

Bacharach Mrh w
Attractive old village, once a marketplace for wine from the whole of the Rheinland, now respected for its own steely Rieslings grown exclusively on very steep slopes. *Grosslage*: Schloss Stahleck.

Bad Cannstadt Würt r w
Suburb of ★Stuttgart known for its mineral water from 18 springs
and its beer festival, as well as for its 80 hectares of vineyards,
planted mainly in Trollinger and Riesling. *Grosslage*: Weinsteige.

Bad Dürkheim Rhpf w (r)
Busy town and spa 25 kilometres west of Mannheim between the
Pfälzerwald (Pfalz Forest) and the vineyards of the Bereich
★Mittelhaardt/Deutsche Weinstrasse. It is the site every September
of the largest wine festival in the world, the Dürkheimer
Wurstmarkt (sausage market). Excellent white wine is made from a
range of vine varieties, although Dürkheim's wines are probably
not quite as fine as the best from neighbouring ★Forst and
★Deidesheim. *Grosslagen*: ★Feuerberg, ★Hochmess and
★Schenkenböhl.

Bad Hönningen, Stadtweingut Mrh
In private hands since 1978, this 8·5-hectare estate is near today's
northern extremity of vine growing on the Rhein. It is planted 50

percent Riesling, but the plan is to expand by 1·5 hectares and have a split of 70 percent Spätburgunder and 30 percent Riesling. Annual production is 6,250 cases, of which 35 percent is *trocken*; 80 percent is sold via the estate's wine bar.
Address: Weinhaus Bernhard Schneider, Hauptstrasse 182, W-5462 Bad Hönningen
Tel: 02635 3116

Bad Kreuznach Nahe w (r)
The largest town in the Nahe and a spa since the 17th century; the southern part of the town with its well-laid-out gardens reflects its pre-1914 heyday. Some of the finest wine of the Nahe is made within the boundaries of the *Grosslage* ★Kronenberg surrounding Bad Kreuznach.

Bad Kreuznach, Staatsweingut: Weinbaulehranstalt Nahe
Estate established in 1900, with an educational and experimental role, owned by the state of ★Rheinland-Pfalz. It has 22 hectares of vineyards in ★Bad Kreuznach and ★Norheim. The estate pioneered controlled fermentation under carbon-dioxide pressure and aims to produce individual cask-matured wines with length and fine acidity. Sales are mainly on the home market.
Address: Rüdesheimerstrasse 68, W-6550 Bad Kreuznach
Tel: 0671 2473

Bad Münster am Stein-Ebernburg Nahe w
Small spa five kilometres south of ★Bad Kreuznach near the distinguished ★Traisen vineyards which back on to high, warmth-retaining rocks. *Grosslage*: ★Burgweg.

Bad Neuenahr-Ahrweiler Ahr r (w)
Principal town in the Ahr valley 30 kilometres south of Bonn. Much damaged in World War II, now skilfully restored and again a centre of tourism. The wine is red, light in weight and flavour. The best comes from Spätburgunder. *Grosslage*: Klosterberg.

Baden w (r)
Most southerly grape-growing region in Germany covering 15,000 hectares and accounting for some 13 percent of the total annual

German wine production. The soil is varied, warm and fruitful. Most of the vineyards lie on gently sloping ground, although near the Schwarzwald some are exceedingly steep. The EC recognizes that the climate in Baden is warmer than that elsewhere in Germany and places the region, for administrative purposes, in wine-producing Zone B, with French regions including Alsace and certain parts of the Loire valley. (All other wine-producing regions in Germany are placed in Zone A, together with the UK and Luxembourg.)

Around 83 percent of the Baden crop is handled by cooperative cellars, including the largest wine-producing cellar in Europe, the ★Badischer Winzerkeller at Breisach, and it is to the cooperatives that credit must be given for the success of Baden wines in Germany. The smaller village cooperatives produce characterful, individual wines and there are a number of private estates that are among Germany's best.

The range of vines grown is large, with Müller-Thurgau, Ruländer and Spätburgunder heading the list. Perhaps because the region extends over 300 kilometres from the river Main to the Swiss border, there is considerable variation in the style of wine from one *Bereich* to another. Baden wines show their grape character well. They are forceful and good value for money. Some are allowed to retain sufficient natural carbon dioxide to make them slightly *spritzig* and most attractive. As yet they are largely unknown outside Germany.

The region, which in many places backs on to the Schwarzwald, is exceptionally pretty and rural, with small vineyards mingling with orchards, and meadows covered in wildflowers. Very definitely worth a detour.

Baden-Württemberg

Federal state in which lie the wine regions Baden and Württemberg. Area under vine is 24,791 hectares. The capital is ★Stuttgart.

Badisch Rotgold

Quality rosé wine made in Baden exclusively from mixing Ruländer (Grauburgunder) and Spätburgunder grapes (not wine). Now out of fashion and little is produced.

Badischer Winzerkeller eG Baden
Vast central cooperative cellar, founded in 1952, taking the crop
from 5,000 hectares spread throughout Baden. Müller-Thurgau
and Spätburgunder are the main grapes, with smaller quantities of
Ruländer, Gutedel and Riesling. Wines of different origin are kept
apart. Over four million cases of sound, good-quality wine are
produced each year, sold mainly in Germany but a small amount
abroad. In addition there are superior 'premium wines'. Highly
impressive large-scale winemaking.
Address: Zum Kaiserstuhl 6, W-7814 Breisach
Tel: 07667 82232

Badstube M-S-R w
Small *Grosslage* of about 51 hectares that includes four of the most
distinguished sites on the Mosel: ★Doctor, ★Graben, ★Alte
Badstube am Doktorberg and ★Bratenhöfchen. The sites are
sloping or very steep indeed and almost 100 percent Riesling. For
marketing reasons wines are often sold under the well-known and
respected *Grosslage* name Badstube, rather than by their individual
site names.

Baiken Rhg w
Einzellage on sloping ground at ★Rauenthal, planted 95 percent
Riesling, that makes splendid, balanced, elegant wines of outstand-
ing quality in great years. *Grosslage*: ★Steinmächer. Growers:
Staatsweingut Eltville, Schloss Schönborn, Simmern.

Balbach Erben, Weingut Bürgermeister Anton Rhh
Important ★Nierstein estate. The Balbach family, engaged in vine
growing since 1650, cleared woods in the 19th century and laid out
the top-quality ★Pettenthal vineyard. Today the estate has holdings
in 17 hectares of prime sites, including ★Hipping, ★Ölberg and
★Bildstock. Vines are 80 percent Riesling. Some 12,500 cases of
good-quality, fresh wines are made.
Address: Mainzerstrasse 64, W-6505 Nierstein
Tel: 06133 5585

Barrique
Wooden cask of approximately 210–225 litres. Maturation in aged

casks of 500 litres or more is common in Germany. Since the early 1970s some producers have experimented in the use of smaller casks of new oak (for both fermentation and storage) which give the wine a particular flavour and bouquet. Although many of these new casks are French and of the exact size found in their region of origin, the term '*barrique*-aged' describes any wine that has spent a period in a new cask of less than 500 litres. Rieslings are unsuitable but Burgunders and other wines with sufficient body and alcohol can benefit from *barrique*-ageing. It is important that the natural fruit of the wine is not hidden by the effect of the untreated wood.

Bart, Weingut Gebr Rhpf
Eighteenth-century, family-owned, 11-hectare estate with holdings at ★Bad Dürkheim (including ★Spielberg, ★Fuchsmantel), ★Ungstein and ★Wachenheim. Many vine varieties are grown, including 50 percent Riesling, nine percent Müller-Thurgau and 13 percent Spätburgunder. Annual production is 4,200 cases (of which 50 percent is *lieblich*), sold 97 percent to private customers.
Address: Kaiserslauterer Strasse 42, W-6702 Bad Dürkheim
Tel: 06322 1854

Base wine
See Grundwein

Bassermann-Jordan, Weingut Geheimer Rat Dr von Rhpf
Estate known to have been in existence in 1250; it came into the hands of the Jordan family in 1816. The 40 hectares are divided among the best sites in the Bereich ★Mittelhaardt/Deutsche Weinstrasse, including ★Grainhübel, ★Hohenmorgen and ★Leinhöhle in ★Deidesheim, ★Jesuitengarten and ★Ungeheuer in ★Forst, ★Reiterpfad, ★Linsenbusch and others in ★Ruppertsberg, etc. Vines are 100 percent Riesling. Wines are matured in oak and the estate aims for fine Riesling acidity and fruit. The wines are extremely elegant and of outstanding quality. Sales are worldwide.
Address: W-6705 Deidesheim
Tel: 06326 6006

Bastei Nahe w
Mainly steep two-hectare *Einzellage* at the foot of the 200-metre-

high rock face near ★Traisen called the Rotenfels, planted entirely with Riesling. The wine has great character and a positive, spicy flavour that comes from the soil. *Grosslage*: ★Burgweg. Growers: Crusius, Niederhausen-Schlossböckelheim Staatliche Weinbaudomäne.

Baumann, Weingut Friedrich Rhh

Estate founded in 1909, with eight hectares in leading sites in ★Oppenheim (such as ★Sackträger, ★Kreuz), ★Nierstein (★Findling, ★Pettenthal) and ★Dienheim, producing a large choice of wines from Riesling (40 percent), Silvaner, Müller-Thurgau and other varieties. They are fresh and lively, matured in wood, and have won many awards. Annual production is 5,000 cases, 60 percent *lieblich*, 20 percent exported.
Address: Friedrich-Ebert-Strasse 55, W-6504 Oppenheim
Tel: 06133 2312

Bayern

A federal state with over 800 breweries and the vine-growing region of Franken. München is the capital.

Bechtheim Rhh w (r)

Village with 628 hectares of vineyards and a famous 11th-century basilica. Bechtheim wine is most often found under the name of its *Grosslage*, ★Pilgerpfad.

Becker, Weingut Brüder Dr Rhh VDP

Ten-hectare estate with holdings at ★Dienheim and ★Ludwigshöhe, planted 45 percent Riesling, 20 percent Scheurebe, 15 percent Silvaner. The wines (60 percent *trocken*) are matured/stored in wood and stainless steel. Annual production is equivalent to 6,900 cases, of which 20 percent is exported. QmP only are listed.
Address: Mainzerstrasse 3, W-6501 Ludwigshöhe
Tel: 06249 8430

Becker, Weingut Gernot Rhh

Five-hectare estate at ★Mettenheim and ★Bechtheim, planted 28 percent Riesling and 14 percent Ruländer (Grauburgunder). The estate participates with some 20 other producers at Mettenheim in

WEINGUT GERNOT BECKER

Rheinhessen

Riesling

1988 er Mettenheimer Goldberg

SPÄTLESE
HALBTROCKEN

Qualitätswein mit Prädikat

Produce of West-Germany

A. P. Nr. 4 300 012 008 89   e 0,75 l
D-6521 Mettenheim · Hauptstraße   alc 14,5 %
                                    vol

the production of Riesling still and sparkling wine under the name 'Casimir'. Annual production is 3,800 cases, 50 percent *lieblich*, 18 percent exported.

Address: Hauptstrasse 10–12, W-6521 Mettenheim
Tel: 06242 2845

Becker, Weingut Weinkellerei J B Rhg
Estate dating from 1893 with 14 hectares of Riesling (82 percent), Spätburgunder (15 percent) and Müller-Thurgau, in ★Walluf, ★Martinsthal, ★Rauenthal and ★Eltville. The Spätburgunder is traditionally made, and some of the Rieslings are fermented as well as matured in cask. Most impressive, concentrated big wines. Annual production is 6,700 cases, of which 80 percent is *trocken*. Ten percent is exported.

Address: Rheinstrasse 5–6, W-6229 Walluf
Tel: 06123 72523

Beeren
Grapes. The structure of the grape has a bearing on winemaking. Many substances that contribute to the aroma are concentrated in

the skin, as is the colour in red grapes. The content of the outer and inner areas of the flesh is not the same, with more sugar and less acid being found near the skin. As a result, the first and second pressings of the same grapes do not share the same chemical make-up and produce noticeably different wines.

Wine grapes vary in size, but small grapes, with their greater proportion of skin to flesh, will have a powerful bouquet if white (such as Scheurebe), and a good colour if red – all things being equal. The tightness with which grapes are packed on the bunch has a direct effect on the rate at which fungal diseases may spread.

Beerenauslese

Prädikat awarded by the control (★Amtliche Prüfung) authorities to wines made from individually selected overripe grapes, probably attacked by *Edelfäule*, and normally intensely sweet. The legal minimum must weights vary from 110–128° Oechsle, depending on where the grapes are grown. In the past, most *Beerenauslesen* contained relatively little alcohol (the legal minimum is 5·5 percent) and much residual sugar. The tendency in the 1990s is to allow the wine to ferment further so that it becomes less sweet. Some successful dry *Beerenauslesen* have also been made.

Usually Riesling produces the finest *Beerenauslesen*, with a high acid content and pronounced yellow-gold colour when young, which can turn to deepest amber in old age. The concentrated flavour of a *Beerenauslese* tends to mask the obtrusive characteristics of some new grape crossings, replacing them with the honey flavour of the *Edelfäule*. Huxelrebe offers a good, cheaper, but much less fine alternative to Riesling *Beerenauslese* and in Germany it is often served nowadays as an aperitif.

Beilstein M-S-R w

Picturesque old wine hamlet a few kilometres upstream from ★Cochem, overlooked by the castle Burg Metternich. A good centre from which to visit the Bereich ★Zell. *Grosslage*: Rosenhang.

Beilstein Würt w r

Attractive town where Trollinger, Limberger, Kerner and Riesling wines can be enjoyed in the Bikini Bar of the municipal swimming pool, as well as in the producers' cellars. *Grosslage*: Wunnenstein.

Bensheim Hess Berg w
Ancient town south of Darmstadt. Steep sites produce Riesling
wines with good acidity, drunk mainly in the region. The style of
Bensheimer wines is similar to that of Rheingau Rieslings but the
quality is usually less exalted. *Grosslage*: Wolfsmagen.

Bensheim, Weingut der Stadt Hess Berg
One of a few town-owned estates in Germany, covering 12
hectares. Planted 75 percent in Riesling and 15 percent in Rotberger
for rosé production. Much of the vineyard has been rebuilt and
most of the production is sold locally.
Address: Am Ritterplatz, W-6140 Bensheim 1
Tel: 06251 14269

Bentzel-Sturmfeder, Weingut Graf von Würt VDP
Estate of 17 hectares occupying all of the sloping Schozacher Roter
Berg *Einzellage*, planted 32 percent Riesling, 22 percent Spätburgunder, 14 percent Samtrot, and others. The wines from heavy soil
undergo a malolactic fermentation (*see* Apfelsäure). They are cask-
matured and long-lived. Annual production is 13,300 cases, 65
percent *trocken*, 60 percent sold to private customers.
Address: Sturmfederstrasse 4, W-7129 Ilsfeld-Schozach
Tel: 07133 7829

Bercher, Weingut Baden VDP
The Bercher family has made wine for over 300 years. It now has
16·5 hectares in ★Burkheim and neighbouring villages, planted 30
percent Spätburgunder, 18 percent Müller-Thurgau, 16 percent
Riesling, ten percent Ruländer (Grauburgunder), plus other
varieties. Quality is high, as are some of the prices; 87 percent of the
wine is *trocken*. Impressive *barrique*-aged Grauburgunder.
Address: Mittelstadt 13, W-7818 Vogtsburg-Burkheim
Tel: 07662 212

Bereich
District. Combination of vineyard sites (*Grosslagen* or *Einzellagen*)
within one region (*Anbaugebiet*) with theoretically more or less
similar growing conditions and wine. In some instances the reason
for a *Bereich* being created has been to help administration rather

than to identify a particular style of wine. Generally, a wine bearing a *Bereich* name must be a quality wine, although in certain areas a *Bereich* name can still be used to describe a table wine. The quality (QbA, QmP) of a *Bereich* wine should be sound but is unlikely to be exciting.

Berg Roseneck Rhg w

Sloping, 100 percent Riesling *Einzellage* on the hill at ★Rüdesheim making top-quality wines with a slightly earthy background flavour. *Grosslage*: ★Burgweg. Growers: Breuer, Staatsweingut Eltville, Groenesteyn, von Hessen, Mumm, Nägler, Ress, Wegeler-Deinhard.

Berg Rottland Rhg w

Einzellage adjacent to Berg Roseneck on the outskirts of ★Rüdesheim producing elegant, fruity, top-quality wines – all from Riesling. *Grosslage*: ★Burgweg. Growers: Altenkirch, Breuer, Staatsweingut Eltville, Groenesteyn, von Hessen, Mumm, Nägler, Ress, Schloss Schönborn, Wegeler-Deinhard.

Berg Schlossberg Rhg w (r)

Steep, slaty, 100 percent Riesling *Einzellage* directly overlooking the confluence of the Nahe and Rhein at ★Rüdesheim. Excellent, finely balanced wines with good acidity. *Grosslage*: ★Burgweg. Growers: Breuer, Staatsweingut Eltville, Groenesteyn, Kesseler, Krone, Mumm, Nägler, Ress, Schloss Schönborn, Wegeler-Deinhard.

Bergdolt, F & G Rhpf

An important 16-hectare estate southeast of ★Neustadt, founded in 1290 and acquired by the Bergdolt family in 1754. Riesling (35 percent), Weissburgunder and Silvaner are the main vine varieties grown. Chardonnay is on trial. The wines are elegant, powerfully flavoured, sometimes with more than 15 percent alcohol. Some are *barrique*-aged. Annual production is 11,000 cases, 80 percent *trocken*. Sales are mainly direct to the consumer in Germany.
Address: Klostergut St Lamprecht, W-6730 Neustadt-Duttweiler
Tel: 06327 5027

Bergstrasse, Staatsweingut Hess Berg
Top-quality *Hessen estate of 37 hectares, dating from the early
part of the century. Vines include 70 percent Riesling, seven percent
Ruländer. The estate is sole owner of the 15-hectare Centgericht site
at *Heppenheim. Some 25,000 cases are produced annually of
fruity, lively wines, 66 percent *trocken*, 97 percent sold in Germany.
Eiswein is a speciality, produced, perhaps uniquely, every vintage
since 1977. (*See also* Eltville, Verwaltung der Staatsweingüter.)
Address: Grieselstrasse 34–36, W-6140 Bensheim
Tel: 06251 3107

Bergsträsser Gebiets-Winzergenossenschaft eG Hess Berg
Cooperative cellar, handling 70 percent of the region's wine, whose
members have holdings in 290 hectares. Vines are 55 percent
Riesling, 18 percent Müller-Thurgau, eight percent each Ruländer
and Silvaner. The wines are full of flavour. Many have undergone a
malolactic fermentation. Most is sold in the region and 41 percent
is *trocken*.
Address: Darmstädterstrasse 56, W-6148 Heppenheim
Tel: 06252 73016

Bergweiler-Prüm Erben, Zach M-S-R
See Pauly-Bergweiler, Weingut Dr

Bernkastel, Bereich M-S-R w
One of five *Bereiche* in the Mosel-Saar-Ruwer. Downstream a few
kilometres from *Trier at *Schweich the steep slopes begin to rise
from the north bank of the Mosel. Here the Bereich Bernkastel
begins and continues on both sides of the river until a little short of
*Zell. The better-quality wines from these vineyards are mainly
offered under their own village and *Einzellage* names. The cheaper
wines are often sold under the *Grosslage* names – Bernkasteler
*Kurfürstlay, Klüsserather *St Michael, Piesporter *Michelsberg.
Generally speaking, any wine called simply Bereich Bernkastel is
likely to be of similar quality to these *Grosslagen* wines. Today,
cheaper versions will probably contain a high proportion of
Müller-Thurgau, but when drunk young they should still be fresh
and crisp in the proper Mosel manner. Bereich Bernkastel Riesling
is likely to be distinctly better.

Bernkastel-Kues M-S-R w

Important wine-producing town on the Mosel. Many of the finest parcels of vineyard of the Mittelmosel, including the Bernkasteler ★Doctor and parts of the Wehlener ★Sonnenuhr, are concentrated around Bernkastel on the right-hand river bank. Ancient half-timbered houses, narrow fairy-tale streets and the pleasure of drinking wine at source attract many tourists. In Kues (on the left bank and over the bridge from Bernkastel) several enormous cellars draw their wine from the whole of the Mosel but mainly from elsewhere. *Grosslagen*: ★Badstube, ★Kurfürstlay.

Besenwirtschaft

See Strausswirtschaft

Besigheim eG, Felsengartenkellerei Würt

A cooperative with a production that is peculiarly Württemberg-isch. Of the 360 hectares that supply grapes, 58 percent is planted in Trollinger, Müllerrebe (Schwarzriesling) and Limberger. Annual production is 283,300 cases, of which 84 percent is *lieblich*. Only one wine, a Limberger QbA *trocken*, is matured in oak.
Address: Am Felsengarten 1, W-7121 Hessigheim
Tel: 07143 5714

Bestes Fass

Best cask. Term used by some growers before 1971 to identify wines from the best of two or more casks of the same description, such as '1953 Oppenheimer Sackträger Riesling Auslese Bestes Fass'. No longer permitted.

Bestimmtes Anbaugebiet

See Anbaugebiet, bestimmtes

Beulwitz, Weingut Erben von M-S-R

This is a 250-year-old estate of 4·5 hectares, taken over in 1983 by Herbert Weis, and planted 100 percent Riesling. All the holdings, including parts of ★Nies'chen, ★Hitzlay and ★Kehrnagel, are at ★Kasel. Half the wine is *lieblich* and much is sold via the Hotel Weis.
Address: Hauptstrasse 1, W-5501 Kasel
Tel: 0651 52128

Bezner-Fischer Würt
See Sonnenhof, Weingut

Bickel-Stumpf, Weingut Franken VDP
Estate on the Main of 7·25 hectares with holdings, at Thüngersheim and Frickenhausen, separated by ★Würzburg. Three-quarters of the vineyards are on steep slopes, planted 35 percent Silvaner, 30 percent Müller-Thurgau, ten percent Riesling and five percent Spätburgunder. Annual production of 5,000 cases is sold mainly to private customers.
Address: Nr 27, W-8701 Frickenhausen
Tel: 09331 2847

Bickensohl Baden w (r)
Part of Vogtsburg in the Bereich ★Kaiserstuhl, producing power-ful, intensely flavoured wines from Ruländer. Drier, crisper versions are sold as Grauburgunder, for which Bickensohl is particularly known. *Grosslage*: ★Vulkanfelsen.

Bickensohl eG, Winzergenossenschaft Baden
Cooperative supplied by 175 hectares. A leader in Germany in the promotion of good, crisp Grauburgunder wine. The holdings are planted 28 percent Müller-Thurgau, 25 percent each Grau- and Spätburgunder, 15 percent Weissburgunder. Some of the Spät-burgunder wines are aged in *barrique*, and, in the modern way of cooperatives in Baden and Württemburg, there is a range of superior quality wine. Sixty percent of the production is *trocken* and three percent is exported.
Address: Neunlindenstrasse 25, W-7818 Vogtsburg-Bickensohl
Tel: 07662 213

Biffar, Weingut Josef Rhpf VDP
Estate with 11 hectares in good sites at ★Deidesheim, ★Wachen-heim, ★Ruppertsberg and ★Niederkirchen, planted mainly in Riesling. A full range of long-lasting, cask-matured wines is offered. *Trocken* wines account for 54 percent of production. Sales are mainly to the consumer.
Address: Niederkircherstrasse 13, W-6705 Deidesheim
Tel: 06326 5028

Bildstock Rhh w (r)
Large *Einzellage* behind the town of *Nierstein on the Rhein. Most of the site is flat, producing good-quality fruity wines. *Grosslage*: *Spiegelberg. Growers: Balbach, Braun, Heyl zu Herrnsheim, G Schneider, Strub, Wehrheim.

Bingen Rhh w (r)
Town at the confluence of the rivers Nahe and Rhein, severely damaged in World War II although some of the old terraced town houses remain. Several large brandy- and wine-producing companies face the Rheingauer *Rüdesheim vineyards across the Rhein. The best-known individual vineyard site is the Binger *Scharlachberg. *Grosslage*: *St Rochuskapelle.

Biologischer Säureabbau
Malolactic fermentation. *See* Apfelsäure.

Birkweiler Rhpf w (r)
Small village on the attractive southern edge of the Pfälzerwald, in an area with several outstandingly good but commercially undervalued estates. *Grosslage*: Königsgarten.

Bischoffingen Baden w r
A village in the heart of the *Kaiserstuhl vineyards devoted to winemaking, with a good, typical Baden village cooperative cellar and an adventuresome, high-class wine producer in Weingut Karl H *Johner. *Grosslage*: *Vulkanfelsen.

Bischof-Klein, Weingut Nahe
Estate of nearly seven hectares with holdings at *Bretzenheim, *Langenlonsheim and *Burg Layen, planted 24 percent Riesling, 21 percent Müller-Thurgau, 15 percent Silvaner. Many awards have been won for the wines, which are 73 percent *lieblich*. Annual production is 5,800 cases, 70 percent sold to private customers.
Address: Naheweinstrasse 62, W-6551 Bretzenheim
Tel: 0671 31301

Bischöflichen Weingüter, Verwaltung der M-S-R
A combination of four estates of ecclesiastical origin, totalling 107

hectares, their vineyards a roll-call of some of the finest of the Mosel-Saar-Ruwer, including Erdener ★Treppchen, Ürziger ★Würzgarten, Trittenheimer ★Apotheke, Kaseler ★Nies'chen and ★Kehrnagel, Ayler ★Kupp, ★Scharzhofberg, Piesporter ★Goldtröpfchen. The vineyards are mainly steep, 97 percent Riesling, with a small plantation of Spätburgunder. The grapes are pressed near the vineyards and the wine is vinified in the central cellar in ★Trier, maturing in wood; 55 percent is *trocken*. Top-quality, elegant and characterful wines, sold all over the world.
Address: Gervasiusstrasse 1, W-5500 Trier
Tel: 0651 43441

Bischofsberg Rhg w
All-Riesling, south-facing, sloping *Einzellage*. One of several good sites at ★Rüdesheim. *Grosslage*: ★Burgweg. Growers: Allendorf, Breuer, Eser, Groenesteyn, von Hessen, Mumm, Nägler, Reinhartshausen, Schloss Schönborn.

Black Forest
See Schwarzwald

Blankenhorn, Weingut Fritz Baden VDP
Estate of 25 hectares in the Bereich ★Markgräflerland, planted 30 percent Gutedel and 25 percent Spätburgunder. Chardonnay was added to the vine varieties in 1991. Around 95 percent of the wine is *trocken*, with good, concentrated flavour.
Address: W-7846 Schliengen
Tel: 07635 1092

Blankenhornsberg Baden
See Freiburg, Staatliches Weinbauinstitut, 'Blankenhornsberg'

Blauer Frühburgunder
See Frühburgunder

Blauer Limberger
See Limberger

Blauer Portugieser
See Portugieser

Blauer Spätburgunder
See Spätburgunder

Blend
See Verschnitt

Blume
Translated literally means 'flower'. As a description of German wine it is positive and refers to the smell of a fresh, balanced and stylish white wine, without any unpleasant overtones or excesses in its make-up. Such a wine is said to have a *schöne* (lovely) *Blume*. A Riesling *Kabinett* from the Mosel, a year after the vintage, might be so described.

Bockenheim Rhpf w (r)
Small town near the Rheinpfalz-Rheinhessen border, with long views over the Rhein plain. Sound, quality wines. *Grosslage:* Grafenstück.

Bocksbeutel
A flagon-shaped green or amber bottle of ancient design used exclusively in Germany for white and red quality wine from Franken and certain areas of north Baden.

Bockstein M-S-R w
Well-known *Einzellage* of the Bereich Saar-Ruwer at ★Ockfen, planted mainly with Riesling – once 24 hectares, now 81 hectares. Stylish wines with a lovely fruity acidity. *Grosslage:* ★Scharzberg. Growers: Fischer, Kesselstatt, Reverchon, Trier Staatliche Weinbaudomäne, Zilliken.

Bodengeschmack
'Taste of the soil'. Certain vineyards and their soils transmit a flavour to the grapes that are grown in them and the flavour is retained when the must becomes wine. Exactly how this happens is not fully understood. Among the wines with a sometimes

pronounced *Bodengeschmack* are some Mosels (slate taste), Nahe wines from ★Traisen and ★Norheim (rhyolite rock) and Franken wines from various soils. In all three, the taste of the soil is regarded as a virtue. *Bodengeschmack* is also known as *Bodenton*. Riesling, in particular, transmits *Bodengeschmack* efficiently.

Bodenheim Rhh w (r)
Small town on the ★Rheinterrasse producing excellent wine from 500 hectares. Some attractive old buildings, including the town hall and old wine cellars. *Grosslage*: ★St Alban.

Bodensee w r
Alias Lake Constance. The vineyards are connected in a somewhat complicated legal way to the regions of Baden, Franken and Württemberg. The steep, high-lying sites are planted with a number of vine varieties including Spätburgunder (frequently made into *Weissherbst*). The Müller-Thurgau from low yields is among the best in Germany. The reflected light and additional heat from the lake help to compensate for a climate of modest warmth in summer.

Bodenton
See Bodengeschmack

Böhlig Rhpf w
Einzellage of nine hectares on mainly level land at ★Wachenheim, making splendid, meaty wines full of strong regional flavour. *Grosslage*: ★Mariengarten. Growers include Bürklin-Wolf.

Bonnet, Weingut-Sektgut Alfred Rhpf
Estate of 25 hectares, belonging to a family of Huguenot descent now in its tenth generation, with holdings at ★Kallstadt (★Stein-acker), ★Bad Dürkheim, ★Forst, ★Wachenheim and other sites. Vine varieties include Riesling (65 percent), plus a wide range of others. The aim is fresh white wines, stored in stainless steel and matured in bottle, and red wines matured in cask. Annual production is 20,800 cases, 45 percent *trocken*, 20 percent exported. Address: Bahnhofstrasse 5, W-6701 Friedelsheim
Tel: 06322 2162

Boppard Mrh w

Riverside town on the Rhein, a major anchorage for pleasure boats and the site of a fine sweep of vineyards – the Bopparder Hamm. Its steep *Einzellagen*, more than 90 percent Riesling, produce racy wines with a good earthy flavour, drunk mainly in the region. *Grosslage*: Gedeonseck.

Botrytis cinerea

See Edelfäule

Botrytiston

Describes the characteristic flavour resulting from *Edelfäule*.

Bottle

Flasche. The typical German wine bottle – ignoring the *Bocksbeutel* of Franken – is tall, slim and elegant and contains 750ml. Since the 18th century, amber-coloured bottles have been used for Rhein wine. Mosel wine has been sold in green bottles for rather longer. In the 1990s many producers are using bottles of foreign (particularly Italian) design or origin for their modern, eye-catching 'products'. There has never been a greater choice of bottle shape and style of label facing the consumer. Clear glass is often used for dry wines, although in the past in Germany it was asssociated mainly with *Weissherbst* and Ruländer. Increasingly, fine sweet wines are sold in 500ml bottles.

Bottle-age

Wines with high acidity (such as Riesling) require more time in bottle to reach their peak of quality than do softer wines (such as Müller-Thurgau). In general, the better the quality the more bottle-age is needed, as these very approximate figures for Riesling's development in bottle show. The first column represents the number of years after the vintage before the wine has reached its peak, the second column shows for how many years thereafter the wine will remain at its best.

QbA, Kabinett	$1\frac{1}{2}$	$1\frac{1}{2}$	Beerenauslese	7	7+
Spätlese	2	2	Eiswein	7	7+
Auslese	5	5	Trockenbeerenauslese	7	7+

These approximate timings can vary widely with different vintages and the conditions under which the wine is stored. Dry wines do not last as long as their medium-sweet equivalents. In spite of these general and rather sweeping comments, well-made, estate-bottled Rieslings of all qualities may give pleasure, and surprise by remaining fresh and attractive, for many more years than those suggested in the table.

Bottle sick

Immediately after bottling a wine will sometimes taste 'tired' and not show at its best. This is said to be the result of the physical disturbance caused by the bottling operation. The malady normally disappears after a few weeks.

Bottling

See Abfüllung

Bötzingen Baden w r

Claims to be the oldest wine-producing community in Baden, with Müller-Thurgau, Spätburgunder and Ruländer the most widely planted vines. *Grosslage*: ★Vulkanfelsen.

Bowlen

Wine cups. Those sold commercially must be based at least 50 percent on wine. If the word 'wine' appears in their description the proportion must reach a minimum of 70 percent. More interesting are the home-made *Bowlen* spiced with woodruff (*Waldmeister*) or those with fruits such as strawberries or peaches. Other ingredients used are sugar, sometimes brandy, and usually sparkling wine added just before serving, well chilled. There are many variations on this very Germanic theme.

Brackenheim-Neipperg-Haberschlacht-Meimsheim eG, Weingärtnergenossenschaft Würt

Cooperative supplied by 270 hectares, planted 21 percent Riesling, 21 percent Trollinger, 12 percent Müllerrebe (Schwarzriesling) and 17 percent Limberger; it is the Limberger for which the area is well known in Germany. Some wines are aged in *barrique*, 70 percent is *halbtrocken*, and a superior range of wines has been developed in

recent years. Annual production is 185,200 cases.
Address: Neippergerstrasse 60, W-7129 Brackenheim
Tel: 07135 4035

Branded wine
See Markenwein

Brandig
'Burnt'. Describes a wine with a high alcohol and a low acid content. This characteristic was very common in wines of the 1959 vintage – a year of excessive heat and drought – but it is sometimes found today in dry wines with more than 13 percent natural alcohol.

Bratenhöfchen M-S-R w
Einzellage at ★Bernkastel producing excellent Riesling. Sometimes a little overshadowed by the more luscious wine of the adjacent ★Graben but nevertheless a top-quality site, whose wines are not overpriced. *Grosslage*: ★Badstube. Growers: Friedrich-Wilhelm-Gymnasium, Kesselstatt, Lauerburg, Pauly-Bergweiler, J J Prüm, St Nikolaus, Vereinigte Hospitien, Wegeler-Deinhard.

Braubach Mrh w
Riverside town, claiming to date from the Stone Age and overlooked by one of Germany's most spectacular castles, the Marksburg. Sound Rieslings from the steepest of sites, not generally as distinguished as those from ★Bacharach upstream. *Grosslage*: Marksburg.

Braun, Weingut Heinrich Rhh VDP
Estate of 30 hectares with holdings at ★Nierstein (including ★Hipping, ★Ölberg, ★Orbel, ★Paterberg, ★Pettenthal, ★Bildstock), ★Oppenheim, ★Ludwigshöhe and ★Dienheim, planted 60 percent Riesling, 15 percent Silvaner. Well known for its cask-matured Rieslings. Half the production is *trocken*.
Address: Glockengasse 9, W-6505 Nierstein
Tel: 06133 5139

Brauneberg M-S-R w
Small village upstream from *Bernkastel. High percentage of Riesling and top-quality wines. *Grosslage*: *Kurfürstlay.

Braune Kupp M-S-R w
Highly rated, small, steep *Einzellage* at *Wiltingen, considered by many to be on a par with nearby *Scharzhofberg. Famous for its Riesling wines of great finesse. *Grosslage*: *Scharzberg. Growers: Gallais, Vereinigte Hospitien.

Braunfels M-S-R w
Steep *Einzellage* on the Saar. Riesling and Müller-Thurgau produce good-quality wines. *Grosslage*: *Scharzberg. Growers: Kesselstatt, Müller-Scharzhof, G-F von Nell, Vereinigte Hospitien, Volxem.

Breisach Baden w r
Small town in south Germany near the Bereich *Kaiserstuhl, known as the home of Europe's largest winery, the *Badischer Winzerkeller.

Breit
Broad. Describes a full-flavoured wine that is low in acidity.

Steep vineyards above Bremm on the Mosel

Bremm M–S–R w (r)
Village of the Bereich ★Zell. Its Calmont *Einzellage* is one of the
steepest (65 percent inclination) in Germany, planted, almost
inevitably, in Riesling. Elegant wines are produced. *Grosslagen*:
Grafschaft, Rosenhang.

Brentano'sche Gutsverwaltung, Baron von Rhg VDP
Estate of 9·3 hectares, family-owned since 1804, with holdings at
★Winkel (including ★Hasensprung, ★Jesuitengarten). Vines are 96
percent Riesling, four percent Spätburgunder. The estate has
romantic associations: its wines were enjoyed by Goethe, Beetho-
ven, von Arnim and his circle, and the attractive estate buildings
include a Goethe museum. The wines are typical of the region:
fruity, fresh and elegant. Annual production is 5,800 cases; 30
percent is exported.
Address: Am Lindenplatz 2, W-6227 Oestrich-Winkel
Tel: 06723 2068

Bretzenheim Nahe w (r)
Village with approximately 100 hectares of vineyard, the home
since 1977 of the central cooperative cellar, the ★Nahe-Winzer
Kellereien, well known locally for its Portugieser red wine,
although the majority of the wines are white. *Grosslage*:
★Kronenberg.

Breuer, Weingut Georg Rhg Charta VDP
Estate of 22 hectares at ★Rüdesheim and ★Rauenthal (sole owners of
the Nonnenberg site). The estate is 70 percent steep slopes, planted
85 percent Riesling. Founder member of ★Charta. Annual production is 7,500 cases of steely, firm wines with good fruit (50 percent is
trocken). An estate with a clear marketing philosophy and the right
high-quality 'product' to back it. Twenty percent is exported.
Address: Geisenheimerstrasse 9, W-6220 Rüdesheim
Tel: 06722 1027

Broker
There are some 400 wine brokers (*Kommissionäre*) who act as links
between grower and buyer. Many broking firms are generations
old and have a formidable knowledge of the vineyard area in which

they operate. They know what the growers have to offer, and their experience of the needs of their customers is the basis on which they survive. Nevertheless, with changes in the structure of the wine trade their role has diminished and they feel themselves an endangered species. At wine auctions in Germany only brokers are allowed to bid and all sales at auctions must, by law, be through them. *See also* Versteigerung.

Brückes Nahe w
Einzellage on mainly sloping land close to *Bad Kreuznach. Its Riesling can produce top-quality, stylish wines in good years. *Grosslage*: *Kronenberg. Growers: August Anheuser, Paul Anheuser, Finkenauer, Plettenberg.

Brudersberg Rhh w
Small *Einzellage* on the *Rheinterrasse near Nierstein which currently overcomes the theoretical disadvantage of young vines through the high quality of the site and a favourable local climate. One of Germany's top vineyards. Sole owner: *Heyl zu Herrnsheim.

Bruderschaft
A brotherhood. There are a number of wine brotherhoods and similar organizations in Germany, supported by wine enthusiasts both in and outside the wine trade, to promote a love and understanding of wine and its culture.

Bruderschaft M-S-R w
Steep *Einzellage* of some 250 hectares at *Klüsserath, not far from *Trier, with a high proportion of Riesling. Much good wine is made, though little that compares with the finest from villages such as *Piesport or *Bernkastel. *Grosslage*: *St Michael. Growers: Friedrich-Wilhelm-Gymnasium, Krebs-Matheus-Lehnert.

Brut
The French word is also used in Germany to describe a sparkling wine with less than 15 grams per litre sugar which will therefore taste dry or very dry depending on the balance of its other constituents. About two percent of German sparkling wine is *brut*.

Brutsekt
Written as one word, *Brutsekt* is the term given to sparkling wine when it has passed through its second fermentation and has not yet had a final sweetening of beet sugar and wine.

Buhl, Weingut Reichsrat von Rhpf VDP
Estate with 54 hectares of vineyards that cover parts of most of the best sites in *Forst, *Deidesheim and *Ruppertsberg. Annual production is 35,800 cases. Fifty percent of the wine is *trocken*; 45 percent is exported.
Address: Weinstrasse 16, W-6705 Deidesheim
Tel: 06326 1851

Bühlertal r w
Small village overlooked by the steep slopes of the Schwarzwald and vineyards planted mainly in Spätburgunder and Riesling. *Grosslage*: Schloss Rodeck.

Bukett
The 'smell' (or 'bouquet') of a wine.

Bukettsorten
Collective noun covering vines that produce wine with a powerful bouquet, such as Scheurebe or Morio-Muskat. The attraction for the consumer of a strongly scented wine is often as a brief change from the more neutral Riesling or Silvaner. Low-grade scented wines tend to cloy quickly, in a way that those with a strong bouquet from varieties such as Traminer and Scheurebe do not. The popularity of the cheaper versions is steadily declining.

Bullay M-S-R w
Typical Lower Mosel village near *Zell with a high proportion of Riesling on steep sites. *Grosslage*: Grafschaft.

Bundesweinprämierung
National wine competition run by the *Deutsche Landwirtschaft Gesellschaft (DLG), open to QbA and QmP estate-bottlings that have successfully passed the regional wine competitions. In 1991 the Bundesweinprämierung was open to wines of the '87, '88 and '89

vintages. 5,516 wines were entered by 902 producers. 2,421 received a *Grosser Preis* (First Prize), 1,952 a *Silberner Preis* (Second Prize) and 712 a *Bronzener Preis* (Third Prize).

Burg
Castle or fortress. EC law allows the word *Burg* to be used as part of a wine name if the wine is made solely from grapes grown and vinified by the estate owned by the *Burg*. In practice, it usually appears on a label as part of a village or community name, such as ★Burg Layen.

Burg Hornberg, Weingut & Schlosskellerei der Güterverwaltung Würt VDP
The 14-hectare wine estate of Burg Hornberg, planted 21 percent Müller-Thurgau, 14 percent each Müllerebe (Schwarzriesling) and Riesling, plus Weissburgunder, Samtrot and others. The romantic castle was the home of Götz von Berlichingen, the one-handed soldier of fortune immortalized in Goethe's play. Annual production is 6,700 cases, of which 60 percent is *trocken*; 20 percent is exported.
Address: Burg Hornberg, W-6951 Neckarzimmern
Tel: 06261 5001

Burg Layen Nahe w
Small wine village just south of ★Bingen, the home of a number of estates whose best sites are at nearby ★Dorsheim. *Grosslage*: ★Schlosskapelle.

Burgberg Nahe w
Small, steep *Einzellage* at ★Dorsheim near ★Bingen, producing well-balanced Rieslings. *Grosslage*: ★Schlosskapelle. Growers: Kruger-Rumpf, Niederhausen-Schlossböckelheim Staatliche Weinbaudomäne.

Burgeff & Co GmbH
One of the oldest sparkling-wine companies in Germany, founded in 1836, now owned by Seagram. Leading brands are Burgeff Grün and Schloss Hochheim.
Address: W-6203 Hochheim

Bürgermeister

Mayor. In Rheinland-Pfalz the mayor of a community heads the committee that decides when the various stages of the harvest may start. Found in the titles of some estates, such as Weingut Bürgermeister Anton Balbach Erben.

Bürgerspital zum Heiligen Geist Weingut Franken VDP

Great Würzburg estate, with 110 hectares planted with Riesling (30 percent), Silvaner and Müller-Thurgau (20 percent each), plus other varieties including Spätburgunder, producing on average 83,300 cases annually. The estate, a charitable institution dating from 1319, supports an old people's home and has a wine bar with places for 425 guests. Its cask cellar is the largest in Germany, with a capacity of 800,000 litres. Winemaking is top quality. Sixty-five percent of the wine is *trocken*; five percent is exported.
Address: Theaterstrasse 19, W-8700 Würzburg
Tel: 0931 3503–0

Burggarten, Weingut am Rhpf

Estate of 5·5 hectares on flat terrain outside *Neustadt, planted 22 percent Weissburgunder, 20 percent Silvaner, and 20 percent Riesling. Modern wines, often with a high alcohol content, including a Ruländer *Beerenauslese* with 16 percent actual alcohol. Eighty percent is *trocken* and some wines are *barrique*-aged. Eighty percent is sold to private customers in Germany.
Address: Burggarten 7, W-6730 Neustadt
Tel: 06327 2770

Bürgstadt Franken w r

Small town by the *Main known for the quality of its serious, tannic red Spätburgunder wine, particularly that from Weingut Rudolf *Fürst. No *Grosslage*.

Burgunder

See Frühburgunder, Grauburgunder, Spätburgunder and Weissburgunder

Burgweg Franken w

Small *Grosslage* that includes the vineyards of *Iphofen.

Burgweg Nahe w
Grosslage of about 900 hectares including top-quality sites such as Schlossböckelheimer ★Kupfergrube and the two-hectare Traiser ★Bastei, as well as some rather ordinary vineyards. The best sites are 100 percent Riesling, though much Silvaner is also still found. The wine often has a strong flavour given to it by volcanic soil.

Burgweg Rhg w (r)
Grosslage of a little under 700 hectares, oddly split in two at the western end of the Rheingau by the smaller ★Steil *Grosslage* in ★Assmannshausen. Wines sold under the name Burgweg are not the cheapest – no Rheingau wine is or should be. When made from Riesling they are full-flavoured, and benefit from a year's bottle-age or more, depending on the quality category.

Burkheim Baden w r
Impressive hilltop village with the usual range of Bereich ★Kaiserstuhl wines sold by the local cooperative cellar and an excellent estate, Weingut ★Bercher. *Grosslage*: ★Vulkanfelsen.

Burkheim, Winzergenossenschaft eG Baden
Village cooperative receiving grapes from 128 hectares, planted 33 percent Müller-Thurgau, 27 percent Ruländer, 27 percent Spätburgunder, plus others. The wines are listed by vine variety and include two series, made from older vines and low yields.
Address: Winzerstrasse 8, W-7818 Vogtsburg-Burkheim
Tel: 07662 725

Bürklin-Wolf, Weingut Dr Rhpf VDP
Great family estate, partly 16th-century, with 100 hectares of top-quality sites at ★Wachenheim, ★Forst, ★Deidesheim and ★Ruppertsberg, planted 75 percent Riesling, 12 percent Müller-Thurgau, plus some Spätburgunder. Annual production is 83,300 cases of wine and *Sekt*. Maturation is in wood. The list includes many fine wines and a premium range of *trocken* Riesling – 'Selection Geheimrat Dr Albert Bürklin'. Sixty-five percent of the wine is dry, with some reds *barrique*-aged. Twenty percent is exported.
Address: Weinstrasse 65, W-6706 Wachenheim
Tel: 06322 8955

Buschenschank
See Strausswirtschaft

Buscher, Weingut Jean Rhh
Enterprising 16-hectare estate. Holdings are all at ★Bechtheim, with 23 percent Riesling, 12 percent Spätburgunder, ten percent Kerner. A superior series of wines is marketed as 'Edition Jean Buscher'; and some of the dry reds are matured in oak from the Odenwald. Fifty-five percent of the total production of 12,500 cases is *trocken*, and sales are 75 percent to the consumer.
Address: Wormser Strasse 4, W-6521 Bechtheim
Tel: 06242 872

Cabinet
See Kabinett

Capsule
A tight-fitting cap enclosing the mouth and part of the neck of a bottle, originally intended to protect the cork. The main job of a capsule today is to complete the 'dressing' of a bottle, but some estates use different length and colour of capsule to denote different qualities of wine. *See also* Lack.

Case
Until the early 1960s German bottled wine was exported in wooden cases, each holding 12 bottles horizontally packed in straw. Today the most usual form of packing is the vertically loaded six- or 12-bottle carton, in which the contents should be stored neck downwards. In this book, the term 'case' when used as a measure of quantity means 12 × 750ml bottles, or nine litres.

Castell Franken w (r)
Village surrounded by vineyards on the slopes of the Steigerwald, producing excellent dry wine from Silvaner and Müller-Thurgau. Most of the holdings are owned by the Castell'sches Domänenamt *(see next entry)*.

Castell'sches Domänenamt, Fürstlich Franken VDP
Great estate on the edge of the Steigerwald, which celebrated its

300th anniversary in 1991. The family of the owner, Fürst zu Castell-Castell, consists of bankers, farmers and foresters as well as vine growers. Sixty-four hectares of vineyards include 30 percent Müller-Thurgau, 25 percent Silvaner, eight percent Kerner, six percent Rieslaner – the last a speciality. Eight *Einzellagen* at Castell and Neundorf are in sole ownership. The wines can be described as earthy and spicy, with good acidity. Annual production is approximately 41,700 cases, five percent exported. The estate is also senior partner in the Erzeugergemeinschaft Steigerwald eV, making wine from its members' 78 hectares, greatly increasing the throughput of its own impressive cellar. Ninety percent of all the wine is *fränkisch trocken*.

Address: Schlossplatz 5, W-8711 Castell

Tel: 09325 601–70

Centgericht Hess Berg w

Einzellage of about 17 hectares solely owned by the Staatsweingut ★Bergstrasse, well known in the region for its Riesling and Ruländer wines – particularly the *Eisweine. Grosslage*: Schlossberg.

Chaptalization

The addition of sugar to must or wine to increase the alcohol level (*see* Anreicherung). A practice developed by Jean Antoine Chaptal (1756–1852) in France.

Chardonnay

Classified as a 'permitted' vine variety for ★Baden-Württemberg and ★Rheinland-Pfalz in 1991 by the EC. Until German Chardonnay clones have completed their trials in some years' time, quality wine can be produced from imported Chardonnay vines only, wine from German clones having to be sold as table wine. It is arguable that the good vineyard sites that Chardonnay needs in order to flourish would be better planted in Riesling: Germany's Riesling wine is incomparable but her Chardonnay is likely to have many rivals.

Charmat-Verfahren

A technique for producing sparkling wine, developed in the 19th century by the French scientist Eugène Charmat. The secondary, sparkle-producing fermentation takes place in bulk instead of in bottle. Today more than 90 percent of German-made sparkling wine is tank-fermented. *See also* Flaschengärung.

Charta

An association of Rheingau growers, founded in October 1984, with rules for the production of its wine that are stricter than those of the 1971 Wine Law. Wine must be 100 percent Riesling, estate-bottled in a special tall, embossed bottle, of enhanced must weight depending on the quality category, and contain between nine and 13 grams per litre residual sugar for all wines up to and including *Spätlese*. The total acid content must be at least 8 grams per litre for QbA and *Kabinett* wines and 7·5 grams per litre for *Spätlesen*. Minimum must weights are 65° for QbA, 78° for *Kabinett* and 88° for *Spätlesen*, measured on the Oechsle scale. The wines must be accepted by the association's tasting panel, which in 1990 passed 184 out of 319 wines. As from the 1991 vintage, Charta wines are not released for sale until 18 months after the vintage.

Christmann, Weingut Arnold Rhpf

Eleven-hectare estate with holdings at ★Gimmeldingen, Königs-bach and ★Ruppertsberg (★Reiterpfad, ★Linsenbusch) planted 62 percent in Riesling. Eighty-five percent of the wine is *trocken*. The 1983 Riesling *Trockenbeerenauslese* had the amazingly high must weight of 243° Oechsle. Annual production is 8,300 cases, five

percent exported.
Address: Peter Koch Strasse 43, Gimmeldingen, W-6730 Neustadt
Tel: 06321 66039

Christoffel Jr, Weingut Jos M-S-R
Estate of 2·8 hectares with holdings at Erden (★Prälat, ★Treppchen),
Ürzig (★Würzgarten), Wehlen (★Sonnenuhr) and Graach (★Dom-
probst). Entirely Riesling. Fine, stylish wines with a natural
sweetness are a speciality.
Address: Moselufer 1–3, W-5564 Ürzig
Tel: 06532 2113

Christus in der Kelter
Christ in the wine press. The representation of Christ in the wine
press has been given many different symbolic and allegoric
meanings in Germany since the 12th century, apart from the
obvious eucharistic connection. There is a fine example in the
Heiligkreuzkapelle above the vineyards of ★Ediger-Eller.

Cie
Kompanie. Company, as in Emil Hammel & Cie.

Cleebronn-Güglingen-Frauenzimmern eG,
Weingärtnergenossenschaft Würt
Cooperative cellar with 300 hectares in the Bereich Württemberg-
isch Unterland southwest of ★Heilbronn. Most of the grapes come
from the large and often steep Michaelsberg site, planted with 25
percent Riesling, 20 percent Müllerrebe (Schwarzriesling) and a
host of other traditional and new vines. In the usual Württemberg
way, 70 percent of the wine (including the reds) is *halbtrocken*.
Annual production is 183,300 cases, sold exclusively in Germany.
Address: Ranspacherstrasse 1, W-7121 Cleebronn
Tel: 07135 5059

Clevner
See Frühburgunder, Traminer

Coblenz
See Koblenz

Cochem M-S-R
Strikingly pretty town and tourist centre (population 6,000) on the
Mosel, in the Bereich ★Zell, overlooked by a dramatically situated
castle. Stylish, racy Rieslings. *Grosslagen*: ★Goldbäumchen,
Rosenhang.

Constance, Lake
See Bodensee

Cooperative cellar
See Winzergenossenschaft

Crusius, Weingut Hans & Peter Nahe VDP
Family-run estate with 9·5 hectares of prime sites including Traiser
★Bastei, ★Rotenfels and Kickelskopf, ★Norheimer Klosterberg,
Schlossböckelheimer ★Felsenberg and at Niederhausen. Seventy-
five percent Riesling, ten percent Müller-Thurgau, ten percent
Weissburgunder, Spätburgunder (for rosé wine). Stylish, firm,
characterful wines, traditionally matured in cask and made under
personal family supervision to a high standard. Fifty percent is

NAHE
1990er
Schloßböckelheimer Felsenberg
Riesling Auslese
– HALBTROCKEN –
alc. 12,0% vol   QUALITÄTSWEIN MIT PRÄDIKAT   750 ml
Erzeugerabfüllung – Produce of Germany – A. P. Nr. 1 775 009 012 91
Weingut Hans Crusius u. Sohn
D-6551 Traisen/Nahe

trocken. Annual production is 7,500 cases, 80 percent sold to private
customers, ten percent exported.
Address: Hauptstrasse 2, W-6551 Traisen
Tel: 0671 33953

Cuvée

Defined under EC law as must or wine, or a blend of different musts or wines, destined to be converted into sparkling wine. The making of a successful *cuvée* requires organized tasting ability of a very high order. It is exacting work from which the palate can gain little pleasure; the satisfaction lies in the consistency of the end result. Some producers, particularly cooperative cellars, have started to market high-quality *cuvées* of still wine from more than one grape variety, in the Bordeaux manner.

Dachsberg Rhg w

Einzellage of 52 hectares above the vineyards of *Schloss Vollrads, producing light wines with fine acidity. *Grosslage*: *Erntebringer. Growers: Allendorf, Brentano, Mumm.

Dahlem Erben KG, Weingutsverwaltung Sanitätsrat Dr Rhh

Estate dating back to 1702, with holdings in 27 hectares at *Oppenheim (including *Sackträger, *Kreuz), *Dienheim and *Guntersblum. Thirty-five percent Riesling, 20 percent Silvaner, 18 percent Müller-Thurgau. Many award-winning wines. Annual production is 19,200 cases, 55 percent *lieblich*, 25 percent exported. Address: Rathofstrasse 21–25, W-6504 Oppenheim
Tel: 06133 2001

Daubhaus Rhg w

Grosslage covering more than 356 hectares at the eastern end of the Rheingau on the river Main, often clearly visible when flying into Frankfurt Airport. Its best-known wine-producing village is *Hochheim. A Rheingau *Grosslage* wine will be a paler reflection of the best wines produced from individual sites within the *Grosslage*. Nevertheless, the quality of wine from the Daubhaus is high. It will probably be more earthy than wine from the central part of the region.

Dauerbegrünung

The practice of growing grasses and clover between vine rows, mainly as a protection against erosion and the compacting of soil by machinery.

Dautel, Weingut Ernst Würt

Eight-hectare estate at Bönnigheim and Meimsheim in the centre of Württemberg, planted 18 percent Riesling, 15 percent Trollinger, 14 percent Müllerrebe (Schwarzriesling), 13 percent Limberger. All the wines are *trocken* (unusual for Württemberg). Some reds and a *Rotling* are *barrique*-aged, and a Riesling is bottled in the Muscadet manner, *sur lie*, without having been removed from the deposit left by fermentation. Annual production is 5,800 cases.

Address: Lauerweg 55, W-7124 Bönnigheim

Tel: 07143 21719

Dautenpflänzer Nahe w

Six-hectare *Einzellage* of the Lower Nahe at *Münster-Sarmsheim. The wines, mainly Riesling, are full-bodied and meaty. *Grosslage*: *Schlosskapelle. Growers: Adelseck, Kruger-Rumpf, Niederhausen-Schlossböckelheim Staatliche Weinbaudomäne.

Deacidification

A relatively high acid content is expected and appreciated in German wines, particularly in those from the northern regions. However, in some years when the grapes are not fully ripe the acidity in the cheaper wines is too high and has to be lowered artificially. Calcium carbonate is used to achieve a chemical deacidification which complements the natural reduction in acidity that normally occurs in winemaking; or, in years of feeble sunshine when the malic acid is particularly high, a double-salt called Acidex is used. The last nationwide poor vintage was 1972, and even in this year many enjoyable wines were produced with the aid of Acidex. In the state of *Rheinland-Pfalz and in the Rheingau, tartaric acid may be added to Riesling and Elbling to reduce acidity by what is known as the Malitex process. Some winemakers rely on malolactic fermentation to soften the acidity in red wine. *See* Apfelsäure.

Deckrotwein

Dark-coloured wine (possibly from Dunkelfelder or Dornfelder) used to deepen the colour of a pale wine of the same quality category. Good producers try to rely on healthy grapes to obtain the required depth of colour, and thus manage without Deckrotwein.

Deidesheim Rhpf w

Attractive small town, recognized for centuries both in Germany and abroad as a source of distinguished wine and the home of a number of fine estates. A high proportion of Riesling in top-quality sites: *Grainhübel, *Herrgottsacker, *Hohenmorgen, *Kieselberg, *Langenmorgen, *Leinhöhle. Two *Grosslagen*: *Mariengarten, *Schnepfenflug an der Weinstrasse.

Deidesheim eG, Winzerverein Rhpf

Cooperative with 477 members in the well-known wine villages of *Deidesheim, *Forst and *Ruppertsberg, with 213 hectares. Vines are 75 percent Riesling, 12 percent Müller-Thurgau. There is a premium range of Riesling wine of which the cooperative has an above average amount for the region.
Address: Prinz-Rupprecht-Strasse 8, W-6705 Deidesheim
Tel: 06326 6016

Deinhard & Co KGaA

Innovative and interesting wine merchant and exporter, founded in the 18th century. Deinhard was one of the earliest producers of sparkling wine in Germany, and at the end of the 19th century acquired its first vineyards. Since then, well-packaged ranges of other wines have been added. Ten percent of the output is *trocken*. Old-established brands are the sparkling wines Lila Imperial, and Deinhard Cabinet and the Mosel still wine, Green Label. *See also* Wegeler-Deinhard.
Address: Deinhard Platz 3, W-5400 Koblenz
Tel: 0261 1040

Deinhard, Weingut Dr Rhpf VDP

Estate dating from the mid-18th century, separate from but occupying the same premises as the Gutsverwaltung *Wegeler-Deinhard Deidesheim. Forty hectares in *Deidesheim (*Grainhübel, *Herrgottsacker, *Kieselberg, *Leinhöhle), *Forst (*Jesuitengarten), *Haardt, *Mussbach and *Ruppertsberg (*Reiterpfad). Vines are 80 percent Riesling, with small amounts of Müller-Thurgau, Scheurebe, Kerner and others. The elegant wines reflect clearly the variations brought about by site, soil and vine variety. Annual production is 25,000 cases; 45 percent is dry.

Address: Weinstrasse 10, W-6705 Deidesheim
Tel: 06325 221

Dellchen Nahe w
Steep, 7·3-hectare *Einzellage* at *Norheim that can produce
absolutely top-quality Riesling wines of character with an attract-
ive flavour that comes from the soil. *Grosslage*: *Burgweg.
Growers: August Anheuser, Paul Anheuser, Bad Kreuznach
Staatsweingut.

Dernau Ahr r w
A village of immensely steep vineyards with an unusually warm
local climate. Noted for the quality of the Spät- and Frühburgunder
and Riesling wines of Weingut *Meyer-Näkel. *Grosslage*:
Klosterberg.

Deutelsberg Rhg w
Grosslage of some 253 hectares in the neighbourhood of *Hattenheim, including part of the Mariannenau island. The name
Deutelsberg is normally used for the lesser wines, but Rieslings
from competent producers will still be well-balanced, stylish,
good-quality wines.

Deutsche Landwirtschaft Gesellschaft (DLG)
Society founded in 1885 along the lines of the Royal Agricultural
Society of Great Britain, to promote good farming practices.
Today the society awards three types of Deutsches Weinsiegel
(wine seal): a yellow seal for dry wines, a green for medium-dry,
and a red for others that meet with its approval. (The standards set
by the DLG tasting panels are higher than those of the *Amtliche
Prufüng authorities.) The DLG also holds an annual national wine
competition, open to quality (QbA and QmP) wines that have
obtained their AP number and have succeeded in an official regional
competition. DLG awards are familiar to German consumers and
valued by many bottlers. *See* Bundesweinprämierung.

Deutsche Weinstrasse
See Weinstrasse

Deutscher Sekt
Quality sparkling wine made from grapes grown in Germany, forming just over ten percent of German sparkling wine production.

Deutscher Tafelwein (DTW)
German table wine. Quality category of German wine, below QbA, with an upper section called *Landwein*. The vineyard area from which a DTW may originate is exactly the same as that which may produce quality wine. There are no areas that may produce table wine only. Whereas a high proportion of French and Italian wine is classified as table wine, only approximately five percent of the total German wine harvest falls into this category. A DTW does not undergo an examination by the AP authorities and therefore does not show an AP number on the label. It must be made from 100 percent German-grown grapes.

Deutsches Eck, Erzeugergemeinschaft M–S–R
A producers' association of 88 members based on the Mosel near ★Koblenz, whose grapes are grown and wines are made to far stricter technical standards than those required by law. They are bottled by estates individually, and considerable quantities of the members' grapes are supplied to merchants ★Deinhard & Co.

Deutsches Weinsiegel
See Deutsche Landwirtschaft Gesellschaft (DLG)

Deutsches Weintor eG, Gebiets-Winzergenossenchaft Rhpf
Huge cooperative cellar near the French border with some 1,300 members delivering grapes from 1,070 hectares of the Bereich ★Südliche Weinstrasse. Storage capacity is 42 million litres, and the cellar is well equipped to produce vast quantities of well-made, agreeable, inexpensive wines, as well as some of better quality. The Dornfelder is well known, and some is aged in *barrique*. The marketing and presentation of the cooperative's wines is modern and professional.
Address: W-6741 Ilbesheim
Tel: 06341 38150

Dexheim Rhh w
Village which probably benefits from having one large *Einzellage* called 'Doktor', a name (but not spelling) it shares with the famous ★Doctor at Bernkastel on the Mosel. *Grosslage*: ★Gutes Domtal.

Dezent
Describes a bouquet or aroma that is restrained, but refined and characteristic.

Dhron M-S-R w
Charmingly situated village linked with ★Neumagen, the source of many Roman relics, forming one community of some 3,000 inhabitants near ★Piesport, with whom it shares some sites. The steep vineyards are planted mainly with Riesling, producing full-flavoured, stylish wines. *Grosslage*: ★Michelsberg.

Diabetikerwein
Diabetes is such a common illness in Germany that it has proved profitable to produce diabetic wines on a wide scale. They should be drunk by genuine diabetics only after medical approval is given. German diabetic wine is subject to a number of restrictions and may contain a maximum of 4 grams per litre residual sugar, 40 milligrams per litre free sulphur dioxide and 12 percent alcohol. Since 1970 the DLG has awarded a yellow seal to diabetic wines that meet its standards, covering about six million bottles annually.

Diedesfeld Rhpf w r
Village just south of ★Neustadt. Müller-Thurgau and Portugieser produce the good-quality wines expected of a Mittelhaardt village; Riesling does even better. *Grosslagen*: Rebstöckel, Pfaffengrund.

Diefenhardt, Weingut Rhg Charta
Estate dating from 1917 but with a 300-year-old cask cellar. Fifteen hectares in ★Eltville, ★Martinsthal and ★Rauenthal, 88 percent Riesling, eight percent Spätburgunder, all on sloping ground. Typical, firm Rheingauer wine. Annual production is 9,500 cases, 50 percent *trocken*, 16 percent exported.
Address: Hauptstrasse 9–11, W-6228 Eltville-Martinsthal
Tel: 06123 71490

Diel, Schlossgut Nahe VDP
Estate owned by the Diel family since 1802, with 12·5 hectares in
★Burg Layen and ★Dorsheim, 70 percent Riesling. The estate has its
own view of winemaking and its outstanding wines are vigorously
marketed at (for Germany) high prices. The dry wines are sold
mainly as QbA or table wine, regardless of their high must weights;
some are *barrique*-aged. Diel is particularly well represented in top
German restaurants, to which approximately 40 percent of the
production is sold.
Address: W-6531 Burg Layen
Tel: 06721 45045

Dienheim Rhh w
★Rheinterrasse village with 550 hectares of vineyards, possibly a
little overshadowed by its neighbour ★Oppenheim, but producing
good, full Riesling and Silvaner wines with grapy characteristics,
well developed. *Grosslagen*: ★Güldenmorgen, ★Krötenbrunnen.

Dirmstein Rhpf w (r)
Attractive old town near the Rheinhessen with approximately 250
hectares of vineyards, planted some 50 percent in Silvaner and
Riesling. Best known in connection with the name of the local
Grosslage, ★Schwarzerde.

DLG
See Deutsche Landwirtschaft Gesellschaft

Doctor M-S-R w
Outstanding *Einzellage* of 3·2 hectares rising steeply above ★Bernkastel. Site, soil and Riesling vine complement each other perfectly. The must weights are usually the heaviest in Bernkastel; the wine is positive, slaty, needing time to show its true quality. One of the best-known *Einzellagen* in Germany. *Grosslage*: ★Badstube. Growers: Heidemanns-Bergweiler, Lauerburg, Thanisch-Knabben, Thanisch-Müller-Burggraeff, Wegeler-Deinhard.

Doktor Rhh w
Einzellage at ★Dexheim in the *Grosslage* ★Gutes Domtal.

Domäne
Domain. Name given to estates (*Weingüter*) owned by old noble families (such as Domänenweingut Schloss Schönborn) or by the Federal States (such as Staatliche Weinbaudomäne Niederhausen-Schlossböckelheim). Many of the state-owned *Domänen* have a training and experimental role as well as operating commercially as winemakers. The word *Domäne* may only appear on a label if the wine was made by the domain exclusively from grapes grown on its own estate.

Domänenamt
Estate office. Found in the title of Fürstlich Castell'sches Domänenamt.

Domblick Rhh w (r)
Grosslage of more than 800 hectares in south Rheinhessen, bordering on the Rheinpfalz. Vineyards vary from level to steep, and face all points of the compass except east. The wines can have a rather strong flavour that comes from the mainly clay soil. On a clear day, from the upper parts of the area, one has a view (*Blick*) of the cathedral (*Dom*) of Worms in the distance – hence *Domblick*.

Domdechaney Rhg w
Probably the best *Einzellage* at the well-known winemaking

community of ★Hochheim, producing full-bodied Riesling wines with big flavour and great elegance. *Grosslage:* ★Daubhaus. Growers: Aschrott, Staatsweingut Eltville, Weingut der Stadt Frankfurt, Ress, Schloss Schönborn, Werner.

Domherr Rhh w
Grosslage in central Rheinhessen covering more than 1,700 hectares. The terrain is mostly sloping or steep, producing good-quality but usually not the finest wine, displaying the traditional Rheinhessen characteristics: soft, agreeable, pleasant fruit flavour. The cathedral (*Dom*) at nearby ★Mainz used to own much land in the area, hence the origin of the name *Domherr* (Canon of the Cathedral).

Domina
High-yielding red grape crossing of Portugieser × Spätburgunder from ★Geilweilerhof, covering 56 hectares, of which 33 hectares are in Franken. Acidity is high, and the tannic wine needs time to develop in cask. When blended with Spätburgunder the result can be potent, well structured and complex.

Domprobst M-S-R w (r)
Distinguished, steep, Riesling *Einzellage* at ★Graach with a small plantation of Spätburgunder. The wine is usually crisper than that from the neighbouring Graacher ★Himmelreich, and less full-bodied. Sometimes spelt 'Dompropst'. *Grosslage:* ★Münzlay.

Growers: Christoffel, Friedrich-Wilhelm-Gymnasium, Heide-manns-Bergweiler, Kees-Kieren, Kesselstatt, J J Prüm, S A Prüm, M F Richter, Selbach-Oster, Studert-Prüm, Thanisch-Knabben, Vereinigte Hospitien, Wegeler-Deinhard, Weins-Prum.

Domthal Rhh
Once a *Gattungslagename*, discarded in 1971. *See also* Gutes Domtal.

Dönnhof, Weingut Hermann Nahe VDP
Nine-hectare estate that came to the fore in the 1980s, with holdings at *Niederhausen (*Hermannshöhle), *Schlossböckelheim (*Fel-senberg), *Oberhausen (sole ownership of Brücke), and at *Bad Kreuznach, planted 75 percent Riesling, Ruländer (Grauburg-under) and others. The wines are characterful, superbly elegant, and well differentiated.
Address: Bahnhofstrasse 11, W-6551 Oberhausen
Tel: 06755 263

Doosberg Rhg
Large *Einzellage* of 153 hectares on mainly level land at *Oestrich that makes good-quality, classic Riesling wines. *Grosslage*: *Gottes-thal. Growers: Allendorf, Altenkirch, Eser, Winzergenossenschaft Hallgarten, Querbach, Ress, Schloss Schönborn, Wegeler-Deinhard.

Dörflinger, Weingut Hermann Baden
Estate of 7·5 hectares with varieties such as the Markgräflerland favourite Gutedel (50 percent), Spätburgunder (14 percent), Müller-Thurgau (nine percent). All the wines are *trocken* and fully fermented, with pronounced acidity.
Address: Mühlenstrasse 7, W-7840 Müllheim
Tel: 07631 2207

Dornfelder
Red grape variety, Helfensteiner (Frühburgunder × Trollinger) × Heroldrebe (Portugieser × Limberger); a very successful crossing from the Württemberg state viticultural institute at *Weinsberg, covering 926 hectares, 79 percent in the Rheinpfalz and Rheinhess-en. From a restricted yield the wine is splendidly dark-coloured,

and ages well in *barrique*. A wine with a good future if poor and cheap versions do not spoil its reputation.

Dorsheim Nahe w
One of the best wine-producing villages of the Lower Nahe, near ★Bingen in the Bereich ★Kreuznach. Outstanding meaty Rieslings from steep sites, usually cheaper than the top-quality wines of the Bereich ★Schloss Böckelheim further south. *Grosslage*: ★Schlosskapelle.

Drathen & Co KB, Ewald Theod M-S-R
Small estate of seven hectares, also internationally known as wine merchants exporting considerable quantities of inexpensive German wine and EC table wine. Founded in 1860, the estate holdings are at ★Neef, ★Alf and ★Bullay.
Address: W-5584 Alf
Tel: 06542 8010

Dreikönigswein
Three Kings Wine. A description that until 1971 could be given to *Eiswein* gathered on January 6 following the main October/November harvest. The word *Dreikönigswein* may no longer appear on the bottle label, although reference to it may be made in advertising material. In practice, it is a rather charming description that now belongs to the past.

Dry
See Trocken

DTW
See Deutscher Tafelwein

Duftig
Finely scented.

Dunkelfelder
Crossing of unknown parentage, planted in 116 hectares. The flesh of the grapes is red and their very dark-coloured wine is used mainly for blending and red *Süssreserve*.

Dünn
Thin, light in alcohol and short of extract.

Durbach Baden w (r)
Attractive village near Offenburg, overlooked by steep vineyards, claiming the highest proportion of Traminer (Clevner) of any wine village in Germany. Well known for its Riesling (Klingelberger), it produces powerful wines and is the home of many good private estates. *Grosslage*: Fürsteneck.

Durchgegoren
Fermented through. A term used to describe wines in which no fermentable sugar remains. Many German wines up to and sometimes including *Auslesen* are stored in bulk *durchgegoren*, although the practice is declining on a number of estates. It avoids the risk of further fermentation and allows a lower sulphur dioxide content. Such wines will usually be sweetened with *Süssreserve* shortly before bottling.

Dürrenzimmern-Stockheim eG,
Weingärtnergenossenschaft Würt
Cooperative south of *Heilbronn supplied by 202 hectares of vineyards planted 24 percent Riesling, 19 percent Limberger and 20 percent Trollinger. Annual production is equivalent to 188,900 cases; 70 percent is *halbtrocken*.
Address: Meimsheimerstrasse 11–13, W-7129 Brackenheim-Dürrenzimmern
Tel: 07135 4078

Duttweiler Rhpf w (r)
Ortsteil of *Neustadt with a good reputation for powerful Weissburgunder and Riesling wines, thanks to a large extent to the efforts of the *Bergdolt estate. *Grosslage*: Pfaffengrund.

Eberbach Rhg
See Kloster Eberbach

Eberstadt eG, Weingärtnergenossenschaft Würt
Modern cooperative northeast of *Heilbronn supplied with grapes

from 160 hectares planted 30 percent Riesling, 30 percent Trollinger, 15 percent Limberger, 12 percent Müllerrebe (Schwarzriesling). The full modern range of Württemberg wines is offered, including a premium range and wines aged in *barrique*. Annual production is 83,300 cases, 60 percent *halbtrocken*, two percent exported.

Address: Lennacherstrasse 25, W-7101 Eberstadt
Tel: 07134 1688

Eckig

Angular. Describes an unbalanced wine with over-accentuated constituents, particularly acidity.

Edelfäule

Noble rot: a fungus that in moist and mild conditions sometimes attacks grapes. If the grapes are already ripe the result is beneficial. The grapes shrivel and the water, sugar and acid content is reduced; but the loss of acids is proportionally greater than that of sugar. The result is highly concentrated juice. Wine made from such grapes will normally have an enhanced must weight. In white wine the colour will be deeper and more golden than usual; in red wine there is a browning and loss of colour. The bouquet of the grape variety is to a greater or lesser extent replaced by an aroma reminiscent of honey. The impression of sweetness of flavour is increased, and the wine tastes smoother and sometimes also a little honeyed. A Riesling *Beerenauslese* will nearly always be made from *Edelfäule* grapes. 1953, 1967, 1975 and 1989 were years in which a considerable amount of *Edelfäule* occurred. In hot, dry years such as 1959 the high general level of ripeness partly compensates for a limited amount of *Edelfäule*.

Edelfirnig

Describes an old wine that carries its years well. The opposite of *firnig*.

Edelsüsse

Noble sweetness. Term for the sweetness left in a wine of high quality as a result of incomplete fermentation, as is the case with *Auslesen*, *Beerenauslesen* or *Trockenbeerenauslesen*. It is often the result of grapes being attacked by *Edelfäule* (noble rot) and will contain enhanced amounts of fructose and glycerin. *Auslesen* to which *Süssreserve* has been added should not, however, be described as *edelsüss*.

Edenkoben Rhpf w (r)

Small but locally important wine town in the Bereich ★Südliche Weinstrasse. More than 500 hectares of vineyards, sprinkled with fig and almond trees, are planted with a wide range of varieties including Riesling, Müller-Thurgau and Silvaner. Good, sound, inexpensive wines. Interesting ★Weinlehrpfad. *Grosslage*: Schloss Ludwigshöhe.

Ediger-Eller M-S-R w

Two ancient and attractive villages linked in the Bereich ★Zell, making elegant fruity wines. *Grosslagen*: Rosenhang and Grafschaft.

eG

Eingetragene Genossenschaft. Registered Cooperative Society, such as Winzergenossenschaft Wachtenburg-Luginsland eG.

Efringen-Kirchen Baden w r

Small town in the Bereich ★Markgräflerland. The most widely grown vine in the immediate locality is the Gutedel. *Grosslage*: Vogtei Rötteln.

Ehrenfelser

White grape variety, a crossing of Riesling × Silvaner from the viticultural institute at ★Geisenheim. Dating from 1929, it is today planted in 523 hectares, mainly in the Rheinpfalz and Rheinhessen. Recommended for good sites that do not quite reach the standards required by Riesling. The yield is greater, the must weight 5–10° Oechsle heavier than that of Riesling and the acidity slightly lower. The grapes can be harvested late in the season to produce *Spätlese* and even higher qualities of elegant, fruity wine that will improve in bottle but develop more quickly than Riesling.

Eigeneswachstum
Own growth. Term used before 1971 to describe wines to which no sugar had been added and which were bottled by the grower. Synonyms were *Eigenbau*, *Eigengewächs* and *Originalabfüllung*.

Einzellage
An individual site, the smallest geographical unit in which vines are planted. Only quality (QbA and QmP) wines may carry an *Einzellage* name, which must always be accompanied by that of a village or community. Some bottlers, believing the large number of *Einzellagen* (2,600) to be confusing, reserve their use exclusively for their best wines.

Eisheiligen
Ice saints. The commemoration days of the 'ice saints' fall between May 11–14. After May 15, known as the *Kalte Sophie*, there is virtually no further risk of frost in the vineyards. The saints include St Pancras, the patron saint of children, and St Boniface, an English missionary who worked in Germany and founded the Abbey of Fulda that later (in 1775) was said to have been connected with the discovery in the Rheingau of the benefits of harvesting grapes late in the season.

Eiswein
Ice wine. Quality category for wines made from grapes naturally frozen at the time of pressing – artificial refrigeration is not permitted in Germany. The water in the grapes remains in the press in the form of ice crystals, concentrating the grape acids and sugar wonderfully. The must weight, measured in degrees Oechsle, has to reach *Beerenauslese* level. As the necessary cold weather (approximately -8°C) seldom occurs before the third week in November, the risk of failure is serious (in the 1985 vintage, some estates did not gather the *Eiswein* crop until February 8 1986). Although *Eiswein* must be made from ripe grapes, it can be produced in less good years when *Beeren-* and *Trockenbeerenauslesen* are out of the question, hence its commercial interest and appeal for the grower.

An *Eiswein* lacks the honeyed tones of a *Beerenauslese*, but its remarkable acidity and great residual sweetness give it a 'zip' and nervosity quite different from the more solid flavour of normally harvested top-quality sweet wines. In the early 1990s dry *Eisweine* have been produced. Comment on their quality is not available, but their curiosity value will be great.

Eitelsbach M-S-R w
Small village, overlooked by its vineyards, near the point where the little river Ruwer decants into the Mosel. Forms part of the city of *Trier. Exceptionally racy and stylish wines in good years, great wines in the best years, mainly Riesling. *Grosslage*: *Römerlay.

Elbling, Weisser
One of the oldest white grape varieties growing in Germany, now restricted almost entirely to the Mosel-Saar-Ruwer, where it occupies 1,177 hectares. Until World War II it was still found in Franken and as a mixed plantation with other vine varieties on the Rhein. On the Mosel above *Trier it produces a high yield (sometimes in excess of 200 hectolitres per hectare) of acidic wine light in body and with a neutral flavour, which is often converted into sparkling wine.

Elegant
A rather subjective wine description which must be the result of personal judgement rather than of chemical analysis. It may usually be correctly applied to a wine in which the bouquet and flavour are perfectly balanced and no one characteristic is too predominant. Normally, light wines with good acidity around which the other constituents are mustered achieve elegance more easily than heavy, alcoholic wines. In German wine, it is found particularly in Rieslings from the Mosel-Saar-Ruwer, Nahe and Rheingau, especially those of *Kabinett* quality. Bigger *Spätlese* wines can also have tremendous style but their power and weight seem to make the description elegant less appropriate.

Ellenz-Poltersdorf M-S-R w
Two villages, linked by a ferry across the Mosel, next to the ancient hamlet of *Beilstein. High percentage of Riesling in most of the vineyards, some Müller-Thurgau, and unusually, a little Elbling. *Grosslagen*: *Goldbäumchen, Rosenhang.

Ellwanger, Weingut Jürgen Würt

Twelve-hectare estate east of Stuttgart planted with 25 percent Riesling, 20 percent Trollinger and 20 percent Kerner, selling mainly to private customers. Some of the wines are aged in *barrique*. Many DLG award-winning wines. Seventy percent (high for the region) is *trocken*. Annual production is 8,300 cases.
Address: Bachstrasse 21, W-7065 Winterbach
Tel: 07181 4525

Eltville Rhg w

Important wine town, home of the Staatsweingut Eltville (*see next entry*). Good-quality Rieslings, similarly priced to those from other leading Rheingau communities. *Grosslage*: ★Steinmächer.

Eltville, Verwaltung der Staatsweingüter Rhg Charta VDP

Collection of fine estates covering 145 hectares in the Rheingau and 37 hectares in the Hessische Bergstrasse (*see* Bergstrasse, Staatsweingut – all owned by Hessen). The holdings in many famous sites include Rüdesheimer ★Berg Roseneck, ★Berg Rottland, ★Berg Schlossberg; Erbacher ★Marcobrunn; Rauenthaler ★Baiken; Hochheimer ★Domdechaney, ★Kirchenstück and ★Hölle. Sole owners of the ★Steinberg vineyard. Eighty-one percent Riesling, 13 percent Spätburgunder. The variety of holdings indicates a wide range of styles but the goal is to produce wines with backbone, elegance and body. The estate is a founder member of ★Charta, and a great producer of *Eiswein*. Experiments are being made in ecological vine growing and winemaking. Total annual production in the Rheingau and Hessische Bergstrasse is 83,300 cases.
Address: Schwalbacherstrasse 56–62, W-6228 Eltville
Tel: 06123 61055

Emrich-Schönleber, Weingut Nahe

Award-winning estate of 11 hectares planted 68 percent Riesling, eight percent each Müller-Thurgau and Kerner. All the holdings are at ★Monzingen – the source of much good wine. Over half are very steep. Annual production is 6,700 cases; 40 percent is *trocken*.
Address: Naheweinstrasse 10, W-6557 Monzingen
Tel: 06751 2733

Enkirch M–S–R w
Village of half-timbered houses and old cellars and, unusually, two parish churches (Protestant and Roman Catholic). The reputation of Enkircher Riesling stands high in Germany but the wine is not often found abroad. *Grosslage*: *Schwarzlay.

Enrichment
See Anreicherung

Erbach Rhg w
Village at the point where a small stream, the Eberbach (of which Erbach is a corruption), joins the Rhein. It has a number of well-known sites including the *Marcobrunn, whose Riesling is among the most full-bodied – and expensive – in the region. *Grosslage*: *Deutelsberg.

Erben
Successors. Placed after the name of a company and forming part of the title, such as Weingut Bürgermeister Carl Koch Erben. It is similar to the English '& Sons'.

Erbslöh'sches Weingut Rhg VDP
Six-hectare estate with holdings planted 100 percent Riesling at *Geisenheim (*Kläuserweg, *Rothenberg and Mönchspfad), with a high 80 percent of the wines being *trocken* and 70 percent sold to private customers.
Address: Erbslöhstrasse 1, W-6222 Geisenheim
Tel: 06722 7080

Erden M–S–R w
Small village which faces its best Riesling vineyards across the Mosel, including the famous *Prälat. *Grosslage*: *Schwarzlay.

Erdig
Earthy. *See* Bodengeschmack.

Ernte
See Harvest

Erntebringer Rhg w
Most widely known *Grosslage* in the Rheingau, covering more than
300 hectares in the neighbourhood of ★Johannisberg, ★Geisenheim
and ★Winkel. Wines sold as Erntebringer are often slightly less
concentrated in flavour than the most positive wines from
individual sites. They have charm and are easy to enjoy, but lack the
distinction of the finest Rheingaus.

Erzeugerabfüllung
Producer-bottled. A term that appears on labels and in wine lists to
indicate that a wine was made and bottled by the grower of the
grapes. Cooperative cellars and *Erzeugergemeinschaften* that buy
their grapes from their members but have no direct control over the
viticulture are also legally entitled to describe their wines as
Erzeugerabfüllungen. Although 'producer-bottled' is not in itself a
guarantee of quality, a good producer will usually sell only his
QmP and better QbA with the description *Erzeugerabfüllung*.

Erzeugergemeinschaft
Producers' association. The formation of such associations became
possible for farmers and vine growers when the German Market
Structure Law came into force in 1969. As far as viticulture is
concerned, they are associations of vine growers who have
combined to link their production to the needs of the market. A
further aim is to act as marketing groups capable of doing business
with large buying organizations on equal terms. Even an estate as
famous as the Fürstlich Castell'sches Domänenamt in Franken
heads a local *Erzeugergemeinschaft*. The names of *Erzeugergemeinschaften* are beginning to appear on wine labels.

Escherndorf Franken w
Charming rustic and well-known village lying at the foot of its
steep, modernized vineyards, planted mainly with Silvaner and
Müller-Thurgau. Powerful wines with lasting flavour. *Grosslage*:
Kirchberg.

Eser, Weingut August Rhg Charta VDP
Well-known estate with 6·2 hectares in ★Oestrich, ★Hattenheim,
★Winkel and ★Rauenthal. Vines are 92 percent Riesling, eight

percent Spätburgunder. Forty percent is *trocken*. Annual production is 4,600 cases, ten percent exported.
Address: Friedensplatz 19, W-6227 Oestrich-Winkel
Tel: 06723 5032

Espenhof, Weingut Rhh
Fifteen-hectare estate in rolling country near ★Alzey with a wide range of vine varieties. Sixty percent of the wine is *trocken* although, unusually, a *lieblich* Grauburgunder is listed. Sales are mainly to private customers.
Address: Hauptstrasse 79–81, W-6509 Flonheim-Uffhofen
Tel: 06734 1007

Essigsäure
Acetic acid. Acceptable at a level of 0·2–0·3 grams per litre in young white wine, and 0·3–0·5 grams per litre in red wine, depending on the method of vinification. An excessive amount of acetic acid, with its sharp taste, is very rare in German wine.

Estate-bottled
Term for which there is no German translation established in law, *Erzeugerabfüllung* or 'producer's bottling' being used by estates, cooperative cellars and producers' associations alike. It is possible that *Gutsabfüllung* may become the official translation of 'estate-bottled'.

Etikett
Label. The first German wine labels were developed at the end of the 18th century. Since then they have become a legal necessity as well as an important aid to the marketing of wine.

Ewig Leben Franken w (r)
Small *Grosslage* based on ★Randersacker.

Extra brut
Describes a sparkling wine with less than 6 grams per litre of residual sugar.

Extra dry/trocken
Describes a sparkling wine with 12–20 grams per litre of residual sugar.

Extract
Term used to describe the non-volatile substances in wine, including sugar, glycerin, acids, minerals and tannin. A wine with low extract will usually be described as hollow and/or short, while a wine high in extract will be full and its flavour will last in the mouth. In theory it might seem that to obtain a scientific, objective judgement of a wine it would only be necessary to determine the extract content. In practice this is not so, and there are many exceptions to the rule that top-quality wines contain more extract than do those of lesser quality.

Eymael, Robert M–S–R
See Mönchof, Weingut

Faberrebe
White grape variety, a crossing of Weissburgunder × Müller-Thurgau from the viticultural institute at *Alzey in the Rhein-hessen, created by Dr Georg Scheu (best known for the Scheurebe). It produces must with a higher weight than Müller-Thurgau and more acidity. Although the grapes ripen very early they can be left on the vine to produce stylish Spätlese wine. Planted in 2,176 hectares, 76 percent in the Rheinhessen, with smaller plantings in the Nahe and Rheinpfalz.

Faber Sektkellerei KG
Founded in 1950, Faber produces approximately 45·5 million bottles of sparkling wine per year. Faber Krönung is the biggest-selling brand of Sekt in Germany.
Address: Niederkircherstrasse 27, W-5500 Trier
Tel: 0651 814–0

Fad
Describes a dull, characterless wine, probably with little acidity.

Falkenstein M-S-R w
Part of the Saar town of *Konz. In the 18-hectare Hofberg
Einzellage, the Friedrich-Wilhelm-Gymnasium makes very attract-
ive, *spritzig*, relatively inexpensive wine. *Grosslage*: *Scharzberg.

Färbertrauben
Colouring grapes: grapes for improving the colour of red wine.
Their must can be made into *Süssreserve* to help both darken and
sweeten otherwise pale, rosé-like 'red' wine for the north German
market. The most promising of such new vines is probably the
Geisenheim-bred, early-ripening Dunkelfelder, planted in 116
hectares, mainly in the Rheinpfalz, Rheinhessen and Baden. *See also*
Deckrotwein.

Fass
Wooden cask. In Germany, in many large cellars, wooden storage
casks have been replaced by vats of stainless steel or other man-
made materials. These are more easily maintained and function
rather like large bottles, keeping the wine fresh and free from
oxidation. Traditionally, Rhein wine used to be sold in *Halbstücke*
(casks) of approximately 610 litres, and Mosel wine in the slightly
smaller but longer *Halbfuder*. Today bulk wine is transported in
large containers, similar to those used for milk. Sales of *Fassweine*
are declining, but remain considerable within Germany. Three-
quarters of the growers who make wine, sell in *Fass* to the wine
trade, which relies on such producers for their commercial blends.
Few wines sold in this way, however, have ever known the feel of
wood, and the term *Fassweingeschäft* (cask trade) is, strictly
speaking, obsolete. *See also* Barrique.

Fassgeschmack
Cask taste, of which there are two entirely different sorts: the
flavour that wine can pick up from tannin in the wood of a new cask
(much sought after in Bordeaux, but until recently regarded as
detrimental in German wine), and the dirty flavour that can appear
in wine that has been stored in a poorly maintained cask where
mould has developed. A wine from the latter sort of cask can easily
be incorrectly thought to be 'corked'.

Fasswein, Fassweingeschäft
See Fass

Federweisser
Partially fermented, still very sweet, cloudy young wine, served in wine bars during the harvest and in large helpings to the grape gatherers. It should be treated with caution as its bubbly nature conceals volatile acids, esters, aldehydes and nasty things from the vineyard that can lead to interrupted sleep, heart problems, diarrhoea and skin complaints – according to some members of the medical profession.

Feilbingert Nahe w
Agricultural village between the Nahe and the Alsenz growing much Silvaner, becoming better known through the wines of Weingut Adolf ★Lötzbeyer. *Grosslage*: Paradiesgarten.

Feine, feinste
Comparative terms meaning fine and finest, used before 1971 to describe superior qualities of *Spätlese, Auslese* and *Beerenauslese* wines, such as *feinste Spätlese*.

Felsenberg Nahe w
Mainly steep *Einzellage* at ★Schlossböckelheim in the Nahe valley. Its Rieslings are attractive, a little earthy, and can be of top quality in a good year. *Grosslage*: ★Burgweg. Growers: Paul Anheuser, Crusius, Dönnhof, Hehner-Kiltz, Niederhausen-Schlossböckelheim Staatliche Weinbaudomäne, Plettenberg.

Feuerberg Rhpf w (r)
Grosslage of just under 1,000 hectares near the town of ★Bad Dürkheim. The whole district has a high reputation for its white wine, but red wine is also produced from Portugieser and much is sold under the *Grosslage* name.

Feurig
Fiery. Describes a red wine rich in alcohol that is thought to warm the blood rapidly, a notion helped by its sanguine colour. Might apply to a red wine from the Bereich ★Kaiserstuhl.

Filigran
Complex: a word much used by some German wine writers in the 1990s. Usually applied to Riesling wines.

Filzen-Hamm M-S-R w (r)
First wine village travelling up the Saar. Its sloping Riesling vineyards produce racy, *spritzig* wines. *Grosslage*: *Scharzberg.

Findling
Mutation of Müller-Thurgau grown in 46 hectares mainly in the Mosel-Saar-Ruwer, producing a lower yield and heavier must weight than the source vine.

Findling Rhh w
Top-quality *Einzellage* at *Nierstein producing a fine range of wines with considerable elegance. *Grosslage*: *Spiegelberg. Growers: Baumann, Guntrum, Heyl zu Herrnsheim, St Anthony, Schneider, Schuch, Sittmann, Strub, Wehrheim.

Finkenauer, Weingut Carl Nahe
Family-owned estate dating from 1828 with 33 hectares, mainly in *Bad Kreuznach (including holdings in *Brückes and *Narren-kappe), and also in *Roxheim, *Winzenheim. Planted 59 percent Riesling, ten percent Müller-Thurgau, eight percent Silvaner, plus other varieties including eight percent Spätburgunder. The cask-matured wines show clearly the characteristics of the grape variety. About 80 percent of the wine, including the *Auslesen*, is *halbtrocken* or *trocken*.
Address: Salinenstrasse 60, W-6550 Bad Kreuznach
Tel: 0671 28771

Firn, firnig
Term used to describe the effect of considerable age on wine, including a darkening of colour in white wine, and oxidation noticeable in the bouquet and on the palate. A somewhat negative description.

Fischer, Weingüter Dr M-S-R VDP
Saar estate of 24·6 hectares with holdings at *Ockfen (including

*Bockstein), *Saarburg and the solely owned 10·4-hectare Herren-berg site at *Wawern. Ninety-eight percent Riesling, two percent Weissburgunder. Lively, fresh Saar wines have a forceful bouquet, and are typical of the best in the area. Sales are mainly to private and export customers.
Address: Bocksteinhof, W-5511 Ockfen
Tel: 06581 2150

Fischerpfad Rhh w
Top-quality vineyard on the *Rheinterrasse at *Alsheim, the best parts of which are planted in Riesling. *Grosslage*: *Rheinblick. Grower: Rappenhof.

Fitz–Ritter, Weingut K Rhpf VDP
Old family estate of 21 hectares, dating from 1785. The vineyard holdings are mainly in *Bad Dürkheim (the estate is sole owner of Dürkheimer Abtsfronhof). Vines are 65 percent Riesling. Annual production is 16,700 cases, 50 percent *trocken*. Dornfelder is aged in *barrique* and the estate has been producing its own *Sekt* since 1837. About 60 percent of the wine is sold to private customers and eight percent is exported.
Address: Leistadterstrasse 1, W-6702 Bad Dürkheim
Tel: 06322 5389

Flach
Flat. A wine with insufficient acidity will taste flat. Not a common fault in German wine but can derive from low-acid vine varieties (such as Bacchus, Auxerrois) if they are allowed to overproduce.

Flasche
See Bottle

Flaschengärung
Fermentation in bottle, as opposed to the more common fermen-tation in vat. *Flaschengärung* is very suitable for the production of small parcels (say, 270 cases) of sparkling wine. For this reason it is the method usually chosen by sparkling-wine producers when making *Lagensekt* (quality sparkling wine from a particular site) for growers. However, almost all the large branded sparkling wines

gain their sparkle in vat. In blind tastings at *Amtliche Prüfung centres, wines fermented in bottle and those fermented in vat have shown no discernible difference in quality that can be related to the method of second fermentation. *See also* Charmat-Verfahren.

Flaschenreife

Bottle ripeness. This term has two meanings. It can refer to the moment when a wine has stabilized and the acidity is at the appropriate level, making it ready or 'ripe' for bottling; or to maturation in bottle.

Flaschenweinverkauf

Sale of wine in bottle. This is the message that is hung outside many cellars in Germany, advertising that wine is sold in bottle to the consumer. It is an increasingly popular form of trading and practically all producer-bottlers sell direct to the public.

Flein Würt w r

Substantial village south of *Heilbronn with a high proportion of Riesling in sloping vineyards, producing *spritzig*, characterful wine. *Grosslage*: Kirchenweinberg.

Flein-Talheim eG, Weingärtnergenossenschaft Würt

Large cooperative near *Heilbronn, supplied by 280 hectares. The usual Württemberg variety Trollinger is not grown, the members' vineyards being planted 50 percent Riesling and 32 percent Müllerrebe (Schwarzriesling). A premium range of wine has been launched (including a Riesling *Spätlese* with 13·5 percent alcohol) and will be developed further. About 75 percent of the wine made is *halbtrocken*.
Address: Römerstrasse 14, W-7101 Flein bei Heilbronn
Tel: 07131 52033

Flonheim Rhh w (r)

A village with 360 hectares of hilly vineyard in the pretty 'Rheinhessische Schweiz', known mainly in connection with its *Grosslage* Adelberg.

Flurbereinigung

The reconstruction and reallocation of vineyards among the growers. The practice is supported by federal and local government, with the aim of increasing the competitiveness of German wine through reduced labour costs and improved wine quality, making wine with strong regional and varietal characteristics. The work of reconstruction, including rebuilding hillsides and abolishing old terracing, offers the chance for the best possible vines to be planted. More than 57 percent of the total area under vine in Germany has been *flurbereinigt*.

Forst Rhpf w (r)

Small but important wine village a few kilometres south of ★Bad Dürkheim, surrounded by top-quality Riesling vineyards. It is the base of a number of well-known estates with holdings in the famous ★Jesuitengarten and ★Ungeheuer sites. *Grosslagen*: ★Mariengarten (for the best sites), ★Schnepfenflug.

Forster Winzerverein eG Rhpf

Cooperative cellar established in 1918, supplied by 65 hectares of vineyards in top-quality sites such as Forster ★Jesuitengarten and ★Ungeheuer. Vines are over two-thirds Riesling, plus Müller-Thurgau and others. Distinguished wines with a considerable reputation, sold in Germany and abroad.
Address: Weinstrasse 57, W-6701 Forst
Tel: 06326 1391

Forstmeister

Head forester, as in Weingut Forstmeister Geltz Zilliken.

Franckenstein Rentamt Weingut, Freiherr von und zu Baden

Fourteen-hectare estate planted 35 percent Riesling, 20 percent Spätburgunder, 15 percent Ruländer (Grauburgunder), 15 percent Müller-Thurgau, all in the Zell-Weierbacher Abtsberg site near Offenburg. Eighty percent of the wine is *trocken*, with well-differentiated grape characteristics.
Address: Weingartenstrasse 66, W-7600 Offenburg
Tel: 0781 34973

Franconia
See Franken

Franken w (r)
The only wine region belonging to the beer-producing state of Bavaria, covering over 5,240 hectares on either side of the river Main and centred on the university city of *Würzburg. More than half the vineyards have been reconstructed and replanted since 1954. Fifty-seven percent of the growers deliver their grapes to the cooperative cellars. The most widely grown grape is Müller-Thurgau, followed by Silvaner and steadily increasing Bacchus. The winters in Franken are often severe, with temperatures sometimes dropping to -25°C. As a result the yield can vary greatly from year to year (in 1982 it was about 170 hectolitres per hectare and in 1985 only about 13 hectolitres per hectare). Half the harvest is processed by cooperative cellars. Among the private growers some have high reputations for wines of outstanding flavour and style. The better 'quality wines' are bottled in the traditional flagon-shaped *Bocksbeutel*.

Wine from Franken is not cheap, and is far more expensive than wine from the southern Rheinpfalz (Bereich *Südliche Wein-strasse). It is, however, good value for money when compared with the price obtained for a simple Mâcon Blanc, for example. It has character in abundance and is never boring. In EC terms it is often dry, with a maximum 9 grams per litre of sugar. When it contains less than 4 grams per litre of sugar it warrants the description *fränkisch trocken* (dry Franken). The slightly earthy flavour, typical of the region, is almost always present, no matter from what grape variety the wine is made.

In spite of the damage caused over the centuries by wars, mediaeval buildings in many of the old towns and villages still stand. In the countryside, inns and cellars provide opportunities to taste and buy wines in seductively rustic surroundings.

Franken eG, Gebietswinzergenossenschaft Franken
Seven cooperative cellars combined in 1959 and this central cellar now handles the crop from 1,400 hectares via 18 pressing stations. Three-quarters of the wine from the typical Franken vine varieties, such as Müller–Thurgau, Silvaner, Bacchus, is *halbtrocken*. The list is

enormous. However, if you wish to buy 29 variations of Bacchus this is the place to come.
Address: W-8710 Kitzingen-Repperndorf
Tel: 09321 70050

Frankfurt am Main, Weingut der Stadt Rhg

The original owners of this 27-hectare estate were Carmelites and Dominicans. The estate was taken over by the city of Frankfurt in 1803. Holdings are in important sites at ★Hochheim (★Domdechaney, ★Kirchenstück, ★Hölle) and the small one-hectare residue of once-extensive vineyards in the suburbs of Frankfurt, the Lohrberger Hang, producing lively Riesling wines. The vineyards are 85 percent Riesling; 30 percent of the wine is *trocken*.
Address: Limpurgergasse 2, W-6000 Frankfurt am Main 1
Tel: 069 2128406

Fränkisch trocken

Franken dry. Describes a Franken wine with less than 4 grams per litre residual sugar.

Freiburg Baden w (r)

University city, severely damaged in World War II but carefully rebuilt. Vineyards covering 650 hectares are in the four *Bereiche* of Breisgau, ★Kaiserstuhl, ★Tuniberg and ★Markgräflerland, and in the city itself.

Freiburg, Staatliches Weinbauinstitut Baden

Founded in 1920, the Freiburg holdings of the state viticultural institute amount to 15 hectares planted with a range of varieties including Müller-Thurgau, Spätburgunder, Gutedel and Riesling. Powerful, balanced wines are aimed for. Approximately 8,300 cases are produced annually; 68 percent is *trocken* and 60 percent is sold directly to the consumer. The Baden-Württemberg state owns four separate estates with an investigative viticultural role: Blankenhornsberg at Ihringen, the largest (*see next entry*), Hecklingen and Durbach, each three hectares, and the holdings at Freiburg itself.
Address: Merzhauserstrasse 119, W-7800 Freiburg
Tel: 0761 40 90 26

Freiburg, Staatliches Weinbauinstitut, 'Blankenhornsberg'

Baden

One of four estates owned by the state of Baden-Württemberg. Founded privately in 1842, it was sold to the state in 1919. Its 24 hectares of vineyards lie on steep volcanic slopes looking across the Rhein to Alsace. The wines (21 percent Spätburgunder, 18 percent Riesling, 16 percent Müller-Thurgau, plus many others) are sold mainly under the name Blankenhornsberg without mention of the *Einzellage*. They are full in weight and flavour and have pronounced acidity. Annual production is 21,700 cases, of which 90 percent is *trocken*.

Address: Blankenhornsberg, W-7817 Ihringen

Tel: 07668 217

Freiherr

Baron. Found in some estate names, such as the Baden estate of Weingut Freiherr von Gleichenstein. A *Freiherr* would inherit the title from a *Reichsfreiherr*, but the *Reichs* or 'imperial' description could not be bequeathed.

Freinsheim Rhpf w (r)

Well-restored walled town whose rolling vineyards mainly supply the local cooperative cellar. The best Riesling and Scheurebe wines are of top quality and relatively inexpensive. *Grosslagen*: ★Kobnert and Rosenbühl.

Freisamer

White grape variety, a crossing of Silvaner × Ruländer from ★Freiburg in Baden, with a small plantation of 56 hectares. Produces a crop of similar yield and must weight to the Ruländer and wine that is neutral in flavour, full-bodied and stylish. If the must weight is less than 80° Oechsle the wine is said to taste 'woody', so overcropping must be avoided and ripeness is all.

Fremersberg, Weingut Klostergut Baden

See Nägelförster Hof, Weingut

Frey & Söhne, Weingut Winfried Rhpf

Award-winning 7·5-hectare estate in the flat country south of

*Neustadt, becoming increasingly known for the high quality of its wine still offered at inexpensive prices. The holdings are planted 30 percent Riesling, 15 percent Ruländer (Grauburgunder), ten percent Spätburgunder, ten percent Gewürztraminer. Annual production is the equivalent of about 5,000 cases, 70 percent *trocken*, 95 percent sold to private customers. Thirteen *Eisweine* (including, unusually, one from the relatively early-ripening Morio-Muskat) and six *Trockenbeerenauslesen* are listed.

Address: Spanierstrasse 1 + 2, Schulstrasse 4, W-6741 Essingen
Tel: 06347 8224

Freyburg S–U w (r)
Attractive and ancient town with terraced vineyards, mainly supplying the local *Winzergenossenschaft.*

Freyburg-Unstrut eG, Winzervereinigung S–U
Cooperative cellar at Freyburg (formerly in East Germany) which takes in grapes from the standard regional varieties (*see* Saale-Unstrut) and sells the wines under the vine variety name. Most are QbA but there is also a range of *Kabinett* and *Spätlese* wines. All are *trocken*, clean, and probably light in extract. Many are filled out through the effect of the chalky soil in which the vines are grown. Yields are low.

Address: Querfurterstrasse 10, O-4805 Freyburg

Friedelsheim Rhpf w (r)

Situated a little east of ★Wachenheim. The wines recall those of the best wine villages in the Pfalz. Good-quality Rieslings. *Grosslagen*: ★Schnepfenflug, ★Hofstück.

Friedelsheim eG, Winzergenossenschaft Rhpf

Cooperative cellar supplied by 139 hectares, whose members' holdings include Forster Bischofsgarten and Wachenheimer ★Gerümpel. Vines are 32 percent Riesling, 15 percent Müller-Thurgau, 15 percent Portugieser, plus a host of other varieties, including Spätburgunder. Seventy percent of the wine is *lieblich*.
Address: Hauptstrasse 93–99, W-6701 Friedelsheim
Tel: 06322 2029

Friedrich-Wilhelm-Gymnasium, Stiftung Staatliches
M-S-R

Distinguished estate, founded in 1563 by Jesuits, with 36 hectares of planted holdings spread along the Mosel (★Dhron, ★Graach, ★Zeltingen-Rachtig, ★Bernkastel) and the Saar (★Oberemmel, ★Ockfen and others). Many of the sites are very steep, planted with 90 percent Riesling, ten percent Müller-Thurgau and Kerner. Storage in oak casks is still valued, and the estate's cellars under ★Trier produce racy wines with restrained sweetness. Annual sales are 33,000 cases, mainly in Germany, but 30 percent exported.
Address: Weberbachstrasse 75, W-5500 Trier
Tel: 0651 73849

Frisch

Fresh. As a result of a vinification that reduces oxidation to a minimum, gentle handling of the wine so as to retain the natural carbon dioxide, and good acid levels, most German wines taste fresh – even after some years in bottle. Applies particularly to Rieslings from the Mosel-Saar-Ruwer, the Rheingau and the best vineyards of the Bereich ★Schloss Böckelheim in the Nahe.

Frostgeschmack

Frost taste. Flavour acquired by unripe grapes attacked by frost in autumn (such as in 1972). It can usually be removed with treatment but not always entirely successfully. The ripeness of grapes used in

Eiswein production, on the other hand, prevents them from developing a taste of frost.

Fruchtig
Fruity. Common description of wine, covering smell and flavour and referring to pronounced grapy characteristics often reinforced by high acidity. A Saar wine, made from ripe grapes but with good acidity, can well be described as fruity.

Fruchtwein
Fruit wine. Wine made from fruits other than grapes, with the addition of water and sugar.

Fruchtzucker
Fruit sugar. Colloquial name for fructose, which tastes twice as sweet as dextrose. However, yeast ferments dextrose more easily than fructose, so the unfermented sugar in a fine sweet wine contains a high proportion of the sweet fructose.

Frühburgunder, Blauer
Red grape variety, an early-ripening mutation of Spätburgunder, covering 38 hectares mainly in Württemberg. It is also known by the synonym 'Clevner' – a name confusingly reserved in the Bereich ★Ortenau in Baden for Traminer. The wine sometimes recalls a blend of Spätburgunder and Gamay.

Frühmesse Rhh w
Large *Einzellage* on slopes at ★Alsheim, producing luscious, stylish Rieslings. *Grosslage*: ★Rheinblick. Growers: Rappenhof, Sittmann.

Fuchs, Weingut Reinhold M-S-R
Small two-hectare estate, downstream from Cochem, planted with 90 percent Riesling. Vinification is deliberately old-fashioned, from the use of a wooden press onwards. The wines are 90–95 percent *trocken* and all improve with bottle-age. Annual production is 1,700 cases, sold 90 percent to private customers in Germany.
Address: Bahnhofstrasse 37, W-5593 Pommern
Tel: 02672 7405

Fuchsmantel Rhpf w
Mainly level *Einzellage*, on the outskirts of ★Bad Dürkheim but
shared with ★Wachenheim, producing good wines typical of the
region. *Grosslage*: ★Schenkenböhl. Growers: Bart, Karst, Probsthof, K Schäfer.

Fuder
Cask of approximately 1,000 litres, used for storage in the Mosel-
Saar-Ruwer. *See* Fass.

Fuhrmann, Karl Rhpf
See Pfeffingen, Weingut

Fürst
Prince, as in Fürst von Metternich-Winneburg'sches Domäne
Rentamt at Schloss Johannisberg.

Fürst, Weingut Rudolf Franken VDP
Estate of 10·6 hectares with holdings mainly at ★Bürgstadt
(Centgericht) and with a small parcel at Grossheubach. The
viticultural work and vineyard management could be said to be at
the technical leading edge. Fifty-five percent is Spätburgunder, and
Riesling and Müller-Thurgau occupy 12 percent of the vineyards.
Top-quality wines, 95 percent *trocken*. Annual production is 7,100
cases of which five percent is exported.
Address: Hohenlindenweg 46, W-8768 Bürgstadt
Tel: 09371 8642

Gallais, Weingut le M-S-R VDP
Small (2·5-hectare) Saar estate with holdings in the 5·8-hectare
★Braune Kupp at ★Wiltingen. Some vines are almost a century old.
Only wines of QmP class are sold under the *Einzellage* name.
Approximate annual production is 1,300 cases, all Riesling, 95
percent *lieblich*. The estate is administered by Weingut Egon
★Müller-Scharzhof.
Address: Verwaltung, Egon Müller-Scharzhof, W-5516 Wiltingen
Tel: 06501 16676

Gattungslagename
Predecessor of the *Grosslage* but much vaguer in geographical definition, abolished by the 1971 Wine Law. It was a site name that could be given to a wine that came, usually, from within ten kilometres of the village name to which the site was attached. Johannisberger (village name) Erntebringer (*Gattungslagename*), for example, could originate in a village as far away as Hallgarten or even further. Today, as a *Grosslage*, ★Erntebringer is more narrowly and precisely defined.

Gau-Bickelheim Rhh
Small town near ★Bad Kreuznach (in the Nahe), since 1967 best known as the home of the large central cooperative cellar that serves the Rheinhessen and Rheingau. *Grosslage*: Kurfürstenstück.

Gau-Bischofsheim Rhh w (r)
Small village with 90 hectares of vineyards set back from the Rhein south of ★Mainz, best known for its Geissel organ built in 1667 and Weingut Oberst ★Schultz-Werner. *Grosslage*: ★St Alban.

Gebhardt Ernst, Weingut/Sektkellerei Franken
Estate founded in 1723, taken over by Georg Jakob Gebhardt in 1761. Fifteen hectares of steep, modernized vineyards in ★Sommerhausen, ★Randersacker and other villages, planted with Silvaner, Müller-Thurgau, Scheurebe, Bacchus, etc. Ninety percent of the wine is *trocken* or *halbtrocken*. *Sekt* has been produced since 1911. Address: Hauptstrasse 21–23, W-8701 Sommerhausen
Tel: 09333 287

Gebiet
District. Not an official EC designation, for which the word is *Bereich*. Appears in *Anbaugebiet* and *Weinbaugebiet*.

Gebietswinzergenossenschaft
District cooperative cellar (*Gebiets*, district; *Winzer*, vine grower; *Genossenschaft*, association). Sometimes known as a *Bezirkswinzergenossenschaft* (*Bezirk* is a synonym for *Gebiet*).

Gebr

Gebrüder. Brothers, as in Weingut Gebr Müller.

Gefällig

Pleasing. A description best applied to ordinary wines that are well made but have few other virtues (such as *Liebfraumilch, Niersteiner *Gutes Domtal).

Geheimrat, Geheimer Rat

Privy councillor. Can appear in estate names as one word, such as Geheimrat Aschrott'sche Erben, or as two, such as Weingut Geheimer Rat Dr von Bassermann-Jordan.

Geil, Weingut Rhh

Estate, now in its seventh generation, with 23 hectares at Eimsheim and *Mettenheim, planted 25 percent Silvaner, 20 percent Riesling, 15 percent Müller-Thurgau. The well-made wines win many awards and are admired for their *spritzig*, fresh style. Annual production is 18,300 cases, of which 30 percent is *trocken*. Ten percent is exported.
Address: Mittelstrasse 14, W-6501 Eimsheim
Tel: 06249 2380

Geil I Erben, Weingut Ökonomierat Johann Rhh

Estate with 25 hectares at *Bechtheim, 70 percent on steep slopes, planted 25 percent Riesling, 15 percent Kerner, 15 percent Müller-Thurgau. The aim is fresh wines with crisp acidity, true to the vine variety. Thirty percent of the wine is *trocken*, sold 90 percent to private customers.
Address: W-6521 Bechtheim
Tel: 06242 1546

Geilweilerhof Rhpf

Home of the federal viticultural institute, the Bundesforschungs-anstalt für Rebenzüchtung, near the village of *Siebeldingen, where the grape varieties Morio-Muskat, Bacchus and Optima were developed.

Geisenheim Rhg w
Famous for its viticultural institute (*see next entry*), Geisenheim produces Riesling wines of distinction, but with a slight additional flavour from the soil. *Grosslagen*: ★Burgweg and ★Erntebringer.

Geisenheim, Weingut der Forschungsanstalt für Weinbau, Gartenbau, Getränketechnologie und Landespflege
Rhg Charta
Part of a complex of world-renowned institutes dealing with all aspects of vine growing and winemaking. Many vine varieties are grown in 24 hectares in Geisenheim (★Kläuserweg, ★Rothenberg, ★Mäuerchen) and at Rüdesheim: 64 percent is Riesling, nine percent Müller-Thurgau, four percent Spätburgunder. The wines are matured in wood and vat, and sold directly to the consumer.
Address: Von-Lade-Strasse 1, W-6222 Geisenheim
Tel: 06722 5021

Geldermann GmbH, Privat-Sektkellerei
Founded in 1838 as producers of champagne, started sparkling-wine production in Alsace in 1904 and in ★Breisach in 1925. The technique used is *Flaschengärung*. A top-quality *Sekt* house.
Address: Am Schlossberg, W-7814 Breisach
Tel: 07667 834–0

Gemeinde
Community or village.

Gemischter Satz
Describes the growing in one vineyard of two or more vine varieties, the grapes being harvested and pressed together. Only in this century have mixed plantations of this sort almost disappeared but the practice is now being revived by a few producers.

Gerbstoff
Tannin. Derives from the skins, pips and stalks of the grape. A low tannin content is characteristic of, and desirable in, German white wine. Many German red wines are now more tannic than they were ten years ago – because of a change in vinification and/or through maturation in untreated new wood. *See* Barrique.

German Wine Academy

Since 1973 this organization has run six-day seminars in English, based at ★Kloster Eberbach in the Rheingau. The basic course covers all aspects of vine growing and winemaking, including many tutored tastings and visits to vine-growing regions. For further information, write to: Reisebüro Bartholomae, Wilhelm-strasse 8, W-6200 Wiesbaden.

Gerümpel Rhpf w

Einzellage at ★Wachenheim producing top-quality, full-bodied wines, mainly from the predominant Riesling grape. *Grosslage*: ★Mariengarten. Growers: Biffar, Bürklin-Wolf, K Schäfer, Wach-tenburg-Luginsland, Wolf.

Geschmeidig

Complimentary description of a wine with low acidity that tastes smooth. Many *Spätlesen* from the ★Rheinpfalz in the 1960s could be described as *geschmeidig*. Today's are crisper and more acidic.

Geschwister

Brother(s) and sister(s), as in Weingut Geschwister Schuch. Sometimes abbreviated to *Geschw*.

Gewürztraminer

Opinion is divided as to the exact relationship of this vine to Traminer, but both names are found in Germany.

Giessen, Weingut Rhpf VDP

Estate of 6·5 hectares with holdings at ★Deidesheim (★Grainhübel, ★Herrgottsacker, ★Langenmorgen, ★Leinhöhle), ★Forst (★Unge-heuer, ★Musenhang) and ★Ruppertsberg (★Reiterpfad), planted 80 percent Riesling. Forty-five percent of the wine is dry. Annual production is 5,800 cases, sold 90 percent to private customers. Address: Weinstrasse 3, W-6705 Deidesheim
Tel: 06326 391

Gimmeldingen Rhpf w

One of several ★Neustadt satellites, producing exciting wines. *Grosslage*: ★Meerspinne.

Glatt
Balanced, with a soft finish – could apply to a *lieblich* Silvaner *Kabinett* wine from the Rheinhessen.

Gleichenstein, Weingut Freiherr von Baden
Estate dating from the 17th century, with buildings going back to the 15th century. Its 21 hectares include 40 percent Spätburgunder and 20 percent Müller-Thurgau. The Spätburgunder is fermented on the skins and matured in cask. Annual production is 15,000 cases, of which four percent is exported; 90 percent is dry.
Address: W-7818 Oberrotweil
Tel: 07662 288

Glühwein
Mulled wine: a hot drink, welcome in winter, based on red wine, water and sugar with lemon peel, cinnamon and cloves.

GmbH
Gesellschaft mit beschränkter Haftung. Describes a private limited company, as in P J Valckenberg GmbH.

Goldbächel Rhpf w
Einzellage of 4·3 hectares on almost flat ground on the outskirts of ★Wachenheim. Planted mainly with Riesling, it produces top-quality wine typical of the Rheinpfalz. *Grosslage*: ★Mariengarten. Growers: Biffar, Bürklin-Wolf, Wolf.

Goldbäumchen M-S-R w
Grosslage on mainly steep, Riesling-planted slopes in the under-valued Bereich ★Zell. Well known in Germany.

Goldlay M-S-R w
Steep *Einzellage* at ★Reil, producing good-quality Rieslings which lack the distinction of the best from ★Wehlen and ★Bernkastel. *Grosslage*: vom ★heissen Stein.

Goldloch Nahe w
Steep *Einzellage* at ★Dorsheim in the Bereich ★Kreuznach, adjacent to the busy Koblenz-Ludwigshafen motorway. Planted mainly

with Riesling (some over 30 years old), it produces top-quality, meaty wine. *Grosslage*: ★Schlosskapelle. Growers: Diel, Kruger-Rumpf, Niederhausen-Schlossböckelheim Staatliche Weinbau-domäne, M Schäfer, Schlossmühle, Tesch.

Goldtröpfchen M-S-R w

Einzellage of some 122 hectares at ★Piesport and ★Dhron, by far the best known of all Mosel sites because its wines are the most widely distributed. Facing southeast, south and southwest, the site is wholly steep and planted with 100 percent Riesling. The wines can be of excellent quality and the best are superb, with a fine powerful flavour and firm acidity. Cheap and genuine Goldtröpfchen is not likely to be found. *Grosslage*: ★Michelsberg. Growers: Bischöfliche Weingüter, Grans-Fassian, Kesselstatt, Krebs-Matheus-Lehnert, Reh (Marienhof), Vereinigte Hospitien.

Goldwingert M-S-R w

Tiny, top-quality, steep, Riesling *Einzellage* at ★Ürzig. *Grosslage*: ★Schwarzlay. Sole owner: Peter Nicolay (★Pauly-Bergweiler).

Göler'sche Verwaltung, Freiherr von Baden VDP

Estate of 14 hectares west of ★Heilbronn planted 60 percent Riesling, with an annual production of approximately 10,800 cases, of which 60 percent is *trocken*. Red wines are made from Limberger and Müllerrebe. Many award-winning wines.
Address: Hauptstrasse 44, W-7519 Sulzfeld
Tel: 07269 231

Gondorf M-S-R w

Wine village not far from ★Koblenz, linked with the adjacent village of ★Kobern. The vineyards are extremely steep, planted almost entirely in Riesling. The best wines are concentrated and full of flavour. Attractive old buildings and much wine-village atmosphere. *Grosslage*: ★Weinhex.

Gottesfuss M-S-R w

Four-hectare steep, slaty *Einzellage* at ★Wiltingen considered by some to be the best Saar site after ★Scharzhofberg. Being much smaller than Scharzhofberg the quality of Gottesfuss wine is more consistent. Growers: Kesselstatt, Reverchon, Volxem.

Gottesthal Rhg w
Grosslage of 321 hectares based on ★Oestrich, with a high proportion of Riesling. The finest wines will always be sold under the names of the *Einzellagen* – ★Lenchen, ★Doosberg and Klosterberg (shared with the *Grosslage* ★Mehrhölzchen) – and the *Ortsteil* ★Schloss Reichartshausen. Good (QbA) Gottesthal wines have the acidity necessary for development in bottle.

Graach M-S-R w
Hardly more than a hamlet in size, Graach is backed by its vineyards on the steep southwest-facing slopes above the Mosel near ★Bernkastel. All its *Einzellagen* (★Domprobst, ★Himmelreich, ★Josephshöfer) are capable of producing some of the finest Rieslings of the Mosel. *Grosslage*: ★Münzlay.

Graben M-S-R w
Top-quality *Einzellage* on the steep, south-southwest-facing hill of 100 percent Riesling vines above the Mosel at ★Bernkastel. The wines are elegant, racy and very 'classy', not the cheapest of Bernkasteler wines but realistically priced. *Grosslage*: ★Badstube. Growers: Friedrich-Wilhelm Gymnasium, Heidemanns-Bergweiler, Lauerberg, Loosen, G-F von Nell, J J Prüm, St Nikolaus, Studert-Prüm, Thanisch-Knabben, Thanisch-Müller-Burggraef, Wegeler-Deinhard.

Graf
Title equivalent to a British earl or a count. Often appears in the names of wine estates, usually of noble origin, such as Weingut Graf von Kanitz.

Gräfenberg Rhg w
Einzellage in a side valley set back from the Rhein at ★Kiedrich, producing very elegant, spicy Riesling wines, particularly in great years. *Grosslage*: ★Heiligenstock. Growers: Groenesteyn, Weil.

Grainhübel Rhpf w
One of the best of the distinguished *Einzellagen* around

★Deidesheim, producing top-quality wine. Its 12 hectares are virtually in the town and (unusually for Deidesheim) 40 percent of the site is steep. The main grape is Riesling. *Grosslage*: ★Mariengarten. Growers: Bassermann-Jordan, Biffar, Winzerverein Deidesheim, Dr Deinhard, Giessen, Kern, Kimich, Spindler.

Grans-Fassian, Weingut M-S-R

Estate of ten hectares with a good and increasing reputation for well-structured, concentrated wines. The holdings are at ★Piesport (★Goldtröpfchen), ★Trittenheim (★Apotheke, ★Altärchen), ★Dhron and ★Leiwen, planted 85 percent Riesling. Some wines are *barrique*-aged (unusual in the Mosel-Saar-Ruwer) and a high (for the region) 50 percent is *trocken*. Annual production is 6,700 cases. Address: Römerstrasse 28, W-5501 Leiwen
Tel: 06507 3170

Grantschen Würt r w

An *Ortsteil* of ★Weinsberg, well known for its Limberger wine and its modern, marketing-orientated cooperative (*see next entry*).

Grantschen eG, Weingärtnergenossenschaft Würt

Cooperative supplied by 114 hectares, planted 27 percent Riesling, 22 percent Trollinger and 21 percent Limberger. The range of bone-dry Riesling and Limberger wines offered as part of the 'Schwarze Serie' (with a black label) is well known in Germany, as is the *barrique*-aged Limberger-Dornfelder *cuvée*, 'Grandor'. Annual production is 108,800 cases, 70 percent *halbtrocken*.
Address: W-7102 Weinsberg
Tel: 07134 3856

Grasig

Grassy. A wine from unripe grapes can taste and smell of greenery. Not unpleasant when young.

Grauburgunder

Synonym for Ruländer, revived in the 1980s and now used to describe a dry, strongly flavoured, crisp wine, made from healthy (no *Edelfäule*) Ruländer grapes. This considerable marketing coup was started by the Winzergenossenschaft Bickensohl in Baden and carried out with particular success in the rest of the region and the Rheinpfalz. Unfortunately *lieblich* Grauburgunder is now also being sold, once again making the selection of German wines less clear than it should be.

Groenesteyn, Weingut des Reichsfreiherrn von Ritter zu Rhg

See Schloss Groenesteyn

Grosser Herrgott M-S-R w

Einzellage at ★Wintrich on the Mosel making stylish, lively Rieslings. *Grosslage*: ★Kurfürstlay.

Grosser Ring

A 'ring' in the English auction world has sinister implications. Not so in Germany, where the *Grosser Ring* (the large ring) consists of 34 fine Riesling-growing estates in the Mosel-Saar-Ruwer, who are all members of the VDP. Each autumn they hold an auction in ★Trier to promote their own wine and the reputation of the wines of the Mosel-Saar-Ruwer. Increasingly active abroad.

Grosskarlbach Rhpf w r

Attractive rural village, devoted to vineyards and orchards. Excellent source of good-quality, meaty white wines to rival the best in the region from *Deidesheim, *Forst and *Wachenheim. *Grosslage*: *Schwarzerde.

Grosslage

A combination of individual sites (*Einzellagen*) within one region (*Anbaugebiet*) producing quality (QbA and QmP) wines of similar style. The name of a *Grosslage* must always be accompanied by that of a village or community. *See* page 16.

Grosslagefrei

Free of a *Grosslage*. In some small areas there are *Einzellagen* but no *Grosslagen*. Common in Franken.

Grosvenor, G & M

Firm of brokers with a portfolio destined for the export market of good, estate-bottled wines, from 30 producers in a number of German wine regions.
Address: Schulstrasse 32, Postfach 63, W-6222 Johannisberg-Geisenheim
Tel: 06722 6087

Grün

Green. Similar to *grasig* but less strong in meaning.

Grundwein

Base wine. Still wine from which sparkling wine is made, and all-important in deciding the quality of the final product. The ideal *Grundwein* will have 9–11° alcohol, a high acid content and no residual sugar. It must be fresh and youthful. As a wine it is austere to the point of unpleasantness, but converted into sparkling wine it becomes balanced and refreshing.

Grüner Silvaner

See Silvaner, Grüner

Güldenmorgen Rhh w
Grosslage of some 430 hectares on the *Rheinterrasse, upstream from *Oppenheim. The name Güldenmorgen was once reserved for an individual vineyard site but now, as a *Grosslage*, it includes within its boundaries such distinguished Oppenheimer sites as *Sackträger and *Kreuz.

Guldental Nahe w
Large vine-growing community on the Naheweinstrasse with a high proportion of Silvaner. *Grosslage*: *Schlosskapelle.

Gült, Weingut Arnsteiner Rhh
A 16-hectare estate much praised by the German wine press, and highly successful in competitions. The holdings are all at *Osthofen and are planted in a wide range of vine varieties, with 25 percent Riesling. Sales are mainly to private customers but ten percent is exported.
Address: Friedrich-Ebert-Strasse 36, W-6522 Osthofen
Tel: 06242 2230

Gunderloch, Weingut Rhh VDP
Estate dating from 1890 with ten hectares around *Nackenheim, including the *Rothenberg site, and in Niersteiner *Paterberg. Vines are 80 percent Riesling, ten percent Silvaner, five percent Müller-Thurgau. The wines are very elegant, well defined and full of character. Some Dornfelder, Grauburgunder and Rivaner (Müller-Thurgau) wines are *barrique*-aged. Approximate annual production is 3,750 cases; 50 percent is *trocken*, 35 percent is exported.
Address: Carl-Gunderloch Platz, W-6506 Nackenheim
Tel: 06135 2341

Guntersblum Rhh w (r)
Small town at the southern end of the *Rheinterrasse, known for fine wines. It has a number of old cellars, patrician houses and the 'Kellerwegfest', a wine festival, at the end of August. *Grosslagen*: *Krötenbrunnen and Vogelsgärtchen.

Günterslay M-S-R w
Steep *Einzellage* at ★Piesport producing good, fresh, fruity
Rieslings, not quite in the class of Piesporter ★Goldtröpfchen.
Grosslage: ★Michelsberg. Growers include Reh (Marienhof).

Guntrum, Weingut Louis Rhh
Estate of 48 hectares in top-quality sites at ★Nierstein (including
★Pettenthal, ★Findling, ★Ölberg, ★Paterberg), ★Oppenheim
(★Sackträger, ★Kreuz) and ★Dienheim and others, planted mainly
in Riesling, Müller-Thurgau and Silvaner. Late-harvesting, and
efficient, modern winemaking, with emphasis on retaining fruity
acidity and varietal characteristics, combine to produce wines of
great refinement. The company dates from 1824, although
Guntrums were active as coopers and brewers in the 14th century.
An estate with clear marketing concepts. Annual production is
34,400 cases.
Address: Rheinallee 62, W-6505 Nierstein
Tel: 06133 5101

Gut
As a noun has several meanings, including that of an estate.
Frequently found as part of the word *Weingut* – wine estate.

Gutedel, Roter
Perhaps the original type of Gutedel, now growing in 44 hectares in
Baden where the price of its white wine from light red grapes falls
between that of Müller-Thurgau and Weissburgunder.

Gutedel, Weisser
An ancient vine variety (known in France as the Chasselas)
producing white grapes for the table and the press house, covering
1,295 hectares, all but three of which are in the Bereich
★Markgräflerland in Baden. It is widely planted in French-speaking
Switzerland where it is known as Fendant. Gutedel is good, but
never great. A wine without complexity.

Gutes Domtal Rhh w
Grosslage of more than 1,300 hectares behind the ★Rheinterrasse at
★Nierstein. It covers the vineyards of 15 villages and 31 *Einzellagen*,

the *Doktor at Dexheim being the best known because of its similarity (in name only) to the famous *Doctor at Bernkastel on the Mosel. After *Liebfraumilch, Gutes Domtal has the widest distribution outside Germany of any Rhein wine. It is always cheap, and drunk within the year following the vintage it can be very pleasant. Unfortunately, with the accepted market price set so low, there seems little incentive to produce quality wine with much character under the name Gutes Domtal.

Gütezeichen Franken
Award first given to Franken quality wines in 1981, under the auspices of the Bavarian government, based on a tasting and analytical examination. Since 1983 only available to wine in *Bocksbeutel*. To qualify, dry wines must be *fränkisch trocken*.

Gütezeichen für Badischen Qualitätswein
Award given by the Baden Winegrowers' Association to quality (QbA and QmP) wines in standard-size (not litre) bottles, that have already won their *AP Nr and achieved high enough marks to qualify for the Gütezeichen. A special yellow certificate can be won by dry wines of *Spätlese* quality and less. The Badisches Gütezeichen is officially recognized by the state of Baden-Württemberg.

Gutsverwaltung
Administration of an estate, as in Gutsverwaltung Wegeler-Deinhard.

Haag, Weingut Fritz M-S-R VDP
Family-owned estate of 5·2 hectares dating from 1605, with steep holdings at Brauneberg (*Juffer, *Juffer-Sonnenuhr), Graach (*Himmelreich) and Burgen. Vines are 95 percent Riesling. The wines are among the finest of the Mittelmosel, usually described as delicate, elegant, intense. Annual production is 5,000 cases; 75 percent is *lieblich*, 30 percent is exported.
Address: Dusemonder Hof, W-5551 Brauneberg
Tel: 06534 410

Haag, Weingut Willi M-S-R VDP
Estate of 3·5 hectares with holdings planted 100 percent Riesling in

steep sites at Brauneberg (*Juffer, *Juffer-Sonnenuhr and others)
and Burgen. Annual production is 2,500 cases; 90 percent is *lieblich*,
and a high 45 percent is exported.
Address: Hauptstrasse 111, W-5551 Brauneberg
Tel: 06534 450

Haardt Rhpf w r
A part of *Neustadt on the vine-friendly slopes of the Pfälzerwald,
known for subtropical plants, dignified old houses and excellent
Riesling wines from Weingut *Müller-Catoir. *Grosslage*:
*Meerspinne.

Hagel
Hail. Hailstorms can cause damage at almost any time – they have
been known to strip vines of leaf and fruit in mid-summer,
destroying the current harvest and severely reducing the following
year's crop. If a hailstorm occurs shortly before the vintage, many
of the grapes may be knocked to the ground. In these circumstances, an early gathering (*Vorlese*) is allowed.

Hagelgeschmack
'Taste of hail'. Hailstones can damage grapes in such a way that they
rot on the vine and later pass on to the wine an unpleasant flavour
(*Hagelgeschmack*), and often excessive volatile acidity as well.

Haidle, Weingut Karl Würt
Seven-hectare estate which takes in must from another 11 hectares.
The estate's holdings at Stetten and Schnait, east of *Stuttgart, are
planted 60 percent Riesling, 15 percent Kerner and ten percent
Trollinger. Both the estate and its wines (80 percent *trocken*) have
received an astounding number of top awards.
Address: Hindenburgstrasse 21, W-7053 Kernen-Stetten
Tel: 07151 42503

Hail
See Hagel

Halbfuder
The Mosel equivalent of the Rhein *Halbstück*, with a capacity of

approximately 500 litres. Its disappearance parallels that of the *Halbstück*, for the same reasons. *See* Fass.

Halbstück
Round (as opposed to oval) wooden cask with a capacity of some 610 litres, used until the mid-1960s for transporting and storing Rhein wine. Still found to a small extent in some cellars, but steadily disappearing because of high maintenance costs and the possible loss of freshness in white wine of relatively low acidity (such as Müller-Thurgau) when stored in wood. *See* Fass.

Halbtrocken
Medium-dry. When describing still (non-sparkling) wine, *halb-trocken* indicates that the sugar content is not more than ten grams per litre greater than that of the total acid content, with a maximum of 18 grams per litre. For those who feel that dry wines from the northern German regions often lack body, and do not want a sweetish wine, *halbtrocken* seems an excellent compromise. It allows the true flavour to be easily tasted and can produce most attractive, balanced results. A *halbtrocken* sparkling wine in the EC can contain between 33 and 50 grams per litre sugar.

Hallgarten Rhg w
Small rural village away from the bustle of the Rhein and protected by the ★Taunus hills that border its northern vineyards. Produces fine Riesling wines. *Grosslage*: ★Mehrhölzchen.

Hallgarten/Rhg eG, Vereinigte Winzergenossenschaft Rhg
Cooperative supplied from 103 hectares, in sites at ★Hallgarten (★Schönhell) and ★Oestrich (★Lenchen, ★Doosberg).
Address: Hattenheimerstrasse 15, W-6227 Oestrich-Winkel
Tel: 06723 7064

Halsschleife
Neck label. It is common for German wine bottles to be dressed with a neck label, showing vintage or other optional information. Some estates (such as ★Schloss Reinhartshausen), however, feel that a neck label does not improve the appearance of their bottles and omit its use.

Hambach an der Weinstrasse Rhpf w (r)

Small picturesque wine town near *Neustadt, well known in the region, producing wines of good quality (including Riesling, Silvaner) but not comparable to the best from a few kilometres further north. The Hambacher Schloss carries great historical significance as a centre of German liberalism. *Grosslagen*: Rebstöckel and Pfaffengrund.

Hammel & Cie Weingut Weinkellerei, Emil Rhpf

Estate of 59 hectares, dating from 1723, producing approximately 59,600 cases a year from its own vineyards. Twenty percent is exported. The estate's holdings, all in northern Rheinpfalz, are planted with a wide range of vine varieties. The aim is to produce pleasant 'drinking' wines, with a gentle acidity and agreeable fruitiness; 35 percent is *trocken*. The Weinkellerei also sells wines from Alsace.

Address: Weinstrasse Süd 4, W-6719 Kirchheim
Tel: 06359 3003

Hammelburg Franken w (r)

Old town in the far north of Franken, on the river Saale, with a tradition of 1,200 years of viticulture. It has some fine old buildings and one of the earliest cooperative cellars in the region. Produces wines of good acidity from Müller-Thurgau and Silvaner. *Grosslage*: Burg.

Hammelburg, Städtlicher Weingut Franken

See Schloss Saaleck

Harmonisch

Balanced. Describes wine in which the constituent parts are in harmony. Fine wines, by definition, must be balanced; lesser wines may be balanced.

Harvest

The German grape harvest (*Ernte* or *Lese*) usually takes place over a period of two months from mid-September onwards. It starts with grapes such as Ortega and Siegerrebe, continues with Müller-Thurgau, Bacchus and Morio-Muskat and finishes with Riesling, the very last of which may not be gathered until the following year if *Eiswein* is being made. *See also* Hauptlese.

Growers have to consider many factors when organizing their harvest, including the rate at which the grapes can be picked and pressed and the risks involved in leaving them on the vine to increase their sugar content. Because of the varying pace at which different grapes ripen, the gathering of *Spätlese* Müller-Thurgau, for example, will often be finished before the main picking of Riesling has begun.

The timing of the harvest is officially controlled and the vineyards are put out of bounds except during the hours when picking is permitted. In recent years mechanical harvesters (*Traubenvollernter*) have appeared in some force in the Rheinpfalz and Rheinhessen. Their use is increasing.

Hasensprung Rhg w (r)

Large, 100-hectare *Einzellage* at *Winkel producing top-quality, refined Riesling wines that are among the best in the region. *Grosslage*: *Honigberg. Growers: Allendorf, Brentano, Eser, von Hessen, Hupfeld, Johannishof, Krayer, Mumm, Querbach, Ress, Schloss Schönborn, Wegeler-Deinhard.

Hattenheim Rhg w

Village with fine old half-timbered houses; produces some of the best Riesling wines in the region. *Grosslage*: *Deutelsberg.

Hatzenport M-S-R w

Small riverside village in the Bereich *Zell, overlooked by steep vineyards planted almost entirely in Riesling. *Grosslage*: *Weinhex.

Hauptlese

Main harvest; takes place when the overall ripeness of the grapes has reached the desired maturity. The main harvest of any one wine will last about seven to ten days, after which it may be followed by a *Spätlese* harvest. Theoretically, all qualities can be picked during the main harvest, with the exception of *Spätlesen*. (In 1989 Weingut Dr *Bürklin-Wolf picked a Riesling *Trockenbeerenauslese* from botrytis-affected grapes on September 27 – before the *Hauptlese*.) Because the weather is not sufficiently cold during the main harvest,

Eiswein-picking will take place long after the start of the *Spätlese* harvest. *See also* Harvest.

Hausen-Mabilon KG, Sektkellerei

Sekt manufacturers and owners of the estate of the same name, producing bottle-fermented high-quality *brut* and extra dry *Sekt* bA from Riesling and Elbling. Annual production is equivalent to 12,300 cases.
Address: Im Staden 124, W-5510 Saarburg
Tel: 06581 3044

Hausen-Mabilon, Weingut M-S-R

Four-hectare estate with steep holdings planted 98 percent Riesling at *Saarburg (*Rausch) and *Ayl (*Kupp). The wines are sold mainly to private customers.
Address: Im Staden 124, W-5510 Saarburg
Tel: 06581 3044

Haustrunk

'Drink of the house'. Usually a low-quality wine provided by a producer from the 'leftovers' of his vintage, free of charge, for the everyday consumption of his workers.

Heckenwirtschaft

Term used in parts of Franken for *Strausswirtschaft*.

Hectare

2·471 acres. The standard unit of measurement of vineyards.

Heddesdorff, Weingut Freiherr von M-S-R

One of the most distinguished estates of the Bereich *Zell, with origins in the 15th century. Four hectares of steep holdings, all at *Winningen, are 100 percent Riesling, producing 3,300 cases of carefully made, often steely wine; 60 percent is *trocken* (a high proportion for the Mosel) and 30 percent is *halbtrocken*. The estate is a founder member of the Erzeugergemeinschaft *Deutsches Eck. Ten percent of the production is exported.
Address: W-5406 Winningen
Tel: 02606 302

Hehner-Kiltz, Weingut Nahe

Estate with 9·2 hectares planted, and with another 3·3 hectares to be added when reconstruction of the vineyards (*Flurbereinigung*) is at last complete. Vines are 75 percent Riesling, ten percent Silvaner, ten percent Spätburgunder. The holdings include parts of Schlossböckelheimer ★Kupfergrube, ★Felsenberg and Königsfels, Niederhäuser ★Hermannshöhle as well as vineyards at Waldböckelheim. The wines are much admired in Germany for their strong, crisp Nahe style. Annual production is at present 4,600 cases, mostly sold to private customers and via the estate's own hotel and restaurant. Sixty percent is *trocken*.

Address: Hauptstrasse 4, W-6558 Waldböckelheim

Tel: 06758 7918

Heidelberg Baden w

Famous old university town astride the river ★Neckar, escaped damage in World War II. Has many old buildings and the vast Heidelberger Fass (cask), dating from 1751, with a capacity of 220,000 litres (314,286 bottles). Produces sound wines from a wide range of vine varieties including Müller-Thurgau, Riesling, Silvaner and Weissburgunder, grown on steep or sloping sites. *Grosslagen*: Rittersberg and Mannaberg.

Heidemanns-Bergweiler, Weingut Dr M-S-R

Estate of 6·5 hectares with holdings in famous sites at ★Bernkastel (such as ★Doctor, ★Alte Badstube am Doctorberg, ★Graben, ★Lay, ★Schlossberg), ★Graach (★Himmelreich, ★Domprobst) and ★Wehlen (including ★Sonnenuhr), planted 95 percent Riesling. Wines are typical of origin, elegant, with good fruity acidity. Annual production is 5,000 cases, 65 percent *lieblich*, 50 percent exported.

Address: Gestade 16, W-5550 Bernkastel-Kues

Tel: 06531 2352

Heilbronn am Neckar Würt r w

Severely damaged in World War II, the rebuilt industrial town as a whole lacks charm, but produces Trollinger and Riesling wines to a very good standard at the Heilbronn-Erlenbach-Weinsberg Co-operative (*see next entry*). *Grosslagen*: Staufenberg, Kirchenweinberg and Heuchelberg.

Heilbronn-Erlenbach-Weinsberg eG, Genossenschaftskellerei Würt

A particularly well-run cooperative cellar of 653 members, receiving grapes from 600 hectares, and producing excellent wines of character and style, of which 75 percent is *lieblich*. Main vine varieties are Riesling and Trollinger. A superior range of wines is produced based on reduced yields and *barrique*-ageing. Sales are exclusively in Germany.

Address: Binswangerstrasse, W-7100 Heilbronn
Tel: 07131 1579

Heiligenhäuschen M-S-R w

Steep *Einzellage* on the edge of the Ruwer vine-growing area, shared by three communities including ★Waldrach. Produces lively, fruity Rieslings in good years. *Grosslage*: ★Römerlay.

Heiligenstock Rhg w

Relatively small (171-hectare) *Grosslage* covering the vineyards of ★Kiedrich. Mainly Riesling.

Heinrich, Weingut GA Würt

Traditional estate with ten hectares at ★Heilbronn planted 26 percent Trollinger, 24 percent Riesling, 12 percent Limberger. Malolactic fermentation (*see* Deacidification) is allowed for both white and red wines when necessary, and a light wine is gathered two weeks before the grapes are fully ripe. Annual production is 7,100 cases, 60 percent *trocken*, sold mainly to private customers.

Address: Roedstrasse 29, W-7100 Heilbronn
Tel: 07131 75948

Heissen Stein, vom M-S-R w

First *Grosslage* of the Middle Mosel, travelling upstream from ★Koblenz. Planted in 628 hectares, much of it on steep slopes, including the ★Goldlay site at ★Reil. The main grape is Riesling.

Heitlinger, Weingut Albert Baden VDP

High-quality 25-hectare estate, of which 60 percent is on steep slopes, planted 45 percent Riesling and 35 percent varieties of Burgunder (Pinot). Modern marketing ideas result in five ranges of

wine (85 percent *trocken*) based on their true (and considerable) quality, rather than the official quality categories. (A Riesling *Tafelwein*, aged in *barrique*, is listed, at a very high price.) Annual production is 15,800 cases, of which three percent is exported.
Address: Am Mühlberg, W-7524 Oestringen-Tiefenbach
Tel: 07259 1061

Helenenkloster M-S-R w
Steep *Einzellage* of 0·8 hectares planted in carefully selected Riesling clones. Now famous for *Eiswein*. Sole owner: M F ★Richter. *Grosslage*: ★Kurfürstlay.

Helfensteiner
Crossing of Frühburgunder × Trollinger from ★Weinsberg, planted in 41 hectares, all but one hectare in Württemberg. Demanding a good site and with an uncertain yield (flowering not always successful), Helfensteiner's future is doubtful.

Henkell & Söhnlein Sektkellereien
Germany's largest drinks enterprise. The best known *Sekt* brands (foreign products are also distributed) are Henkell Trocken (the most exported *Sekt* made in Germany) and Söhnlein Brilliant.
Address: Biebricher Allee 142, W-6200 Wiesbaden
Tel: 06121 63230

Half-timbered houses in the town of Heppenheim

Heppenheim Hess Berg w
Town 28 kilometres north of *Heidelberg, with some attractive
half-timbered buildings. The wines are lively, made mainly from
Riesling. Largest producer is the local cooperative, the *Bergsträsser Gebiets-Winzergenossenschaft. *Grosslage*: Schlossberg.

Herb
Austere. Sometimes used in restaurants as a synonym for *trocken*.
Elsewhere generally describes the effect of tannin in red wine,
without residual sugar.

Hermannsberg Nahe w
Small *Einzellage* on the slopes at *Niederhausen producing
charming Riesling wines of great finesse. *Grosslage*: *Burgweg.
Sole owner: *Niederhausen-Schlossböckelheim Staatliche
Weinbaudomäne.

Hermannshof Rhh
See Schmitt, Weingut Hermann Franz

Hermannshöhle Nahe w
One of the best *Einzellagen* on the Nahe, at *Niederhausen, steep
and 100 percent Riesling. In a good vintage, great wine of immense
elegance is made. *Grosslage*: *Burgweg. Growers: August
Anheuser, Dönnhof, Hehner-Kiltz, Niederhausen-Schlossböckelheim Staatliche Weinbaudomäne, J Schneider.

Heroldrebe
Red grape variety, a crossing of Portugieser × Limberger. Like the
Helfensteiner it originated in *Weinsberg. Can yield as much as 140
hectolitres per hectare of light red wine of no special quality. Needs
to be picked late in the season, to avoid an unripe flavour and an
excess of tannin. Good as *Weissherbst*. Planted in 220 hectares, over
half in the Rheinpfalz.

Herrenberg Franken w (r)
Small *Grosslage* at Castell producing full-bodied Silvaner and
Müller-Thurgau, and a little red wine. Growers include *Cas-
tell'sches Domänenamt.

Herrenberg-Honigsäckel eG, Winzergenossenschaft Rhpf

Cooperative of 176 hectares whose members' holdings – at *Ungstein, *Kallstadt (*Saumagen) and elsewhere – are planted 32 percent Riesling, 22 percent Portugieser, 17 percent Müller-Thurgau and other varieties. *Lieblich* wines account for 65 percent of the production.

Address: Weinstrasse 12, W-6702 Bad Dürkheim-Ungstein

Tel: 06322 1450

Herrenberg, Weingut Serriger M-S-R

See Simon, Bert

Herrenberger M-S-R w

Steep *Einzellage* of outstanding quality at *Ayl on the Saar, exclusively Riesling. In good vintages the wine shows great class: it is stylish, well structured and will keep for years. *Grosslage*: *Scharzberg. Sole owners: *Bischöfliche Weingüter.

Herrgottsacker Rhpf w

Largest (120 hectares) *Einzellage* at *Deidesheim. Produces racy Rieslings, lighter than some in the district but stylish, with a balance more often found in the Rheingau. *Grosslage*: *Mariengarten. Growers: Bassermann-Jordan, Biffar, Bürklin-Wolf, Winzerverein Deidesheim, Dr Deinhard, Giessen, Kern, Kimich, Mosbacher, Mossbacher-Hof, Spindler, Wegeler-Deinhard, Wolf.

Hersteller

The producer of a wine, not the grower of the grapes. Often found as 'hergestellt in': 'produced in'.

Herxheim am Berg Rhpf w (r)

Village on a plateau in the northern Rheinpfalz with one of the oldest nature reserves in the region. Good, solid, meaty wines. *Grosslage*: ★Kobnert.

Herxheim am Berg eG, Winzergenossenschaft Rhpf

Cooperative supplied by 154 hectares on rolling slopes below the Pfälzerwald in the north of the region, planted 20 percent Riesling, 18 percent Silvaner, 15 percent each Müller-Thurgau and Portugieser. Good quality *lieblich* wines predominate, and there is also a premium range.

Address: Weinstrasse, W-6719 Herxheim am Berg
Tel: 06353 7348

Herzhaft

Hearty. In Germany, describes a wine with pronounced flavour and bouquet, and usually good acidity. A term that might be applied, for example, to a Riesling from ★Münster-Sarmsheim in the Nahe, or from ★Lorch in the Rheingau.

Hessen

Federal state encompassing the vine-growing regions of the Rheingau and Hessische Bergstrasse. The capital is ★Wiesbaden. Not to be confused with Rheinhessen in Rheinland-Pfalz. Area under vine is 3,293 hectares.

Hessen, Weingut Prinz von Rhg Charta VDP

Fifty-hectare estate taken over by the Prince and Landgrave of Hessen in 1958, 88 percent Riesling, in well-known sites at ★Rüdesheim (★Berg Rottland, ★Bischofsberg), ★Geisenheim (★Kläuserweg, ★Mäuerchen), ★Johannisberg, ★Winkel (★Hasensprung, ★Jesuitengarten), ★Rauenthal, ★Eltville and ★Kiedrich (★Sandgrub). The estate has a clear marketing strategy and many of its wines are intended to accompany food. Annual production is 33,300 cases, 60 percent *lieblich*, five percent exported.

Address: Grund 1, W-6222 Geisenheim
Tel: 06722 8172

Hessische Bergstrasse w (r)

Small wine-producing region, with 389 hectares under vine. Riesling covers 212 hectares. Müller-Thurgau is widely planted in the north near Darmstadt. The vineyard holdings are exceptionally small and *Dauerbegrünung* is almost universal. Here vine growing is very much a weekend occupation, and 84 percent of the harvest is delivered to the two cooperative cellars. For all that, the wines can be excellent and compare in quality with many from the Rheingau, to which they are similar in style. They are seldom found outside the region.

Heuchelberg-Kellerei eG Würt

Important innovative cooperative with a cask cellar built from sandstone retrieved from the rubble of ★Heilbronn in 1945. Holdings of 335 hectares are planted 36 percent Riesling, 21 percent Trollinger, 11 percent Müllerrebe (Schwarzriesling) – much in the Grafenberg *Einzellage*. All the modern trends are here united – *barrique*-ageing, production of premium wines, environmentally friendly viticulture, and the planting of Chardonnay and (less usually) Cabernet Sauvignon. Thirty percent of the wine is *trocken* and 50 percent is *halbtrocken*.
Address: Weingärtnergenossenschaft, Neippergerstrasse 25, W-7103 Schwaigern
Tel: 07138 9702–0

Heyl zu Herrnsheim, Weingut Freiherr Rhh VDP

By journalistic general agreement, the top estate in the Rheinhessen, with 24 hectares in the best ★Nierstein sites (★Pettenthal, ★Hipping, ★Ölberg, and the solely owned ★Brudersberg). Planted 60 percent Riesling, 17 percent Müller-Thurgau, 14 percent Silvaner. The range has been simplified with only the best wines being sold with a site name. Approximate annual production is the equivalent of 13,900 cases. The wines are full of character and 60 percent is *trocken*. Sales 85 percent in Germany. The estate is a pioneer in Germany of ecological viticulture, and a founder member of its supporting national association.

Address: Mathildenhof, Langgasse 3, W-6505 Nierstein
Tel: 06133 5120

Heymann-Löwenstein, Weingut M-S-R

Estate of 3·8 hectares at ★Winningen (★Uhlen), planted 100 percent
Riesling. The quality of the wines bears little relationship to any
preconceived ideas that might be suggested by the official quality
categories. An '89 *Beerenauslese trocken* is beautifully balanced in
spite of its 16·5 percent of alcohol, and the QbAs are remarkable.
Annual production is 2,500 cases, 99·5 percent *trocken*. Highly

priced, but good-value wines, imaginatively packaged.
Address: Bahnhofstrasse 10, W-5406 Winningen
Tel: 02606 1919

Himmelreich M-S-R w
Steep, southwest-facing *Einzellage* of nearly 90 hectares at *Graach.
The site forms part of the great sweep of vineyards that stretches
from *Bernkastel to *Zeltingen-Rachtig. Among Mosel wines,
those from the Graacher Himmelreich seem full, fruity, with a
stylish acidity. Prices are similar to those of nearby Wehlener
*Sonnenuhr. *Grosslage*: *Münzlay. Growers: Christoffel, Fried-
rich-Wilhelm-Gymnasium, Fritz Haag, Heidemanns-Bergweiler,
Kees-Kieren, Kesselstatt, Lauerburg, Loosen, Pauly-Bergweiler, J J
Prüm, S A Prüm, M F Richter, St Nikolaus, Studert-Prüm,
Thanisch-Knabben, Thanisch-Müller-Burggraef, Vereinigte Hospitien, Wegeler-Deinhard, Weins-Prüm.

Himmelreich M-S-R w
Like the site of the same name at Graach (*see previous entry*), the
Himmelreich *Einzellage* at *Zeltingen-Rachtig forms part of the
continuous vineyard that stretches from *Bernkastel to Zeltingen-
Rachtig. Classic Mosel Riesling wines, although the general
standard is probably not quite so high as that set by the Graacher
Himmelreich. *Grosslage*: *Münzlay. Growers: Friedrich-Wilhelm-
Gymnasium, Mönchof, Peter Nicolay (Pauly-Bergweiler), Sel-
bach-Oster, Vereinigte Hospitien.

Hipping Rhh w
Mainly steep *Einzellage* overlooking the Rhein at *Nierstein,
producing top-quality wines of depth and much flavour. *Grosslage*:
*Rehbach. Growers: Balbach, Braun, Heyl zu Herrnsheim, H F
Schmitt, Schmitt'sches Weingut, G Schneider, Sittmann, St
Anthony, Strub.

Hitzlay M-S-R w
Einzellage on the rural river Ruwer at *Kasel. Like most of the Kasel
sites, capable of producing tremendously fresh, well-constructed
wine in good years. *Grosslage*: *Römerlay. Growers: Beulwitz,
Karlsmühle, Kesselstatt, Wegeler-Deinhard.

Hochfarbig

High-coloured. Describes a white wine which may be oxidized, or made from grapes whose colour in the skins has entered into the must (possibly from Ruländer, Siegerrebe or Roter Traminer grapes) or from grapes that have been attacked by *Edelfäule*. Thus *hochfarbig* can be either negative or positive in meaning.

Hochgewächs

See Riesling-Hochgewächs

Hochheim Rhg w

Small town five kilometres east of *Mainz, with 225 hectares of vineyard – one of the largest Rheingau wine-producing communities. The best sites (*Domdechaney, *Hölle, *Kirchenstück) produce powerful Rieslings with a distinct earthy flavour. The English word *'hock' derives from Hochheim. *Grosslage*: *Daubhaus.

Hochmess Rhpf w

Small *Grosslage* of some 100 hectares on the northern edge of *Bad Dürkheim, including the well-known *Spielberg site. The best wines are sold under the *Einzellage* names but the quality of wine produced by the *Grosslage* as a whole is high. The Riesling and Scheurebe wines are often excellent.

Hock

Abbreviation for Hochheimer, originally described wines from *Hochheim but became a generic term for all white Rhein wine. The heading 'Hocks and Moselles' still appears on many restaurant, and a few merchants', wine lists in the UK. Hock is defined by the EC as (1) any German table wine that bears the description 'Rhein'; (2) a German quality wine from any of the following regions: Ahr, Hessische Bergstrasse, Mittelrhein, Nahe, Rheingau, Rheinhessen, Rheinpfalz. Hock must also be produced from Riesling or Silvaner, or their derivatives.

Hoensbroech, Weingut Reichsgraf & Marquis zu Baden VDP

Estate of 17 hectares near *Heidelberg, including sole ownership of the Michelfelder Himmelberg site. Vines are 35 percent

Weissburgunder, 20 percent Riesling, 15 percent Ruländer (Grauburgunder), and Spätburgunder. All the wines are fully fermented except the richest *Auslesen*. Some *barrique*-ageing. Annual production is 10,000 cases, a high 70 percent of which is sold to hotels and restaurants.
Address: W-6921 Angelbachtal-Michelfeld
Tel: 07265 381

Hofkammerkellerei Stuttgart, Württembergische Würt VDP
Estate owned by King Carl, Duke of Württemberg, based in new buildings at Germany's largest baroque castle, Schloss Monrepos. The holdings (42 hectares) are on six subsidiary estates in various parts of the region, planted 47 percent Riesling, 14 percent Limberger, 24 percent Trollinger, and other varieties. Around 85 percent of the wine is *trocken* and virtually all is sold locally.
Address: Schloss Monrepos, W-7140 Ludwigsburg
Tel: 07141 31085

Hofstück Rhpf w (r)
Grosslage that covers some 1,250 hectares of scattered vineyards near ★Deidesheim and ★Ruppertsberg. Most of the sites are on level land on clay or sandy soil, producing good-quality white wines from the standard Rheinpfalz vine varieties (Riesling, Müller-Thurgau, etc) and red from Portugieser.

Hohenbeilstein, Schlossgut Würt VDP
Nine-hectare estate southeast of ★Heilbronn, planted 23 percent Trollinger, 20 percent Riesling, 15 percent Müllerrebe (Schwarzriesling), ten percent Limberger. Weissburgunder is fermented and aged in *barrique* and Limberger is matured in *barrique*, both with attractive results. Production is 85 percent *trocken* and 60 percent is sold to private customers.
Address: W-7141 Beilstein
Tel: 07062 4303

Hohenberg, Weingut Rhpf VDP
Ten-hectare estate at the foot of the Pfälzerwald, planted 44 percent Riesling, plus Weissburgunder, Spätburgunder, St Laurent and

others. The steep sites are partly terraced. Tannic, cask-matured red wines, and the refreshing (mainly dry) whites win many national prizes. *Barriques* are an essential part of the winemaking – not a sideline. Annual production is 5,000 cases, 100 percent *trocken*.
Address: Dr Heinz Wehrheim, Weinstrasse 8, W-6741 Birkweiler
Tel: 06345 3542

Hohenlohe Langenburg'sche Weingüter, Fürstlich
Würt and Franken
Estate of 18 hectares, planted 30 percent Müller-Thurgau, 15 percent Riesling, 14 percent Kerner and other varieties. Sole owners of the ten-hectare Karlsberg and Schmecker sites at Weikersheim in Württemberg as well as Tauberrettersheimer Königin in Franken. Annual production is 10,000 cases, all sold in Germany.
Address: W-6992 Weikersheim

Hohenlohe-Öhringen'sche, Fürst zu Würt VDP
Estate first mentioned in 1360, with 20 hectares in the sloping Verrenberger Verrenberg site (sole ownership) and the Verrenberger Goldberg. Vines are 53 percent Riesling, 15 percent Limberger, ten percent Spätburgunder, plus others. The wines are *trocken* and contain less than 2 grams per litre sugar. They are matured in wood, some in *barriques*, even Riesling and now Chardonnay. Annual production is 15,000 cases.
Address: W-7110 Öhringen im Schloss
Tel: 07941 7081

Hohenmorgen Rhpf w
One of the best *Einzellagen* at ★Deidesheim, producing top-quality, weighty Rieslings from sloping ground. *Grosslage*: ★Mariengarten. Growers: Bassermann-Jordan, Bürklin-Wolf.

Hölle Rhg w
Einzellage at ★Hochheim, overlooking the river Main. The wines from the heavy soil are analytically similar to those of the nearby ★Kirchenstück *Einzellage*, but taste fuller and a shade less elegant. *Grosslage*: ★Daubhaus. Growers: Aschrott, Staatsweingut Eltville, Weingut der Stadt Frankfurt, Hupfeld, Künstler, Ress, Schloss Schönborn, Werner.

Hölle Rhg w
Sloping *Einzellage* at ★Johannisberg making balanced, classic Rheingau Riesling wines. *Grosslage*: ★Erntebringer. Growers: von Hessen, Hupfeld, Johannishof, Mumm, Wegeler-Deinhard.

Höllenberg Rhg r
Impressive, steep *Einzellage* overlooking the village of ★Assmannshausen, planted mainly in Spätburgunder. The wine is stylish and shows the vine characteristics well. Somewhat expensive. *Grosslage*: ★Steil. Growers: Allendorf, Kesseler, König, Krone, Mumm, Ress, Schloss Schönborn.

Holzgeschmack
'Taste of wood.' The flavour that may be picked up by a wine that has been stored in a new cask, which can be either a good or a bad thing, depending on the structure of the wine, and the personal opinion of the taster.

Homburg am Main Franken w (r)
A village with too many vine varieties and a magnificent but partly derelict vineyard (Kallmuth) with an incline of 70 percent in parts, producing, *inter alia*, well-structured wines from Silvaner. No *Grosslage*.

Honigberg Rhg w
Grosslage covering some of the best Rheingau sites. Production of good-quality Riesling is endemic in Honigberg, so a Riesling sold under the *Grosslage* name will be closely related to wines sold with an *Einzellage* name. Good value for money but not cheap.

Honigsäckel Rhpf w
A relatively small *Grosslage* of about 170 hectares covering three sites near the village of *Ungstein (Weilberg, Herrenberg and Nussriegel). Full-bodied wines, typical of the region, from varied soil on steep or gentle slopes. The Scheureben are particularly good.

Hövel, Weingut von M–S–R VDP
Important Saar estate, nearly 200 years old, with cellars dating back to the 12th century. A holding in the *Scharzhofberg and sole ownership of the Hütte in *Oberemmel, totalling 11 hectares of steep vineyards, 98 percent Riesling, two percent Weissburgunder. Annual production is 6,600 cases (70 percent exported) of cask-matured, high-quality (mainly *lieblich*) wines with good acidity.
Address: Agritiusstrasse 5–6, W-5503 Konz-Oberemmel
Tel: 06501 15384

Hubertuslay M–S–R w
Mainly steep *Einzellage* at *Kinheim producing good-quality, charming Riesling wines, possibly lacking the personality of the best of the region. *Grosslage*: *Schwarzlay. Growers: Kees-Kieren, Mönchof, Peter Nicolay (Pauly-Bergweiler).

Huesgen GmbH, Adolf M–S–R
Wine merchants, established in 1735, exporting estate bottlings and their own of QbA, DTW and EC table wine.
Address: Am Bahnhof 54, W-5580 Traben-Trabach
Tel: 06541 9281

Hupfeld Erben, Weingut H Rhg Charta VDP
Estate of 11 hectares with holdings at ★Johannisberg (such as
★Hölle), ★Winkel (★Hasensprung, ★Jesuitengarten), ★Mittelheim,
★Oestrich (★Lenchen), planted 90 percent Riesling, six percent
Spätburgunder. Best known outside Germany for its ownership of
Weingut ★Königin Victoria Berg.
Address: Rheingaustrasse 113, W-6227 Oestrich-Winkel
Tel: 06723 3307

Huxelrebe
White grape variety, a crossing of Weisser Gutedel × Courtillier
musqué by Dr Georg Scheu of ★Alzey, dating from 1927. If the
vine is prevented from its tendency to overcrop the must will be
above average in weight, with more acidity than Müller-Thurgau.
Because of the high sugar content of the grapes the wine will often
reach potential *Auslese* quality, with a light Muskat bouquet.
Successful as a dry wine, the sweeter *Auslesen* and *Beerenauslesen* are
cheaper alternatives to Riesling – but not as good. Planted in 1,684
hectares, mainly in the Rheinhessen and Rheinpfalz.

Hybride
Hybrid vine – *see* Rebsorte.

Ice saints
See Eisheiligen

Ice wine
See Eiswein

Ihringen Baden w r
Village in the Bereich ★Kaiserstuhl, producing positive, powerful
wines from a variety of vines, including Silvaner (for which
Ihringen is well known), Müller-Thurgau, the Burgunder (Pinot)
family, and Riesling. *Grosslage*: ★Vulkanfelsen.

Ihringen eG, Kaiserstühler Winzergenossenschaft Baden
Cooperative supplied by 410 hectares in the warmest part of
Germany, planted 34 percent Silvaner, 24 percent Spätburgunder,
22 percent Müller-Thurgau and 13 percent Ruländer. Since 1989 a

range of cask-matured wines has been produced from a low yield, from vines that are at least 20 years old. *Barriques* are used for ageing Spät- and Weissburgunder. Annual production is 294,400 cases, 40 percent *trocken*, 45 percent *halbtrocken*, sold mainly to supermarkets and grocery chains in Germany.
Address: Winzerstrasse 6, W-7817 Ihringen
Tel: 07668 622

Immich-Batterieberg, Carl Aug M-S-R

Six-hectare estate with sites at ★Enkirch, including sole ownership of the steep 1·3-hectare Batterieberg vineyard, planted 100 percent Riesling. Annual production is 2,900 cases of elegant, racy wine, 55 percent *trocken*, eight percent exported.
Address: Im alten Tal 2, W-5585 Enkirch
Tel: 06541 9376

Ingelheim am Rhein Rhh r (w)

Small town known for many years for its agreeable Spätburgunder *Weissherbst* and red wine. The acidity in the best of the white wines recalls the Rheingau. *Grosslage*: Kaiserpfalz.

Innere Leiste Franken w
Steep site at ★Würzburg; one of the relatively few internationally
known Franken *Einzellagen*. Produces splendid, rather earthy
Riesling wines with a firm, positive style. *Grosslage*: Marienberg.
Growers: Bürgerspital, Juliusspital, Würzburg Staatlicher
Hofkeller.

Intergrierter Weinbau
Viticulture that takes into account the whole field of technical
information necessary for the minimum use of chemicals in a
vineyard. Related to ★Ökologischer Weinbau.

Interspecific crossing
See Rebsorte

Invertzucker
Invert sugar. A mixture of glucose and fructose which until 1971
could be used with water to enrich and deacidify cheaper wines.
Achieved notoriety in the early 1980s for having been used in the
falsification of wine.

Iphofen Franken w
Fine old town with many noble and ecclesiastical wine-related
buildings dating back to the 16th century. Silvaner, Müller-
Thurgau and other vines produce top-quality wines, full of flavour
and character. *Grosslage*: ★Burgweg.

Istein, Schlossgut Baden VDP
Seven-hectare estate of the rural district of Lörrach near Basel,
planted 35 percent Gutedel, 25 percent Spätburgunder, 15 percent
each Riesling and Weissburgunder. The wines have good body and
the Spätburgunder receives high praise in Germany. All the wines
are *trocken*, sold mainly to private customers.
Address: Weingut des Landkreises Lörrach, W-7859
Efringen-Kirchen
Tel: 07628 1284

Jahrgang
Vintage. Not used in the sense of 'harvest', for which the German

word is *Ernte*, but simply to denote wine of any one year. (*See* pages 31–34 for vintage information.)

Jahrgangssekt
Vintage, quality sparkling wine. A vintage may be given to a quality sparkling wine if at least 85 percent of the grapes used to make its base wine comes from the year stated. *Jahrgangssekt* is not necessarily either better or worse than non-vintage sparkling wine, but in the eyes of the consumer it can have a certain added appeal and individuality.

Jesuitengarten Rhg w
Einzellage close to the river Rhein at *Winkel producing well-balanced wines, mainly from Riesling. *Grosslage*: *Honigberg. Growers: Allendorf, Brentano, von Hessen, Hupfeld, Krayer, Ress, Wegeler-Deinhard, Zwierlein.

Jesuitengarten Rhpf w
Only six hectares in extent, this *Einzellage* at *Forst has a reputation for refined, well-balanced Riesling wines. More elegant and less fat in flavour than some from the Rheinpfalz, their quality is undenied. The site is widely known outside the region. *Grosslage*: *Marien-garten. Growers: Bassermann-Jordan, Buhl, Bürklin-Wolf, Winzerverein Deidesheim, Dr Deinhard, Forster Winzerverein, Mossbacher-Hof, Spindler, Wolf.

Johannisberg Rhg w
Through its *Schloss* (castle), one of the most famous German wine-producing villages, lying in a fold in the vineyards. The *Grosslage*, *Erntebringer, is probably the best known in the region. Distinguished Riesling wines.

Johannisberg, Bereich Rhg w (r)
The Rheingau region and the Bereich Johannisberg cover exactly the same territory – a little under 3,000 hectares, alongside the Rhein and Main rivers between *Lorchhausen and Wicker, beyond *Wiesbaden. Johannisberg has been known for many years as a wine-producing village and its name has become legally attached to the whole of the *Bereich*. The use of the name Bereich Johannisberg

for still wine has been limited, as in many instances the *Grosslage* name (eg ★Erntebringer, ★Burgweg, ★Steinmächer) preceded by the appropriate village name has seemed more attractive. Nevertheless, the name has proved popular as a description for sparkling wine made from grapes grown in the district.

Johannisberg, Schloss Rhg
See Schloss Johannisberg

Johannishof, Weingut Rhg Charta
Estate dating from 1680, with 18 hectares of modernized, 100 percent Riesling vineyards in ★Johannisberg (★Hölle), ★Winkel (★Hasensprung, ★Jesuitengarten) and ★Geisenheim (★Kläuserweg). Annual production is 12,500 cases, of which 30 percent is *trocken* and 30 percent is exported.
Address: W-6222 Johannisberg
Tel: 06722 8216

Johner, Weingut Karl H Baden
Estate of 3·3 hectares planted with 42 percent Spätburgunder, 38 percent Weissburgunder and 18 percent Müller-Thurgau (Rivaner). All the wines, which are much praised by the German press, are aged in *barrique*. They are weighty, surprising, fascinating, and French-influenced, both in their vinification and their 'packaging'.
Address: Gartenstrasse 20, W-7818 Vogtsburg-Bischoffingen
Tel: 07662 6041

Josefinengrund, Weingut M-S-R
Estate owned by Franz ★Reh & Sohn.

Josephshof, Der M-S-R
See Kesselstatt, Weingut Reichsgraf von

Josephshöfer M-S-R w
Small, prestigious *Einzellage* at ★Graach, owned by Weingut Reichsgraf von ★Kesselstatt. Six hectares, 90 percent steep, produce stylish, elegant wines that benefit from maturation in bottle. *Grosslage*: ★Münzlay.

Jost, Weingut Toni Mrh and Rhg VDP
Family-owned estate, established in 1832, with ten hectares on steep or sloping sites at ★Bacharach and ★Steeg in the Mittelrhein and at ★Walluf and ★Martinsthal in the Rheingau. Vines are 75 percent Riesling, Müller-Thurgau and others, 15 percent Spätburgunder. Thirty percent of the wine is *trocken*. Annual production is 5,700 cases. Much is sold in the estate's wine bar; 20 percent is exported. Address: Hahnenhof, Oberstrasse 14, W-6533 Bacharach
Tel: 06743 1216

Juffer M-S-R w
One of the best-known steep *Einzellagen* on the Mosel, at ★Brauneberg. Produces complex Riesling wines, less steely than some from ★Bernkastel and more gentle in flavour. Very appealing and can certainly be of top quality. *Grosslage*: ★Kurfürstlay. Growers: Fritz Haag, Willi Haag, Karp-Schreiber, Paulinshof, Pauly-Bergweiler, St Nikolaus, M F Richter.

Juffer-Sonnenuhr M-S-R w
Small, south-southeast-facing, steep Riesling *Einzellage* at ★Brauneberg, surrounded by the larger Juffer site. Very stylish, top-quality wines. *Grosslage*: ★Kurfürstlay. Growers: Fritz Haag, Willi Haag, Karp-Schreiber, Paulinshof, Pauly-Bergweiler, M F Richter, Thanisch-Knabben, Thanisch-Müller-Burggraef.

Julius-Echter-Berg Franken
Einzellage at *Iphofen producing wines with firm acidity and much flavour from Riesling, Silvaner and Müller-Thurgau. *Grosslage*: *Burgweg. Growers: Juliusspital, Popp, Ruck, Wirsching.

Juliusspital-Weingut Franken VDP
Great *Würzburg charitable estate, dating from 1576, owned by the Julius hospital. Its 163 hectares of vineyards include holdings in many of Franken's most famous sites: Würzburger *Stein, Escherndorfer *Lump, Rödelseer *Küchenmeister, and at *Iphofen and *Randersacker. Vines are 35 percent Silvaner, 22 percent Müller-Thurgau, 18 percent Riesling, plus many other vine varieties including a small amount of Spätburgunder. Maturation in cask (some over 100 years old) in a 150-metre-long cellar helps to produce wines with depth and body. Annual production is 83,300 cases, two percent is exported. The wines can also be tasted in the estate's own wine bar.
Address: Klinikstrasse 5, W-8700 Würzburg
Tel: 0931 3084–147

Jung
Young. Implies freshness if applied to a QbA and immaturity in the case of a fine wine.

Jungfernwein
Literally 'virgin wine'; wine from the first harvest of a newly planted vineyard. The term, no longer an official description in Germany, is applied in the Italian South Tyrol to wines from second generation grapes which set after the main crop.

Jungwein
Young wine. Defined by the EC as a wine with an incomplete fermentation, not yet separated from its yeast deposit.

Kabinett
Before 1971 spelt 'Cabinet', originally a description given to wines considered to be particularly fine and worthy of storage in a grower's private cellar, or Cabinet. Since 1971 *Kabinett* has been the legally established term for the first category of *Prädikat* (QmP)

wine, usually the lightest in alcohol of all German wines. The old spelling is still permitted as a brand name for sparkling wines, such as Deinhard Cabinet, Schloss Wachenheim Grün-Cabinet, Schloss Koblenz Cabinet.

Kageneck'sche Wein- & Sektkellerei GmbH, Gräflich von

A subsidiary, but independent, company of the *Badischer Winzerkeller known mainly for high-quality single-vine *Sekt* bA from Baden, sold under the brand name Schloss Munzingen. Address: Kupfertorstrasse 35, W-7814 Breisach
Tel: 07667 83126

Kaiserstuhl, Bereich Baden w (r)

The warmest and driest *Bereich*, facing the vineyards of Alsace across the Rhein. Although the wines are not widely known outside Germany, the Spätburgunder and Grauburgunder in particular have a good reputation in their homeland. The volcanic soil gives the white wine a positive flavour that is easily recognized.

Kalb Franken w

Well-known *Einzellage* on the slopes at *Iphofen producing stylish, firm, Müller-Thurgau and Silvaner wines. *Grosslage*: *Burgweg. Growers: Popp, Wirsching.

Kallfelz, Weingut Albert M-S-R

A 95 percent Riesling estate of five hectares at Zell-Merl, which took over the five-hectare estate of the Lehr- und Versuchsanstalt des Landkreises Cochem-Zell in neighbouring Bullay in 1990 (20 percent of which was planted, unusually, in Weissburgunder). The estate now operates a system under which further vineyards are leased from part-time growers who continue to tend the vines themselves. None of the wines from this grouping is sold as *Erzeugerabfüllungen*, whether this description would be justified or not. Many are offered without their *Einzellage* names.

Address: Hauptstrasse 60–62, W-5583 Zell-Merl

Tel: 06542 2713

Kallstadt Rhpf w (r)

The northernmost of the string of top-quality Rheinpfalz villages. Splendid, full-flavoured, essentially fruity wines from Riesling, Silvaner, Scheurebe and other varieties, similar in price to wines from *Forst and *Deidesheim further south. *Grosslagen*: *Kobnert and *Feuerberg.

Kallstadt eG, Winzergenossenschaft Rhpf

Small cooperative cellar founded in 1902 whose members own 190 hectares of vineyards at *Kallstadt (*Saumagen, *Steinacker and others). Vines are 25 percent Riesling, with Silvaner, Portugieser, Müller-Thurgau and others. *Lieblich* wines make up 65 percent of production.

Address: Weinstrasse 126, W-6701 Kallstadt

Tel: 06322 8654

Kalte Ente

'Cold duck': a corruption of *Kalte Ende*, the cold end to a meal. A drink which, sold commercially, must contain at least 25 percent sparkling wine or *Perlwein*. Other ingredients are still wine, lemon peel and sugar to taste. In home-made *Kalte Ente* the proportion of sparkling wine will probably be much higher and will be added, very chilled, immediately before serving.

Kalte Sophie

See Eisheiligen

Kammer M-S-R w
Tiny *Einzellage* (under 0·5 hectares) surrounded by the famous
Brauneberger ★Juffer. Sole owners: ★Paulinshof.

Kanitz, Weingut Graf von Rhg Charta VDP
Estate dating from the 13th century or earlier with 13·5 hectares of
vineyards, all on steep sites at ★Lorch. Vines are 95 percent Riesling,
organically manured. The wines are elegant and full of flavour; 68
percent *trocken*. They can be tasted in the wine bar in the estate's
16th-century buildings. Annual production is 10,000 cases, of
which ten percent is exported.
Address: Rheinstrasse 49, W-6223 Lorch
Tel: 06726 346

Kanzem M-S-R w
One of a number of very small, pretty, rustic villages on the Saar
that can make superb Riesling wines in good years. *Grosslage*:
★Scharzberg.

Kanzemer Berg, Weingut M-S-R VDP
Small, 5·5-hectare, high-quality estate, dating from the 16th
century or earlier, with a holding in the modernized steep
Kanzemer ★Altenberg site, 95 percent Riesling. Superb, flowery
wines with lingering fruity acidity, which last for years in bottle.
Annual production is 2,700 cases, 33 percent *trocken*.
Address: Weinstrasse 11, W-5511 Kanzem
Tel: 06501 16709

Kanzler
White grape variety, a crossing of Müller-Thurgau × Silvaner
from Dr Scheu of ★Alzey, planted in 93 hectares, mainly in the
Rheinhessen and Rheinpfalz. In ★Sachsen the vine is also known
as Jakobsteiner. The yield is often small but the must weight is
usually higher by about 20° Oechsle than that of Müller-Thurgau.
The harvest can take place after the Müller-Thurgau has been
picked, resulting in full-bodied wines, sometimes of *Auslese* quality
or higher.

Kappelrodeck Baden r w
A Schwarzwald village in the Bereich *Ortenau, well known in
Germany for its good and competitively priced Spätburgunder.

Kappelrodeck eG, Winzergenossenschaft Baden
One of several well-known village cooperatives in the Bereich
*Ortenau, receiving grapes from 127 hectares, planted 70 percent
Spätburgunder and 20 percent Müller-Thurgau. About 60 percent
is *halbtrocken* but the good, *trocken*, true-to-type Spätburgunder is
more to international taste. Some is aged in *barrique*. Annual
production is 83,300 cases, two percent exported.
Address: W-7594 Kappelrodeck
Tel: 07842 1735

Karlsmühle Lorenzhof, Weingut M-S-R
Estate of 9·5 hectares with a charmingly sited hotel at *Mertesdorf
and additional holdings at nearby *Kasel (including *Nies'chen,
*Hitzlay). The vineyards are 90 percent Riesling and 80 percent
steep. Half the production is *trocken* and sales are mainly to private
customers, although ten percent is exported.
Address: Mühlengrund 1, W-5501 Mertesdorf bei Trier
Tel.: 0651 5123

Karp-Schreiber, Weingut Christian M-S-R
Six-hectare estate with holdings at *Brauneberg (*Juffer), 70
percent Riesling, 30 percent Müller-Thurgau, Kerner and others.
Annual production is 2,500 cases of racy, fruity wines of which up
to 40 percent is *trocken*. Ten percent of all wines is exported. Many
successes in regional and national competitions.
Address: Hauptstrasse 1181, W-5551 Brauneberg
Tel: 06534 236

Karst & Söhne, Weingut Johannes Rhpf VDP
Ten-hectare estate owned by the Karst family, growers for 250
years. Holdings are at *Bad Dürkheim (*Spielberg, *Fuchsmantel), 72 percent Riesling, also 12 percent highly successful Scheurebe
and eight percent Spätburgunder. All the wines are matured in
cask. Annual production is 5,000 cases, 50 percent *trocken*, 25
percent exported.

Address: Burgstrasse 15, W-6702 Bad Dürkheim
Tel: 06322 2103

Karthäuserhofberg M-S-R w

Steep *Einzellage* of some 19 hectares at *Eitelsbach on the Ruwer, solely owned by the *Rautenstrauch'sche Weingutsverwaltung. *Grosslage*: *Römerlay.

Käsberg Würt r

Well-known, very steep, partially terraced, south-facing, irrigated *Einzellage* above the Neckar at *Mundelsheim, planted very densely, mainly in Trollinger.

Kasel M-S-R w

Small village in the compact little Ruwer valley, making top-quality Riesling wines in good years. *Grosslage*: *Römerlay.

Kees-Kieren, Weingut M-S-R

Estate of 4·5 hectares including holdings at *Kinheim (*Hubertus-lay), *Graach (*Domprobst and *Himmelreich) and *Kesten, planted 100 percent Riesling. Well-structured, often *spritzig* wines.
Address: Hauptstrasse 22, W-5550 Graach
Tel: 06531 3428

Kehrnagel M-S-R w

One of several excellent *Einzellagen* at *Kasel, mainly steep and planted with Riesling and Müller-Thurgau. Racy, elegant wines, especially the Rieslings. *Grosslage*: *Römerlay. Growers: Beulwitz, Bischöfliche Weingüter, Kesselstatt, Simon, Wegeler-Deinhard.

Kellerbesichtigungen

Cellar visits. For details on visiting cellars, *see* pages 35–36.

Kellerei

The word *Kellerei* is commonly used in two ways. It is either a cellar situated above ground, or it is a merchant's (as opposed to a producer's) cellar. In the second meaning *Kellerei* is used for the whole of a merchant's business. It is reported that over half the wine produced in *Rheinland-Pfalz is sold via *Kellereien*.

Kellermeister

Cellar master. Responsible for the winemaking and all cellar activity, including teaching apprentices. Today, the younger generation of cellar masters will almost certainly have trained at a viticultural institute.

Kendermann GmbH, Hermann

Export house, established in 1947. Leading brands are Black Tower Liebfraumilch and a QbA Mosel, Green Gold. Represents a number of top estates outside Germany. Annual sales in excess of two million cases.
Address: Am Ockenheimer Gruben 35, W-6530 Bingen
Tel: 06721 7010

Kern, Weingut Dr Rhpf

Estate dating in its present form from the start of the 19th century, with six hectares in top-quality sites in ★Deidesheim (including ★Herrgottsacker, ★Kieselberg, ★Langenmorgen, ★Leinhöhle, ★Grainhübel), ★Ruppertsberg (★Linsenbusch, ★Reiterpfad) and in ★Forst (★Ungeheuer). Planted with 75 percent Riesling, 12 percent Kerner, and others. The emphasis is on *trocken* wines, many sold in the estate's wine bar.
Address: Schloss Deidesheim, W-6705 Deidesheim
Tel: 06326 260

Kerner

White grape variety, a crossing of Trollinger × Riesling from the viticultural institute in ★Weinsberg. From five hectares in 1964, plantings had increased to 7,409 hectares by 1988 and Kerner is now found in all 13 wine-producing regions. It grows well in middle-quality sites, suitable for Silvaner, and can ripen late into the season, producing wine in all the quality (QmP) categories. The crop is large and the must weight usually 10–15° higher on the Oechsle scale than that of Riesling. Its acidity often causes it to be likened to Riesling, although its flavour is less fine. It is fruity, with a slight Muskat bouquet. A constituent of many ★Liebfraumilch wines.

Kernig

Term used to describe a wine that has good body and acidity.

Associated particularly with Rheingau Rieslings, often with a certain amount of bottle-age.

Kesseler, Weingut August Rhg
Estate of 15 hectares at ★Assmannshausen (★Höllenberg) and at ★Rüdesheim (★Berg Schlossberg), planted 50 percent Spätburgunder, 40 percent Riesling and, unusually for the Rheingau, ten percent Silvaner. The 100 percent *trocken* wines are impeccably made and true to type. Prices are accordingly high. Annual production is 8,300 cases.
Address: Lorcherstrasse 16, W-6224 Assmannshausen
Tel: 06722 2513

Kesselstatt GmbH, Weingut Reichsgraf von M-S-R
Great estate dating in its present form from 1820, although it has operated as a *Weingut* for more than 600 years. Consists of four estates, all owned by the Reh family, at ★Graach ('Der Josephshof'), ★Piesport ('Domklausenhof'), ★Kasel ('St Irminenhof') and ★Oberemmel ('Abteihof'), 98 percent Riesling and covering 66 hectares in some of the best sites of the Mosel-Saar-Ruwer: Graacher ★Josephshöfer (sole owner); Piesporter ★Goldtröpfchen and Trittenheimer ★Apotheke on the Mosel; Kaseler ★Nies'chen on the

QUALITÄTSWEIN
MIT PRÄDIKAT

AP. NR. 3561077-13-90
PRODUCE OF
GERMANY

750 ml e

Alc. 9.0% vol

MOSEL · SAAR · RUWER

1989 JOSEPHSHÖFER*
RIESLING AUSLESE

ERZEUGERABFÜLLUNG

REICHSGRAF von KESSELSTATT
D-5500 TRIER

Ruwer; and Wiltinger ★Braunfels, ★Gottesfuss and ★Scharzhofberger on the Saar, among others. Annual production equivalent to 50,500 cases, 49 percent exported; 27 percent is *trocken*.
Address: Liebfrauenstrasse 10, W-5500 Trier
Tel: 0651 75101

G C Kessler and Co

Oldest sparkling-wine producers in West Germany, at Esslingen near Stuttgart, established in 1826 by Georg Christian von Kessler, who had worked with the Champagne house Veuve Clicquot Ponsardin. Wine sold under the Kessler label is made by *Flaschengärung* (bottle fermentation) and that of the subsidiary company, Gebrüder Weiss, by vat fermentation.

Address: Marktplatz 21–23, W-7300 Esslingen

Tel: 0711 359956

Kesten M-S-R w

Old village near *Brauneberg, whose good Riesling wines are not often found abroad other than under the *Grosslage* name Bernkasteler *Kurfürstlay. A high proportion of Riesling is grown.

KG

Kommanditgesellschaft. Limited partnership, as in Sektkellerei Hausen-Mabilon KG.

KGaA

Kommanditgesellschaft auf Aktien. Partnership based on shares, as in Deinhard & Co KGaA.

Kiedrich Rhg w

Small, attractive village on the slopes above *Eltville. There has always been a close bond between the vine growers of the region and the remarkable parish church of St Valentin (although it was an Englishman, John Sutton, who restored the church and organ to their present splendour in the 19th century, and established the locally famous choir). Best-known sites are *Gräfenberg and *Sandgrub. *Grosslage*: *Heiligenstock.

Kieselberg Rhpf w

Good *Einzellage* in *Deidesheim, making excellent Riesling wines. *Grosslage*: *Mariengarten. Growers: Bassermann-Jordan, Biffar, Buhl, Winzerverein Deidesheim, Dr Deinhard, Kern, Kimich, Spindler.

Kimich, Weingut Jul Ferd Rhpf VDP
Estate of 9·5 hectares with holdings (80 percent Riesling) at
*Deidesheim (*Grainhübel, *Leinhöhle, *Langenmorgen, *Herr-
gottsacker), *Forst (*Ungeheuer, *Pechstein) and *Ruppertsberg
(*Reiterpfad, *Linsenbusch) – some of the best sites in the region.
The wines are mainly cask-matured; 45 percent is *trocken*. Sales are
mostly to private customers.
Address: Weinstrasse 54, W-6705 Deidesheim
Tel: 06326 342

Kinheim M-S-R w
Ancient wine village near *Traben-Trabach; the vineyards were
established by Benedictine monks in the 12th century. The sites face
south and southeast, planted mainly with Riesling, and produce
stylish, elegant wines. *Grosslage*: *Schwarzlay.

Kirchberg Franken w
Kirchberg is one of the most common site names in Germany. The
small, 1·5-hectare Kirchberg site at Castell produces excellent,
powerfully flavoured, earthy wines. *Grosslage*: *Herrenberg.
Growers include Castell'sches Domänenamt.

Kirchberghof, Weingut Baden
Twelve-hectare estate north of Freiburg with terraced vineyards
planted 34 percent Spätburgunder, 28 percent Müller-Thurgau and

other varieties. About 85 percent of the wine is *trocken*, some is *barrique*-aged. Annual production is 7,300 cases, 60 percent sold to private customers.
Address: W–7832 Kenzingen-Bombach
Tel: 07644 1261

Kirchenstück Rhg w
One of the best small *Einzellagen* at ★Hochheim, producing elegant wines, exclusively from Riesling, with fine, balanced acidity. *Grosslage*: ★Daubhaus. Growers: Aschrott, Staatsweingüt Eltville, Weingut der Stadt Frankfurt, Künstler, Ress, Schloss Schönborn, Werner.

Kirchheim Rhpf w (r)
The name of this small village is usually found on inexpensive wines, linked to that of the *Grosslage* ★Schwarzerde.

Kitzingen Franken w (r)
Town 19 kilometres southeast of ★Würzburg with attractive old buildings, and for centuries a centre of the Franken wine trade. The eighth-century Benedictine abbey claims one of the oldest (more than 1,000 years old) cellars in Germany. Wines with grip, from Silvaner and Müller-Thurgau. *Grosslage*: Hofrat.

Kläuserweg Rhg w
One of several excellent *Einzellagen* at ★Geisenheim, on sloping ground, producing full-bodied Riesling wines with firm acidity. *Grosslage*: ★Erntebringer. Growers: Forschungsanstalt Geisenheim, von Hessen, Mumm, Ress, Wegeler-Deinhard, Zwierlein.

Klein
Small. A *kleiner Wein*, perhaps an Elbling from the Bereich ★Obermosel, can be a pleasant drink when young but will be light in alcohol and lack extract.

Klingelberger
Name sometimes used in the Bereich ★Ortenau in Baden for the Riesling grape, after the one-time Klingelberg site at ★Durbach in which it was planted.

Klingenberg Franken r w

Small town 23 kilometres south of Aschaffenburg on the Main, first mentioned in connection with vine growing in AD 776. Well known in Germany for its soft red wine (Portugieser, Spätburgunder). Also produces Müller-Thurgau. No *Grosslage*.

Klingenberg, Weingut der Stadt Franken

Estate of 17 hectares, 70 percent on steep slopes, planted 45 percent Spätburgunder, 21 percent Müller-Thurgau, 20 percent Portugieser. About 80 percent of the wine is dry and 65 percent finds enthusiastic private customers.
Address: Wilhelmstrasse 107, W-8763 Klingenberg
Tel: 09372 2438

Klören, Weingut Michael Nahe

Estate with 5·6 hectares of holdings at *Laubenheim and *Langenlonsheim, planted 36 percent Riesling, Weissburgunder, Silvaner, Ruländer (Grauburgunder) and others, producing lively wines full of flavour and, sometimes, a taste of the soil. Annual production is 2,900 cases, sold mainly to private customers.
Address: Am Steinkreuz 17, W-6531 Laubenheim
Tel: 06704 500

Kloster

Monastery or convent. In law, *Kloster* can be included in the title of an estate if the wine is made in the *Kloster*'s own cellar from its own estate-grown grapes. The Cistercian, Carthusian and Benedictine orders have all been involved in vine growing in Germany, but the most famous wine-connected *Kloster* today is undoubtedly the Cistercian Kloster Eberbach in the Rheingau (*see next entry*).

Kloster Eberbach Rhg

Cistercian monastery dating from the 12th century in a valley above *Hattenheim. Today, like the Cistercian Clos de Vougeot in Burgundy, it is very much the spiritual home of vine growing in the region. It is open to the public and provides a venue for many activities promoting wine. It is also the base for the *German Wine Academy.

Kloster Liebfrauenberg Rhpf w (r)

Large *Grosslage* covering some 1,900 hectares in the Bereich
★Südliche Weinstrasse, mainly on gently sloping or flat land north
and east of Bad Bergzabern. The wines are inexpensive and usually
sold with Steinweiler providing the village name.

Klostergut St Lamprecht Rhpf

See Bergdolt, F & G

Klüsserath M-S-R w

Long, narrow village on the ★Mittelmosel, stretching for 250
hectares between the ★Brüderschaft *Einzellage* and the river. Good-
quality Riesling wines. *Grosslage*: ★St Michael.

Knyphausen, Weingut Freiherr zu Rhg Charta VDP

Estate founded in the 12th century by the Cistercians from ★Kloster
Eberbach, acquired by the Knyphausen family in 1818. There are 18
hectares including holdings at ★Erbach (★Marcobrunn, ★Siegels-
berg), ★Hattenheim (★Wisselbrunnen) and ★Kiedrich, 96 percent
Riesling, four percent Spätburgunder (mainly for *Weissherbst*).

Storage is in stainless steel. Annual production is 11,700 cases – only the top wines in each QmP category bear a site name, as from the '90 vintage.
Address: Klosterhof Drais, W-6228 Eltville
Tel: 06123 62177

Kobern M-S-R w

Charming old village near *Koblenz in the Bereich *Zell. Very steep vineyards planted mainly with Riesling give powerfully flavoured, fruity wines. *Grosslage*: *Weinhex. *See* Gondorf.

Koblenz Mrh and M-S-R w

Founded in the first century after Christ as 'Confluentes', Koblenz stands at the meeting point of the Rhein and Mosel. Badly damaged in World War II, the old part of the town has been expertly restored. Near the centre of the town is the 0·2 hectare of one of the smallest *Einzellagen* in Germany, the Schnorbach-Brückstück, planted mainly in Müller-Thurgau. In the Ehrenbreitsteiner Kreuzberg site, in a charming side valley of the Rhein, good Mittelrhein Riesling wines are made. Koblenz is an important administrative centre for the local wine trade and is the home of vineyard owners, wine exporters and *Sekt* producers *Deinhard.

Kobnert Rhpf w (r)

Grosslage of some 1,500 hectares that spreads north from the village of *Kallstadt. As throughout the Bereich *Mittelhaardt/Deutsche Weinstrasse the quality of wine is good, the range of vine varieties wide and the soil varied.

Koch Erben, Bürgermeister Carl Rhh

Estate of 12 hectares, planted with 40 percent Riesling, 20 percent Silvaner, 12 percent Müller-Thurgau, plus other varieties, at *Oppenheim (including *Sackträger, *Kreuz) and *Dienheim. Storage is in wood and vat, and 30 percent of the annual production of 6,700 cases is *trocken*. The wines mature well in bottle, and ten percent is exported.
Address: Wormser Strasse 62, W-6504 Oppenheim
Tel: 06133 2326

Koehler-Ruprecht, Weingut Rhpf VDP
Ten-hectare *Kallstadt estate, including holdings in *Steinacker
and *Saumagen. Vines are 60 percent Riesling, plus Kerner and
others, producing concentrated wines full of flavour and character.
Spätburgunder is also grown. Maturation is in oak casks and only
QmP are sold in bottle. Traditional high-quality winemaking is
combined with interesting innovations (such as *barrique*-aged
Trockenbeerenauslese with over 16 percent alcohol). About 80
percent is *trocken*. Because of the microclimate, *Auslese* can be made
every year from one or more of the vine varieties. Annual
production is 6,800 cases, five percent exported.
Address: Weinstrasse 84, W-6701 Kallstadt
Tel: 06322 1829

Kommissionär
See Broker

König, Weingut Robert Rhg VDP
Six-hectare estate in the steep vineyards of *Assmannshausen
(*Höllenberg) planted 95 percent Spätburgunder, five percent
Riesling, Portugieser, Frühburgunder and the unusual Rotberger.
The Spätburgunder, matured in cask, receives much praise in
Germany and, being a serious red wine, is *trocken*. Annual
production is a low 2,700 cases.
Address: Landhaus Kenner, W-6220 Rüdesheim-Assmannshausen
Tel: 06722 1064

Königin Victoria Berg Rhg w
Small, five-hectare Riesling *Einzellage* at *Hochheim, named after
Queen Victoria and owned by the Weingut Königin Victoria Berg.
Grosslage: *Daubhaus.

Königin Victoria Berg, Weingut Rhg
Estate concentrated entirely in one site, owned by Weingut H
*Hupfeld Erben. The Königin Victoria Berg (*see previous entry*), to
which Queen Victoria allowed her name to be officially given in
1857, following a visit to *Hochheim in 1850, produces approximately 3,300 cases a year of firm, full-bodied Riesling wines with a
positive, earthy character.

Address: Weingut Hupfeld, Rheingaustrasse 113, W-6227 Oestrich-Winkel
Tel: 06723 3307

Königsbach-Neustadt eG, Winzergenossenschaft Rhpf
Cooperative supplied by 161 hectares at Königsbach and *Ruppertsberg, planted 40 percent Riesling, 20 percent Müller-Thurgau. Sixty percent of the production is *lieblich*, perhaps to meet the taste of German supermarket customers.
Address: Deidesheimerstrasse 12, W-6730 Neustadt-Königsbach
Tel: 06321 66079

Königschaffhausen eG, Winzergenossenschaft Baden
An innovative cooperative supplied by 168 hectares in the Bereich *Kaiserstuhl, with 38 percent Müller-Thurgau, 30 percent Spätburgunder and 20 percent Ruländer. *Barriques* are very successfully used for some of the *Burgunder (Pinot) wines, for maturation and, less commonly in Germany, for vinification. Annual production is 125,000 cases, 98 percent sold in Germany, 35 percent *trocken*.
Address: W-7833 Endingen-Königschaffhausen
Tel: 07642 1003

Königswinter Mrh w
Today a tourist attraction, Königswinter, near Bonn, is known to have produced wines since the 11th century. Its small – and only – *Einzellage*, Drachenfels, accounts for more than half the 19-hectare viticultural area of the state of *Nordrhein-Westfalen, producing Müller-Thurgau and Riesling wines with pronounced acidity. *Grosslage*: Petersberg.

Konsumwein
Wine for everyday drinking. The term is not defined in law but refers to cheap wine blended to a particular style.

Kontrollzeichen
As from September 1 1992, every wine bottled in Germany will have to bear a control sign, a sufficient and precise number of which will be issued for each bottling. Details are yet to be published but the scheme will probably be similar to that operating in Austria.

Konz M–S–R w (r)
Town at the confluence of the Saar and Mosel. A high proportion of Riesling is grown, producing fruity, racy wines in a number of good ★Ortsteilen. *Grosslage*: ★Scharzberg.

Korkgeschmack
Corked. Term used to describe wines with an unclean smell. The causes are not fully understood but they include infection of the cork on the tree by fungus, incorrect storage and inadequate cleaning of cellar equipment.

Körper
Body. In any one region a wine with more than average ★extract and possibly alcohol is said to have good *Körper* or to be *körperreich* – a description which is the opposite of *klein*.

Köstlich
Delicious. A subjective description of wine.

Kratzig
Describes a wine that 'scratches' (*kratzt*) the throat through too much volatile acid. Such a wine would be in very poor condition and liable to deteriorate further.

Krayer, Weingut Dr Karl-August Rhg Charta
Estate with 4·3 hectares of holdings at ★Oestrich (★Lenchen), ★Winkel (★Hasensprung, ★Jesuitengarten) and ★Mittelheim. Ninety-five percent Riesling; five percent Spätburgunder in the Hasensprung. Sixty percent of production is *trocken*.
Address: Gänsgasse 10, W-6227 Oestrich-Winkel 2
Tel: 06723 2508

Krebs, Ferdinand, J Matheus-Lehnert, Weingüter M–S–R
Two small estates which sell their separate bottlings together. The first has holdings at ★Klüsserath, ★Neumagen, ★Trittenheim and ★Dhron, the second at ★Piesport (★Goldtröpfchen) and ★Dhron. The total holding covers 4·5 hectares; 80 percent is steep and 90 percent is Riesling. Seventy percent of the cask-matured wine is *lieblich*. Annual production is 4,200 cases.

Address: Folzerweg 20, In der Zeil 1, W-5507 Neumagen-Dhron
Tel: 06507 2237

Kreuz Rhh w
An *Einzellage* shared by ★Oppenheim and ★Dienheim, next to the
equally distinguished and well-known ★Sackträger site. *Grosslage*:
★Güldenmorgen. Growers: Baumann, Dahlem, Guntrum, Koch,
Staatsweingut Oppenheim, Rappenhof, Schmitt'sches Weingut,
Sittmann.

Kreuznach, Bereich Nahe w
Bereich that covers the vineyards of what used to be known as the
Lower Nahe (Untere Nahe) from Bingerbrück upriver to ★Bad
Kreuznach. The *Bereich* name is probably used more for administra-
tive purposes than as a description of wine. The type of simple
quality wine likely to be sold as Bereich Kreuznach will usually be a
little more full in flavour than a wine from the adjacent Bereich
★Schloss Böckelheim.

Kreuzwertheim Franken w r
Small, attractive town bordering on Baden with a range of
★*traditionelle Rebsorten* and some good-quality, long-lasting wines
from Bacchus. No *Grosslage*.

Krone Assmannshausen, Weingut Rhg
Estate of 4·5 hectares, 100 percent Spätburgunder, owned by the
beautiful and famous hotel of the same name. *Barriques* are used
although no mention of the fact is made in the price list. Eighty
percent of the wine is *trocken*. The wines are expensive and highly
regarded in Germany.
Address: Rheinuferstrasse 10, W-6220 Rüdesheim-
Assmannshausen
Tel: 06722 2525

Kronenberg Nahe w
Grosslage of 1,300 hectares surrounding the town of ★Bad
Kreuznach. The top-quality sites concentrate on Riesling but many
other grapes are grown on a wide variety of soils. The best Riesling
wines will normally be sold under an *Einzellage* name, but a

Kronenberg wine should still show the blend of body and racy flavour expected from the Nahe.

Krötenbrunnen Rhh w (r)
Large *Grosslage* covering nearly 1,800 hectares. It encompasses some of the vineyards of the well-known wine villages of ★Dienheim, ★Guntersblum, ★Alsheim and ★Uelversheim, as well as four of the sites at ★Oppenheim – Schlossberg, Schloss, Paterhof, Herrengarten. The Krötenbrunnen name is mainly used for inexpensive, simple quality wine (QbA), very much on the same level as that from the adjacent *Grosslage* ★Gutes Domtal.

Krötenpfuhl Nahe w
Small *Einzellage* at ★Bad Kreuznach planted mainly in Riesling, from which excellent, positive stylish wines are made. *Grosslage*: ★Kronenberg. Growers: August Anheuser, Paul Anheuser, Finkenauer.

Kröv M-S-R w
Village near ★Traben-Trabach, probably best known outside the region for the wines of its *Grosslage* ★Nacktarsch.

Kruger-Rumpf, Weingut Nahe
Estate of 15 hectares with holdings at ★Dorsheim (including ★Goldloch) and ★Münster-Sarmsheim (including ★Dautenpflänzer, ★Pittersberg), planted 70 percent Riesling, ten percent Silvaner, and others including Chardonnay. The estate is one of a number in the Nahe valley that have had a particularly good press in recent years. Annual production is 7,100 cases of which 85 percent is *trocken* and five percent is exported.
Address: Rheinstrasse 47, W-6538 Münster-Sarmsheim
Tel: 06721 43859

Küchenmeister Franken w (r)
Einzellage at ★Rödelseer producing spicy wines, full of flavour, that can rise to considerable heights in a good vintage. *Grosslage*: Schlossberg. Growers: Juliusspital, Popp, Wirsching.

Künstler, Weingut Franz Rhg Charta

Six-hectare estate with all the holdings at *Hochheim (*Hölle, *Kirchenstück and others) planted 84 percent Riesling, ten percent Spätburgunder. Firmly structured Rieslings are characteristic and the Spätburgunders are much praised in Germany.

Address: Freiherr-von-Stein Ring 3, W-6203 Hochheim
Tel: 06146 5666

Kupferberg & Cie, KGaA, Christian Adalbert

Established in 1850 as producers of sparkling wine, Kupferberg quickly moved into the export market, selling, in particular, a 'Sparkling Hochheimer Domdechaney', an early forerunner of *Lagensekt*. At the same time, in the 1850s, the brand 'Kupferberg Gold' was launched. About two-thirds of Kupferberg's production gains its sparkle in vat, one-third in bottle. For the latter, the yeast deposit from the second fermentation is removed by filtration, avoiding the regular and expensive shaking of each bottle to force the deposit onto the cork for later removal. With Champagne Bricout et Koch S A R L, Avize, Kupferberg is owned by Racke of *Bingen. Annual production is over one million cases.

Address: Kupferberg-Terrasse, W-6500 Mainz
Tel: 06131 555

Kupfergrube Nahe w

Undoubtedly one of the finest Riesling *Einzellagen* of the Nahe, and therefore of the whole of Germany. It was created by convict labour in the early part of this century, and literally hewn out of the rocky hillside. In the best years great wines of incredible distinction and complexity are made from the 100 percent steep slopes. Rightly expensive. *Grosslage*: *Burgweg. Growers: Hehner-Kiltz, Niederhausen-Schlossböckelheim Staatliche Weinbaudomäne, Plettenberg.

Kupp M-S-R w

Riesling *Einzellage* at *Ayl on the Saar, 100 percent steep and capable of producing great wines in fine vintages. *Grosslage*: *Scharzberg. Growers: Bischöfliche Weingüter, Hausen-Mabilon, G-F von Nell.

Kupp M-S-R w
One of two good *Einzellagen* on the Saar of the same name, the small, mainly steep Kupp at ★Wiltingen produces elegant Riesling wine. *Grosslage*: ★Scharzberg. Growers: Bischöfliche Weingüter, Kesselstatt, Vereinigte Hospitien.

Kurfürstlay M-S-R w
Large *Grosslage* of more than 1,600 hectares including the top-quality wine-producing village of ★Brauneberg. Wines sold under the Kurfürstlay name should be of adequate quality, reflecting the expected fresh Mosel characteristics, but are unlikely to be very distinguished.

Kurz
Short. Describes a wine in an off-vintage, with a lower than usual level of tartaric acid and much malic acid (*see* Apfelsäure), which is likely to have a flavour that does not last in the mouth. A 'short' white wine can still be refreshingly agreeable.

Lack
Lac or varnish. Originally a resinous substance secreted by an insect, the *Coccus lacca*, which yields a fine, red dye. Before the arrival of the capsule, coloured wax seals (*Siegellack*) were used to protect the corks in bottled wine. The different-coloured capsules used by Schloss Johannisberg today for its various qualities of wine are still referred to as *Rotlack*, *Grunlack*, etc.

Lactic acid
See Milchsäure

Lage
Site: a vineyard that has been recorded in the official vineyard register (the *Weinbergsrolle*). The smallest unit is the *Einzellage*, which should be not less than five hectares in size, although there are many exceptions. A *Grosslage* comprises a number of *Einzellagen*. Only quality (QbA or QmP) wines may bear site names. If they do, at least 85 percent must come from the site stated. In the case of a QbA the remaining 15 percent must have originated in the same region, or for a QmP in the same *Bereich*.

Lagensekt
Quality sparkling wine from an *Einzellage* or *Grosslage*. There is an increasing interest in Germany in sparkling wines bearing site names, often offered by well-known estates. *Lagensekt* is usually made by a specialist contract cellar, using a second fermentation in bottle (*Flaschengärung*) to produce the sparkle. *See also* Markensekt, Rieslingsekt.

Lahn Mrh w
Small river that joins the Rhein at Lahnstein, just below ★Koblenz. The vineyards, now much reduced in size and number, are planted mainly with Riesling.

Lahr, Weingut der Stadt Baden
A privately owned estate of 8·8 hectares bought from the town of Lahr in 1979 with half of its vineyards on terraced slopes. It is planted 27 percent Müller-Thurgau and 19 percent Spätburgunder. The plantation of the Burgunder (Pinot) family will be enlarged. Annual production is some 5,400 cases of which 80 percent is *trocken*.
Address: Weinbergstrasse 3, W-7630 Lahr
Tel: 07821 25332

Laible, Weingut Andreas Baden

Long-established family-owned estate of 3·8 hectares with holdings on the granite hilly slopes around ★Durbach. Vines are 30 percent Riesling, 28 percent Traminer (Gewürztraminer), 18 percent Spätburgunder, etc. The estate has new cellars, set in the midst of the vineyards, and produces a low yield of fresh, full-bodied and often slightly *spritzig* wine, 40 percent *trocken* and sold mainly to private customers in Germany.

Address: Bühl 71, W-7601 Durbach

Tel: 0781 41238

Landau in der Pfalz Rhpf w (r)

Attractive town in the Bereich ★Südliche Weinstrasse, suffered much through wars and political upheavals over the centuries. Wines are sound but seldom outstanding when compared to the finest in the region. *Grosslage*: Königsgarten.

Landenberg, Weingut Freiherr von M-S-R

Hoteliers, wine merchants, and owners of 8·5 hectares of steep vineyards at Ediger-Eller and Senheim, planted 90 percent Riesling and, unusually, with a small parcel of Gewürztraminer. Annual production is 6,700 cases, five percent exported, 65 percent *lieblich*.

Address: Moselweinstrasse 60, W-5591 Ediger-Eller 2

Tel: 02675 277

Landgräflich

Belonging to a landgrave, as in Landgräflich Hessisches Weingut at Johannisberg, now known as Weingut Prinz von Hessen. A landgrave was a count of a country district (his urban counterpart was a burgrave).

Landwein

'Country wine': a category of German table wine created in 1982, the equivalent of *vin de pays*, with a natural alcohol content (before enrichment) at least 0·5 percent higher than the minimum set for *deutscher Tafelwein*. A *Landwein* cannot be sweeter than *halbtrocken* (that is, it will contain at most 18 grams per litre sugar). It is a rustic wine, to be enjoyed in large quantities, accompanying food. Its commercial success is limited.

Lang, Weingut Hans Rhg Charta

Fourteen-hectare estate with holdings in ★Kiedrich (★Sandgrub), ★Hallgarten and ★Hattenheim (★Wisselbrunnen, ★Nussbrunnen). Eighty percent Riesling, ten percent Spätburgunder. *Barriques* are used for vinification and maturation of Spätburgunder. Eighty percent of the wine is *trocken*; 20 percent is exported.

Address: Rheinallee 6, W-6228 Eltville-Hattenheim

Tel: 06723 2475

D · 6228 HATTENHEIM · RHEINGAU

WEINGUT

HANS LANG

ERZEUGERABFÜLLUNG

RHEINGAU

Riesling

1990

TROCKEN

A. P. Nr. 31 045 011 91

QUALITÄTSWEIN
PRODUCE OF GERMANY

alc 11,5 % vol   750 ml

Langenlonsheim Nahe w

Small agricultural town between ★Bad Kreuznach and ★Bingen. Old-established estates produce good, well-structured wines, seldom found outside Germany. *Grosslage*: Sonnenborn.

Langenmorgen Rhpf w
Small, seven-hectare *Einzellage* on the slopes at ★Deidesheim,
making excellent Riesling wine. *Grosslage*: ★Mariengarten.
Growers: Bassermann-Jordan, Bürklin-Wolf, Winzerverein Deidesheim, Giessen, Kern, Kimich.

Laubenheim Nahe w
Expanded village with 100 hectares of vineyard. The best of the
Riesling, Silvaner and Müller-Thurgau are inexpensive and very
good at the price. *Grosslage*: Schlosskapelle.

Laubenheim Rhh w
Small town, now within the boundaries of ★Mainz. *Grosslage*:
★St Alban.

Lauda, Staatliche Weinbauversuchsgut Baden
Six-hectare estate in the Badisches Frankenland, established in 1930,
and owned by the state of Baden-Württemberg. Many vine
varieties are grown, including Müller-Thurgau, Kerner, Bacchus
and Weissburgunder. Some are on trial as part of research into
resistance against frost. Thirty-five percent of the wine is *trocken*.
Address: Rebgutsstrasse 80, W-6970 Lauda-Königshofen
Tel: 09343 1210

Lauerburg, Weingut J M-S-R
Four-hectare Mosel estate, in the Lauerburg family since 1700.
Holdings are 100 percent Riesling in top-quality sites at Bernkastel
(★Bratenhöfchen, ★Graben, ★Lay). Annual production is 3,800
cases, 50 percent *lieblich*, 25 percent exported.
Address: Graacherstrasse 24, W-5550 Bernkastel-Kues
Tel: 06531 2481

Laufen Baden w (r)
Pleasant village in the rural Bereich ★Markgräflerland with a high
proportion of Gutedel, handled by the cooperative cellar and,
unusually for the district, by a number of private estates. *Grosslage*:
Burg Neuenfels.

Lauffen am Neckar Würt r w
Small town ten kilometres southwest of *Heilbronn with 550
hectares of vineyard, especially well known in the region for its
gentle Schwarzriesling wine, but other red and white vine varieties
are also grown. *Grosslage*: Kirchenweinberg.

Lay M–S–R w
Small *Einzellage* at *Bernkastel, planted exclusively in Riesling.
Grosslage: *Badstube. Growers: Heidemanns-Bergweiler, Kessel-
statt, Lauerburg, Pauly-Bergweiler, J J Prüm, St Nikolaus,
Thanisch-Knabben.

Lebendig
Lively. Describes a fresh wine with good acidity and often a
noticeable amount of carbon dioxide (*spritzig*).

Leer
Literally 'empty'. Describes a wine that is thin, characterless, with
insufficient body.

Lehmen M–S–R w
One of many small villages in the Bereich *Zell producing sound,
crisp Riesling wines from very steep vineyards. *Grosslage*:
*Weinhex.

Lehranstalt
Teaching institute. Germany's teaching institutes for viticulture
and winemaking are respected throughout the world. Among the
best known are those at *Geisenheim and *Weinsberg.

Lehrensteinsfeld Würt w (r)
A village, east of *Heilbronn, particularly known in the region for
its Riesling wines. *Grosslage*: Salzberg.

Leicht
Light. EC regulations define a light wine as having not more than
15 percent alcohol, but in the real world about 12 percent would be
the upper limit.

Leinhöhle Rhpf w

Mainly sloping *Einzellage* at ★Deidesheim from which full-bodied top-quality Riesling wines are made. *Grosslage*: ★Mariengarten. Growers: Bassermann-Jordan, Biffar, Buhl, Winzerverein Deidesheim, Dr Deinhard, Giessen, Kern, Kimich, Spindler, Wolf.

Leiningerland eG, Winzerkeller Rhpf

Cooperative cellar supplied with grapes from 90 hectares, from villages in the north of the Rheinpfalz, planted 23 percent Müller-Thurgau, 16 percent Riesling, 12 percent Scheurebe. Of the annual production of 66,700 cases, 69 percent is *lieblich* and six percent is exported.
Address: Asselheimer Strasse 22, W-6718 Grünstadt
Tel: 06359 3094

Leiwen M-S-R w

Small, pleasant village in the ★Mittelmosel producing sound but not top-quality wines. Home of the merchants Carl ★Reh. *Grosslage*: ★St Michael.

Lemberger

See Limberger, of which it is an alternative spelling.

Lenchen Rhg w

Large, 145-hectare, mainly level *Einzellage* at ★Oestrich making flowery, balanced Rieslings with finesse and body. *Grosslage*: ★Gottesthal. Growers: Allendorf, Eser, Winzergenossenschaft Hallgarten, Hupfeld, Krayer, Querbach, Ress, Wegeler-Deinhard.

Lenz-Dahm, Weingut M-S-R

Small 3·8-hectare estate and wine merchants with holdings at ★Pünderich; 100 percent Riesling. Fermentation at low temperatures, no *Süssreserve*, minimum use of sulphur dioxide are the proclaimed characteristics of the winemaking. The marketing policy is clear and 70 percent of the wine is *trocken*.
Address: Hauptstrasse 3, W-5587 Pünderich
Tel: 06542 22950

Lergenmüller, Werner Rhpf
Thirty-hectare estate at Hainfeld in the Bereich ★Südliche Wein-
strasse with a range of vine varieties including 30 percent Riesling.
Barriques are used for fermentation and maturation of Weiss-
burgunder and the maturation only of Spätburgunder, St Laurent
and Dornfelder. *Sekt* is produced from the estate's own wine.
Address: Weinstrasse 16, Cyriacus Hof, W-6741 Hainfeld
Tel: 06323 5128

Lese
See Harvest

Lesegut
The grapes from which wine is made. Most often found in the
phrase ★'*Aus dem Lesegut*'.

Leutesdorf Mrh w
Attractive Rhein village with many half-timbered houses. Mainly
Riesling is grown in the steep, decomposed slate and sandstone
vineyards, producing strongly flavoured wines. *Grosslage*: Burg
Hammerstein.

Liebfrauenkirche Rhh
The Church of Our Lady in Worms: the vineyard from which the
world-famous ★Liebfraumilch originally came adjoins the Gothic
church. The vineyard is largely on the site of an old convent – a
writer in the early 19th century noted that the soil was much mixed
with rubble and therefore somewhat artificial. Today it forms the
Liebfrauenstift-Kirchenstück *Einzellage*, itself part of the ★Lieb-
frauenmorgen *Grosslage*.

Liebfrauenmorgen Rhh
Grosslage of more than 1,000 hectares scattered around the cathedral
city of ★Worms in the extreme south of the Rheinhessen. Vineyards
are on level or slightly sloping land. The name Liebfrauenmorgen
shares its origin with ★Liebfraumilch: both relate to the Liebfrauenkirche (Church of Our Lady) in Worms. A *Morgen* is an obsolete
measure of land.

Liebfrauenstift-Kirchenstück
See Liebfrauenkirche

Liebfraumilch
Also spelt Liebfrauenmilch meaning the 'milk of Our Lady', after the vineyard of the *Liebfrauenkirche in Worms from which the wine originally came. A white QbA, produced mainly in the Rheinhessen and Rheinpfalz, to a lesser extent in the Nahe and theoretically also in the Rheingau. It must derive predominantly from Riesling, Silvaner, Müller-Thurgau, or Kerner and should taste of these wines. It may not, however, bear a grape name and must contain more than 18 grams per litre of residual sugar (the upper limit for *halbtrocken* wines). Liebfraumilch is the most widely exported of German wines, and since the early 1970s has become among the cheapest – a wine loved by millions, deplored by the critics. In as much as it is a German quality wine, Liebfraumilch should be at least pleasant and agreeable. Annual production is the equivalent of over 12 million cases, decreasing in the early 1990s.

Lieblich
Medium-sweet. Technically describes any wine with 18–45 grams per litre residual sugar. Can often be legitimately applied to Rheinhessen QbA with low acidity and a gentle, sweet flavour. Such wines contain relatively little alcohol and are, for many, the archetypal German wines, so much appreciated (especially as *Liebfraumilch) on the export market.

Liebrecht'sche Weingutsverwaltung, Oberste Rhh VDP
Thirteen-hectare estate with holdings in modernized vineyards at *Bodenheim, planted with over 50 percent Riesling, 25 percent Silvaner and six percent Kerner. Rieslings are particularly distinguished but all the wines do well at the national (*DLG) competitions. Annual production is 7,600 cases (half *lieblich*), sold mainly to the consumer but also exported.
Address: Rheinstrasse 30, W-6501 Bodenheim
Tel: 06135 2301

Lieser M-S-R w
Small village near *Bernkastel-Kues making racy, elegant wines. It

takes its name from the stream that flows into the Mosel. The castle at Lieser is the family seat of the vineyard-owning von Schorlemer family. *Grosslage*: ★Kurfürstlay.

Limberger, Blauer

Red grape variety, also spelt Lemberger, occupying 611 hectares almost all in Württemberg (also widely grown in the Burgenland [Austria] where it is known as Blaufränkisch). It ripens late in the season, shortly after the Spätburgunder, compared to which its wine is lighter, has a higher acid content and is usually inferior in quality. Often sold in Germany blended with Trollinger.

Lingenfelder, Weingut H & R Rhpf

Fifteen-hectare estate, planted with 38 percent Riesling, eight percent Scheurebe, 15 percent Spätburgunder and other varieties, at ★Freinsheim and ★Grosskarlbach. The wines have character, depth of flavour and structure – both red and white are equally successful. Arguably the *barrique*-aged Spätburgunder is among the best in Germany.

Address: Hauptstrasse 27, W-6711 Grosskarlbach
Tel: 06238 754

Linsenbusch Rhpf w (r)

Large, 175-hectare, level *Einzellage* at ★Ruppertsberg, in which various vine varieties are grown. *Grosslage*: ★Mariengarten. Growers: Bassermann-Jordan, Buhl, Bürklin-Wolf, Winzerverein Deidesheim, Kern, Kimich, Ruppertsberger Winzerverein, Spindler, Wegeler-Deinhard.

Linz Mrh w

Exceptionally attractive market town, a good spot from which to visit the northern Mittelrhein. Sound Riesling wines, now produced on a small scale. *Grosslage*: Rheinburgengau.

Longuich M-S-R w

Small village east of ★Trier, near the upstream boundary of the ★Mittelmosel, making distinguished, fruity Rieslings. *Grosslage*: Probstberg.

Loosen, Weingut Ökonomierat Dr M-S-R

Small but high-quality eight-hectare estate with holdings at ★Erden
(★Prälat, ★Treppchen), ★Wehlen (★Sonnenuhr), ★Graach (★Him-
melreich) and ★Ürzig (★Würzgarten), planted 97 percent Riesling.
Three percent is Müller-Thurgau whose wine, unusually for the
Mosel-Saar-Ruwer, is aged in *barrique*. Some vines are 70 years old
and ungrafted. Annual production is 5,400 cases, 60 percent
exported. Ninety percent of the QbA is *trocken*, 84 percent of the
QmP is *lieblich*.
Address: St Johannishof, W-5550 Bernkastel
Tel: 06531 3426

Lorch Rhg w

Village in the Rhein gorge, opposite the vineyards of the
Mittelrhein, at the downstream end of the Rheingau. Riesling
predominates. The cost of vineyard land is about 20 percent of that
at nearby ★Assmannshausen but the wine quality is good; prices are
similar to those from villages such as ★Johannisberg and ★Winkel,
although the wines probably cannot quite compete with the finest
in the region. *Grosslage*: ★Burgweg.

Lorchhausen Rhg w

Attractive village immediately adjacent to the vineyards of the
Mittelrhein, producing light, elegant Riesling wine. *Grosslage*:
★Burgweg.

Lorettoberg Baden w
Grosslage south of ★Freiburg in the Bereich ★Markgräflerland.
Many vine varieties (especially Gutedel) and a high proportion of
simple quality wine (QbA), made to modern high standards of
vinification. Much of the wine is sold by the vast ★Badischer
Winzerkeller at Breisach.

Lötzbeyer, Weingut Adolf Nahe
Six-hectare estate in agricultural land south of the river Nahe at
★Feilbingert, planted 50 percent Riesling. Many awards at the
★DLG competitions.
Address: Kirchstrasse 6, W-6767 Feilbingert
Tel: 06708 2287

Löwenstein, Weingut Fürst Rhg Charta VDP
Twenty-hectare estate at ★Hallgarten, leased by ★Schloss Vollrads,
with 97 percent Riesling holdings in the ★Schönhell, Hendelberg
and Jungfer sites. Characterful, flavoury, stylish, wines of which 66
percent is *trocken* and only two percent *lieblich*. Annual production
is 14,200 cases, 28 percent exported.
Address: Schloss Vollrads, W-6227 Oestrich-Winkel
Tel: 06723 660

Löwenstein, Weingut Fürst Franken/Baden VDP
Estate of 26 hectares shared between Franken and Baden, that has
been producing wine since the 12th century, acquired by the
Löwenstein-Wertheim-Rosenberg family nearly 200 years ago.
Very steep sites, including the terraced Homburger Kallmuth by
the river Main. Vines are 38 percent Silvaner, 17 percent Müller-
Thurgau, 19 percent Spätburgunder and others, producing tra-
ditional *trocken* Franken wines, and a small amount of red wine sold
in Burgundy bottles.
Address: Rathausgasse 5, W-6983 Kreuzwertheim
Tel: 09342 6505

Ludwigshöhe Rhh w
Small and relatively unknown village on the ★Rheinterrasse – an
area that almost guarantees wines of above average quality.
Grosslage: Vogelsgärten and Krötenbrunnen.

Lump Franken w
Steep, well-known *Einzellage* at ★Escherndorf making powerful, soft, Silvaner and Müller-Thurgau wines. *Grosslage*: ★Kirchberg. Growers: Juliusspital, Schäffer.

Maikammer Rhpf w (r)
Small town with many old houses in the north of the Bereich ★Südliche Weinstrasse, well known in the region. Sound but not top-quality wines. *Grosslage*: Mandelhöhe.

Main
River 483 kilometres long that flows into the Rhein at ★Mainz. En route it provides an erratic line around which the Franken vineyards are planted. It also passes the small but important sites at ★Hochheim in the Rheingau.

Mainz Rhh
Capital of ★Rheinland-Pfalz and the headquarters of many institutions concerned with wine. It lies mainly in the Bereich ★Nierstein and much of its sound wine is sold under the *Grosslage* names of ★St Alban and ★Domherr. It is also the birthplace of the printer Johannes Gutenberg.

Mainzer Weinbörse
A fair held each year in ★Mainz for the wine trade by members of the ★VDP in Rheinhessen, Rheinpfalz, Nahe, Mosel-Saar-Ruwer, Mittelrhein, Franken, Rheingau, Baden and Württemberg. It is an important event in the German wine-trade year.

Maische
The pulp and juice of the grape, after it leaves the crusher and before it is pressed.

Maischeerhitzung
A method of heating red grape must to obtain more colour, followed mainly for economic reasons by cellars with a large production of ordinary wine. Wines treated in this way mature quickly – and in fact are usually ready for drinking immediately after bottling.

Maischegärung

Fermentation together of the pulp and juice (and perhaps stems) of red grapes, almost essential for producing red wine destined for ageing in bottle.

Malic acid

See Apfelsäure

Männle, Weingut Andreas Baden

A 6·2-hectare estate, one of a number of first-class producers on the granite slopes above ★Durbach, and sole owners of the Bienengarten *Einzellage*. The holdings are planted 30 percent each Spätburgunder and Riesling, 18 percent Müller-Thurgau, 15 percent Traminer and others. Sales are mainly to the consumer. Seventy percent of the wine is *trocken*.
Address: Heimbach 12, W-7601 Durbach
Tel: 0781 41486

Männle, Weingut Heinrich Baden

Five-hectare estate planted 38 percent in Spätburgunder (a high proportion for the region), plus Müller-Thurgau, Ruländer, Weissburgunder, Scheurebe and a range of other varieties. A third of the wine is *trocken* and customers value the red cask-matured wine from Spätburgunder highly. Sales are mainly directly to the German consumer.
Address: Sendelbach 86, W-7601 Durbach
Tel: 0781 41101

Marcobrunn Rhg w

One of the best-known *Einzellagen* in the Rheingau, covering some five hectares near ★Erbach and benefiting greatly from an underground water supply. The mainly Riesling wines need time in bottle to show their very considerable best, and are more expensive than those from neighbouring sites. *Grosslage*: ★Deutelsberg. Growers: Staatsweingut Eltville, Knyphausen, Oetinger, Reinhartshausen, Schloss Schönborn, Simmern.

Mariengarten Rhpf w

Grosslage of some 400 hectares situated in the heart of the Bereich

*Mittelhaardt/Deutsche Weinstrasse. It covers vineyards in three well-known wine villages – *Wachenheim, *Forst and *Deidesheim. A high percentage of Riesling is grown. Although the *Grosslage* wines are not expected to be in the same class as those from the best *Einzellagen*, they should still show similar characteristics of Riesling style with a slightly earthy Rheinpfalz flavour.

Marienhof, Weingut M-S-R
Estate owned by Franz *Reh & Sohn.

Marienthal, Staatliche Weinbaudomäne Ahr
The *Rheinland-Pfalz state-owned cellars in the Ahr valley, with 16 hectares of vineyards. Vines are 61 percent Spätburgunder and 10 percent Portugieser. Wines are matured in cask and have a loyal following, but their relatively low alcohol and tannin content limits their appreciation abroad. Half is *trocken*.
Address: Klosterstrasse, W-5487 Marienthal
Tel: 02641 4083

Markant
Describes a well-made wine with pronounced and typical characteristics, such as a good *Würzburger Stein Riesling.

Markensekt
Quality sparkling wine sold under a brand name. Most German sparkling wine is *Markensekt*, and the number of consumers who ask for a sparkling wine with a regional or site name (*Lagensekt*) is still relatively small. Unlike the wine lover who will want, and find, endless variations in still wine, the German sparkling-wine drinker prefers consistency of price and quality. For him, geographical origin is unimportant. He will ask for a *Rieslingsekt* when he wants a good sparkling wine, but it, too, will probably bear a brand name, such as Deinhard Lila Imperial, Jubilar Brut from Rilling or Riesling Brut from Kupferberg.

Markenwein
Branded wine: wine sold under a (usually) registered name by one company or group of companies. The aim is to supply the same style of wine year after year, even if the blend varies from one

market to another. The large number of branded wines exported from Germany reflects the attempts over many years to overcome the difficulties of the German language, particularly in English-speaking countries. Some of the best-known brand names are applied to a range of wines (such as Goldener Oktober). Others, such as Black Tower and Green Label, are more closely associated with one wine. The efforts of the leading brand owners on the export markets, and the financial support they have given to their wines, prepared the way for the commercial success of cheaper wines in the 1980s.

Markgräflerland, Bereich Baden w (r)
Bereich that stretches from ★Freiburg to Lörrach near the Swiss border. Its wines are well known in southern Germany, especially those made from Gutedel.

Markgräfler Winzergenossenschaft eG, Erste Baden
Cooperative cellar at Schliengen, the first to be built in Markgräf-lerland, in 1908. Grapes are received from 208 hectares, planted 50 percent Gutedel, 20 percent Spätburgunder, and 20 percent Müller-Thurgau. Sixty percent of the wine is *trocken* and over 40 percent is sold directly to the consumer.
Address: Am Sonnenstück 1, W-7846 Schliengen
Tel: 07635 1094

Martinsthal Rhg w
Small, out-of-the-way village at the ★Wiesbaden end of the Rheingau producing admirable Riesling wines, somewhat over-shadowed by those of neighbouring ★Rauenthal. *Grosslage*: ★Steinmächer.

Matheisbildchen M-S-R w
Einzellage at ★Bernkastel producing full-bodied, firm Riesling wines. *Grosslage*: ★Badstube.

Matheus-Lehnert, Weingut J M-S-R
See Krebs, Ferdinand, J Matheus-Lehnert, Weingüter

Mäuerchen Rhg w
Mainly level *Einzellage* on the outskirts of ★Geisenheim, producing
elegant, fruity wines. *Grosslage*: ★Burgweg. Growers: Forschungsanstalt Geisenheim, von Hessen, Schloss Schönborn, Zwierlein.

Maximin–Grünhaus M-S-R w
Small hamlet on the Ruwer. All its excellent 32 hectares of mainly
Riesling vineyard is owned by the Carl von ★Schubert'sche
Gutsverwaltung. *Grosslage*: ★Römerlay.

Maximinhof M-S-R
See Studert-Prüm, Stephan

Mayschoss Altenahr, Winzergenossenschaft Ahr
Oldest cooperative cellar in Germany, founded in 1868. Its 284
members supply grapes from 110 hectares planted with 45 percent
Spätburgunder, 35 percent Riesling. Light, gentle red wines and
firm whites are sold almost exclusively in Germany; 25 percent is
trocken. Annual production is 100,000 cases.
Address: Bundesstrasse 42, W-5481 Mayschoss
Tel: 02643 7326

Meaty
Describes a full-bodied, rich but not sweet wine, with sufficient
acidity to balance the weight. Might be applied to a *halbtrocken*
Riesling *Spätlese* from the Rheinpfalz in a good year.

Meddersheim Nahe w
Very much a Riesling-growing village of the upper reaches of the
Nahe. Most of the grapes are delivered to the excellent Winzergenossenschaft ★Rheingrafenberg, named after the *Einzellage* of the
same name. *Grosslage*: Paradiesgarten.

Medium-dry
See Halbtrocken

Meersburg Baden w r
Beautiful old walled town on the banks of the ★Bodensee and a
major tourist attraction. Steep, lakeside vineyards produce light-

weight Spätburgunder, well-balanced Ruländer and some of the best, lively Müller-Thurgau in Germany. *See also next entry.*

Meersburg, Staatsweingut Baden

Estate of some 55 hectares established in 1802, owned by the state of Baden-Württemberg; now run by a young management team and said to be one of the few profitable state cellars in Germany. The vineyards are mainly on the shores of the *Bodensee. Vines are 45 percent Spätburgunder, 35 percent Müller-Thurgau and others (the Spätburgunder was recorded as growing at Meersburg as a single vine in 1705). Annual production is some 41,700 cases, of which 50 percent is *trocken*; five percent is exported.
Address: Seminarstrasse 6, W-7758 Meersburg
Tel: 07532 6085

BADEN BODENSEE

STAATSWEINGUT
MEERSBURG

1991
MEERSBURGER
RIESCHEN
RULÄNDER

QUALITÄTSWEIN
ERZEUGERABFÜLLUNG
10,5 %   A.P.Nr. 102/02/90
vol   D-7758 Meersburg   0,75l

Meerspinne Rhpf w (r)

Grosslage of some 795 hectares at the southern end of the Bereich *Mittelhaardt/Deutsche Weinstrasse. Until recently, the reputation of its wines was overshadowed by those of the adjacent *Grosslage* *Hofstück with its sites at *Deidesheim.

Mehrhölzchen Rhg w

Grosslage of nearly 350 hectares in the central Rheingau covering individual sites at *Hallgarten and *Oestrich. As usual in the region, the finest wines are sold under the site names. The *Grosslage* name is used for sound but not top-quality wine. A very high proportion of Riesling is grown.

Mehring M-S-R w

Village on the Mosel some kilometres downstream from *Trier, overlooked by its steep or sloping vineyards. In the steep sites, Riesling makes flowery, firm wines with good acidity. *Grosslagen*: *St Michael for the better, south-southwest-facing sites; Probstberg for the rest.

Meissen S w (r)

The historic, china-manufacturing town with a long history of vine growing. A leader in the 18th and early 19th centuries in the production of and trading in German wine. Presently shares the problems of its region, *Sachsen. No *Grosslage*.

Mertesdorf M-S-R w

Small Ruwer village whose best-known wines are sold under the name of its satellite hamlet *Maximin-Grünhaus. Prestigious Riesling wines of great elegance. *Grosslage*: *Römerlay.

Messer, Weingut Georg Rhpf

'The Messer-Method reaches beyond a mere technical process. Rather it lays claim to a wholeness, stretching organically across the whole sphere of the culture of the vine and the development of the vine.' This 20-hectare estate takes marketing very seriously and offers its wines (90 percent *trocken*, ten percent *halbtrocken*) at prices to match the remarkable packaging. Annual production is 12,500 cases, of which 16 percent is exported.
Address: Hauptstrasse 47, W-6719 Weisenheim am Berg
Tel: 06353 1015

Mettenheim Rhh w

Village at the southern end of the *Rheinterrasse with some 300 hectares of vineyards. *Grosslagen*: *Krötenbrunnen, *Rheinblick.

Meyer-Näkel, Weingut Ahr

Seven-hectare estate planted 80 percent Spätburgunder, five percent each Frühburgunder, Portugieser, Dornfelder, and Riesling. The red wines are tannic, and 20–30 percent of the Spätburgunder is *barrique*-aged. All are well worth tasting and command high prices in Germany. Two *trocken* Spätburgunder *Beerenauslesen* are listed. Annual production is 3,500 cases, 90 percent *trocken*, five percent exported.

Address: Haardtbergstrasse 20, W-5487 Dernau

Tel: 02643 1628

Meyer Wineries GmbH, Peter

Wine merchants heavily involved in exports to the UK and USA, concentrating on ★Liebfraumilch and inexpensive QbA. Owners of the von Schorlemer estates.

Address: Cusanusstrasse 14, W-5550 Bernkastel-Kues

Michelmark Rhg w

Einzellage at ★Erbach making Riesling wines with pronounced fruity acidity that benefit from bottle-age. However, as with so many vineyards much enlarged in 1971, its wines are of uneven quality. *Grosslage*: ★Deutelsberg. Growers: Knyphausen, Nikolai, Oetinger, Reinhartshausen, Tillmanns.

Michelsberg M-S-R w

One of the best-known *Grosslagen* in Germany, covering more than 1,300 hectares in the neighbourhood of ★Piesport. Some of the individual sites, such as ★Piesporter Treppchen and ★Trittenheimer Altärchen, extend over 200 hectares or more; others cover less than a hectare. The quality varies greatly, with much rather ordinary Müller-Thurgau wine being made and sold as Piesporter Michelsberg. However, as soon as the word Riesling appears on the label, the wine should have good Mosel style and fruit. No top-quality wine will be sold under the name Michelsberg.

Milchsäure

Lactic acid. Not normally present in must but formed during alcoholic fermentation and, infrequently in German wine, by a malolactic fermentation (*see* Apfelsäure).

Mild
Describes a wine that is balanced but has relatively low acidity. It is
not a quality definition and is neutral in implication. Might well be
applied to a Müller-Thurgau from the Bereich *Südliche Weinstrasse (Rheinpfalz). It is often used as an alternative to *lieblich*.

Milz, Weingut M-S-R VDP
The Milz family has been making wine since 1520. Today the 7·5-
hectare estate has holdings at *Neumagen, *Dhron, *Trittenheim
(*Altärchen, *Apotheke) and *Ockfen and enjoys sole ownership
of the 0·8-hectare Neumagener Nusswingert, the 0·5-hectare
Trittenheimer Felsenkopf and the 0·25-hectare Trittenheimer
Leiterchen – all three sites very steep and 100 percent Riesling. The
cask-matured wines have won many prizes; 30 percent is *lieblich*.
Address: Laurentiushof, W-5559 Trittenheim
Tel: 06507 2300

Mittelhaardt/Deutsche Weinstrasse, Bereich Rhpf w (r)
Bereich that covers some of the best vineyards in Germany. The
number of good producers away from its most famous villages is
increasing, and the quality of the wines is very high. Most are sold
under the *Einzellage* or *Grosslage* name. The *Bereich* name is rarely
found on a label.

Mittelheim Rhg w
Small village joined to its neighbour *Winkel, looks across the
Rhein to *Ingelheim in the Rheinhessen. The proportion of
Riesling grown is high. *Grosslagen*: shares *Honigberg with
Winkel; the remainder is in *Erntebringer.

Mittelhölle Rhg w
Small *Einzellage* planted exclusively in Riesling, producing elegant,
long-lasting wines. *Grosslage*: *Erntebringer. Grower: Mumm.

Mittelmosel M-S-R
Middle Mosel: area almost the same as that covered by the Bereich
*Bernkastel.

Mittelrhein w (r)

Region of 731 hectares whose steep vineyards closely follow the course of the Rhein upstream from ★Königswinter, just south of ★Bonn. The attractive terraced vineyards have almost all been rebuilt in recent years to form uninterrupted, more easily worked slopes. The romantic and sometimes dramatic scenery is well known to many visitors, but the wine seldom leaves the region except in the back of tourists' cars or as branded *Sekt*. In the early 1990s tourism in the region is on the decline and so is viticulture. Riesling covers 75 percent of the area under vine and its wine can reach great heights, although generally the quality is not so distinguished as that from the neighbouring Rheingau, of which it often seems a slightly more steely, earthy version. North of ★Braubach the wine resembles that from the Lower Mosel. Mittelrhein Riesling makes excellent sparkling wine.

Mittlere Nahe

Area covering the best vineyards of the Nahe between ★Bad Kreuznach and ★Schlossböckelheim. Not an official wine designation, but a description used in the region.

Mönchhof, Weingut M-S-R VDP

Five-hectare, 100 percent Riesling estate, owned by the Eymael family since 1802. The steep holdings are at ★Ürzig (★Würzgarten),

★Erden (★Prälat, ★Treppchen), ★Zeltingen-Rachtig (★Himmel-reich), ★Wehlen and ★Kinheim (★Hubertuslay). Of the annual production of 5,000 cases of slaty, cask-matured wines, 40 percent is exported.
Address: W-5564 Ürzig
Tel: 06532 2116

Monsheim Rhh w
Wine village with some 16th and 18th-century houses near the border with the Rheinpfalz, and a technically advanced cooperative cellar. *Grosslage*: ★Domblick.

Monzingen Nahe w
Village with wines once thought to be of sufficient quality to warrant shipment to the East Indies and back to encourage maturation. Vineyards are steep with a high proportion of Riesling. *Grosslage*: Paradiesgarten.

Morgen
A measure of land, now obsolete, that varied from region to region but was usually a little less than an acre (·405 hectare): thought to have equalled the amount of land that a man could plough in a morning (*Morgen*). The word is still recalled in site names such as Güldenmorgen and Hohenmorgen.

Morio-Muskat
White grape variety, a crossing of Silvaner × Weissburgunder, grown on 2,242 hectares mainly in the Bereich ★Südliche Weinstrasse, where the vine was developed, and in the Rheinhessen. The yield can be large and the wine often forms part of commercial blends, to which its pronounced bouquet brings a certain attraction. Unfortunately, the wood and the young branches of the vine are particularly attractive to deer, rabbits and hares. The area under Morio-Muskat (just over two percent of the whole) is decreasing. The particularly strong bouquet and flavour can become cloying and the wine lacks true distinction.

Mosbacher, Weingut Georg Rhpf
Estate of 8·5 hectares with holdings in most of the best sites at ★Forst

(★Ungeheuer, ★Pechstein, ★Musenhang), ★Deidesheim (★Herr-gottsacker) and ★Wachenheim. The percentage of Riesling is high (80 percent) and the wines achieve many successes at regional and national competitions. Cask-matured, Riesling *trocken* wines are much in demand, 90 percent sold to private customers in Germany.
Address: Weinstrasse 27, W-6701 Forst
Tel: 06326 329

Mosel

Famous wine river that rises in the Vosges mountains and flows some 500 kilometres later into the Rhein at ★Koblenz, having been joined en route by many tributaries including the Ruwer and the Saar. The 130 or so picturesque wine villages that line its banks are easily reached from the Koblenz-Trier motorway or from the Hunsrück Hohenstrasse (B327). Minor roads follow both sides of the river closely for most of the distance from Trier to Koblenz, and part of the riverside journey can also be made by train.

Mosel-Saar-Ruwer w

The best known internationally of Germany's wine-producing regions, with 12,760 hectares under vine – mainly Riesling (55 percent), Müller-Thurgau (22 percent), Elbling (nine percent) and Kerner (seven percent). Many of the vineyards are on very steep, slaty sites that provide ideal ripening conditions for Riesling. Because of the difficult terrain, viticultural costs are far greater than in the flat or rolling countryside of the Rheinhessen or Rheinpfalz. However, in recent years most of the old walled terraces that could only bear a small number of vines have been replaced by more economically worked vineyards, and over 70 percent of the vine-growing area has now been modernized. The crop from 40 percent of the region is delivered to cooperative cellars. The balance is either sold in bulk to the wine trade or bottled by the grower. There are many distinguished estates, most of them upstream from ★Zell, either on the Mosel itself or on its tributaries, the Saar and the Ruwer. A Riesling wine from the Mosel-Saar-Ruwer has a high level of tartaric acid which gives it style, freshness and the possibility of developing well in bottle over many years. A 'good' year will be one in which these characteristics are pronounced and much late-picked (*Spätlese*) wine can be made.

Moselland eG M-S-R
Rapidly growing cooperative cellar with over 5,200 members, who deliver to it each year (from 3,000 hectares) approximately 25 percent of the Mosel-Saar-Ruwer grape harvest. Vines are 55 percent Riesling, ten percent Elbling, 25 percent Müller-Thurgau. Pleasant wines, and good value for money. About 42 percent of the wine is exported, much to the United Kingdom.
Address: W-5550 Bernkastel-Kues
Tel: 06531 570

Moseltaler
A name created in 1986 for quality wines from the Mosel-Saar-Ruwer made from Riesling, Müller-Thurgau, Elbling and Kerner, which are typical of the region. They must contain between 15 and 30 grams per litre residual sugar, and have a total acidity of at least 7 grams per litre.

Mossbacher-Hof, Weingut Rhpf VDP
Eleven-hectare estate with holdings in important *Einzellagen* at ★Forst (★Ungeheuer, ★Pechstein, ★Musenhang, ★Jesuitengarten) and ★Deidesheim (★Herrgottsacker), planted with a high proportion of Riesling (90 percent); 85 percent of the wine made is *trocken*. Elegant acidity is a characteristic. Annual production is 6,300 cases of which two percent is exported and 80 percent sold directly to the consumer.
Address: Weinstrasse 23, W-6701 Forst
Tel: 06326 264

Most, Mostgewicht
See Must

Muffig
Musty. Wines that have been stored in unclean containers or bottled with corks that have also been incorrectly stored can develop a dirty smell. If the fault is not too serious the smell can be removed by treatment in bulk.

Mülheim M-S-R w
Village on the Mosel with a high proportion of Riesling in its

vineyards, making attractive, characterful wines. *Grosslage*: ★Kurfürstlay.

Müller GmbH and Co KG, Rudolf M-S-R

Wine merchants, sparkling-wine producers and owners of the Müller-Burggraef part of Weingut Dr H ★Thanisch and of Weingut Müller-Burggraef itself. Best known of the Rudolf Müller wines is the widely exported 'Bishop of Riesling', a Bereich Bernkastel Riesling QbA. Annual production is 830,000 cases of still wine, 583,000 of *Sekt*.

Address: W-5586 Reil
Tel: 06532 610

Müller, Weingut Gebr Baden

Six-hectare estate under new management since the 1990 vintage. The holdings (70 percent in steep sites) at ★Ihringen (★Winkler-berg) and at ★Breisach, are planted 30 percent Spätburgunder, 30 percent Riesling, 20 percent Weissburgunder, and other varieties. All the wines are *trocken*, some Spätburgunder are *barrique*-aged. Annual production is 4,200 cases. No exports.

Address: Richard-Müller-Strasse 5, W-7814 Breisach
Tel: 07667 511

Müller-Catoir, Weingut Rhpf

A much and rightly praised 17-hectare estate with holdings at

*Neustadt, *Gimmeldingen, and *Haardt planted 50 percent Riesling, 15 percent Scheurebe, and others. The wines are beautifully structured and taste balanced, even when they have more than 15 percent natural alcohol. No *barriques*, no malolactic fermentation (*see* Apfelsäure), no *deacidification, virtually never any enrichment (*see* Anreicherung), low yields, resulting in good acidity and enough alcohol, produce characterful wines that are among the best in Germany. Annual production is 10,800 cases, of which 50 percent is *trocken*; ten percent is exported.
Address: Mandelring 25, W-6730 Neustadt
Tel: 06321 2815

Müller-Scharzhof, Weingut Egon M-S-R VDP

Great estate, owned by Egon Müller, dating in its present form from 1797 but with origins reaching back over 700 years. Its 8·5 hectares of top-quality Saar vineyards include seven hectares in the heart of the superb *Scharzhofberg. Two hectares of the Scharzhofberg holding is planted in ungrafted Riesling, and only QmP in good vintages is sold under the Scharzhofberger name. Of the total area under vine, 95 percent is Riesling.

The wines are known for their great finesse and ability to last in bottle; 95 percent is *lieblich*. Approximate annual production of bottled wine is 4,600 cases, sold in Germany and abroad.
Address: W-5511 Wiltingen
Tel: 06501 17232

Müller-Thurgau

White grape variety, the great workhorse vine of Germany, covering some 23,881 hectares in all 13 wine-growing regions. Named after its developer, Professor Dr Müller from the Thurgau in Switzerland, it was originally thought to be a crossing of Riesling × Silvaner but is now considered to be a crossing of two clones of Riesling. It regularly produces a large crop, usually with low acidity, early in the autumn. The low acid content and the tendency of the grapes to rot makes a late harvest difficult.

Müller-Thurgau cannot compare in quality with Riesling but it makes perfectly sound, agreeable wine, usually of no great distinction. Where the yield is kept below 80 hectolitres per hectare the improvement in the wine is marked. However, it is more often used as the backbone of cheap commercial blends, when it is best drunk within a year or so of being bottled before it loses its youthful freshness.

Müllerrebe
Red grape variety, a mutation of Spätburgunder, also deceptively known as Schwarzriesling and found in France as Pinot Meunier. Planted in 1,685 hectares, mainly in Württemberg, it produces wine with a good deep colour but not of the quality of Spätburgunder.

Müllheim Baden w (r)
Town in the Bereich *Markgräflerland. Winemaking from 400 hectares, predominantly in the hands of cooperative cellars. Well known for the Gutedel grown in sloping vineyards. *Grosslage*: Burg Neuenfels.

Mumm'sches Weingut, G H von Rhg
Estate of 54·2 hectares, established in the early 19th century, lying above *Schloss Johannisberg. The estate is sole owner of the 3·8-hectare Hansenberg and four-hectare Schwarzenstein sites at *Johannisberg, and also has holdings at *Rüdesheim (including *Berg Rottland, *Berg Schlossberg, *Berg Roseneck), *Assmannshausen (*Höllenberg) and *Geisenheim, planted with Riesling and Spätburgunder. All the wines are cask-matured and aim to achieve the typical Rheingau Riesling virtues of elegance, good acidity and fruit.
Address: Schulstrasse 32, W-6222 Geisenheim
Tel: 06722 8012

Mundelsheim Würt r w
Prosperous-looking, picturesque village with often-photographed, steep, sometimes terraced, south-facing vineyards. Sixty percent is planted in red vine varieties (Trollinger, Schwarzriesling and Spätburgunder). *Grosslage*: Schalkstein.

Mundelsheim eG, Weingärtner-Genossenschaft Würt
Cooperative supplied by 575 (mainly part-time) grape growers from 175 hectares, 50 hectares in steep, terraced sites (including

*Käsberg), planted 30 percent Trollinger, 15 percent Müller-Thurgau. Legal restrictions on how much wine can be sold each year (and therefore, produced) make it difficult for the cooperative to satisfy its customers' needs. Annual production is 158,000 cases, sold exclusively in Germany.
Address: W-7121 Mundelsheim
Tel: 07143 5196

Münster-Sarmsheim Nahe w
A small village some three kilometres south of *Bingen, which produces good-quality Riesling wine, particularly from its *Dautenpflänzer *Einzellage*. The 'Sarmsheim' does not appear on the label. *Grosslage*: *Schlosskapelle.

Münzlay M-S-R w
Grosslage of more than 500 hectares around *Zeltingen-Rachtig, *Graach and *Wehlen, on both sides of the river Mosel. Most of the vineyards are very steep, producing a relatively small crop from Riesling grown on slaty soil. The best wines will normally be offered under the individual site names (such as Wehlener *Sonnenuhr, Zeltinger *Sonnenuhr, Zeltinger *Himmelreich). Wine that is sold carrying only the *Grosslage* name, Münzlay, should still be quite stylish, but will probably lack the finesse of one of the wines bearing an *Einzellage* name on the label.

Musenhang Rhpf w
Sloping *Einzellage* at *Forst making top-quality, stylish, meaty Riesling wines. *Grosslage*: *Mariengarten. Growers: Bassermann-Jordan, Winzerverein Deidesheim, Forster Winzerverein, Giessen, Mosbacher, Mossbacher-Hof, Wolf.

Muskat
Name applied to many different and sometimes unrelated vine varieties. Some are European in origin, others are hybrids. Both red and white Muskat grapes are possible. The common factor of all Muskat wine is a distinctive bouquet that can range from the flowery and delicate to the overblown and sickly. The most widely grown Muskat in Germany is Morio-Muskat. Gelber Muskateller, with 45 hectares, is found mainly in Baden (characterful, balanced

wines) and Franken has over half of the 21 hectares of Muskat-Ottonel.

Mussbach Rhpf w (r)
Small community on the Deutsche ★Weinstrasse, immediately north of ★Neustadt. The vineyards, including the large Eselshaut *Einzellage*, are as flat as a billiard table but can produce some magnificent wines in the highest quality categories up to *Trockenbeerenauslese*. *Grosslage*: ★Meerspinne.

Must
Grape juice. Its quality is judged by weight, which for practical purposes means its sugar content (and thus its potential alcohol) and its degree of acidity. Must weight (*Mostgewicht*) is measured in Germany against the Oechsle scale. The legal minimum must weight for each quality of German wine ranges from 44° Oechsle (in all regions except Baden) for *deutscher Tafelwein* to 150° for a *Trockenbeerenauslese*. From must, wine and *Süssreserve* are made.

Nachfolger
Successors. An alternative to ★*Erben*, forming part of a company title, as in Weingut Bürgermeister Willi Schweinhardt Nachf. May be abbreviated to *Nachf.*

Nackenheim Rhh w
Small town on the Rhein, near ★Mainz. The area under vine is not large but the red sandstone produces excellent wine with character and style. *Grosslagen*: ★Spiegelberg, ★Gutes Domtal.

Nacktarsch M-S-R w
Relatively small *Grosslage* of some 400 hectares in the ★Mittelmosel, devoted entirely to the vineyards of the village of ★Kröv and its *Ortsteil* Kövenig. A high proportion of Riesling is grown on extremely steep sites and the wine, like that from the neighbouring villages, has all the welcome Mosel characteristics of freshness and fruitiness. None of the individual Kröver site names is as well known, particularly to the German consumer, as that of Nacktarsch – a memorable name which, if translated, means exactly what you would expect.

Nägler, Weingut Dr Heinrich Rhg VDP

Estate with 6·9 hectares of holdings in ★Rüdesheim (including ★Berg Rottland, ★Berg Schlossberg, ★Berg Roseneck, ★Bischofsberg, Drachenstein). Vines are 87 percent Riesling, eight percent Ehrenfelser, five percent Spätburgunder. Yield is strictly limited. Annual production is 4,580 cases, of which 50 percent is *trocken*, and 14 percent is exported.
Address: Friedrichstrasse 22, W-6220 Rüdesheim
Tel: 06722 2835

Nägelsförster Hof, Weingut Baden VDP

Seventeen-hectare estate at ★Varnhalt with Cistercian origins, which encompasses Weingut Klostergut Fremersberg founded by Franciscans – an order to which François Rabelais surprisingly belonged. All the holdings are on steep and partly terraced slopes, planted 60 percent Riesling, 20 percent Spätburgunder, five percent Chardonnay. Annual production is 10,000 cases, part bottled in *Bocksbeutel*; 90 percent is *trocken*.
Address: W-7570 Baden-Baden 22
Tel: 07221 24053

Nahe w (r)

Region of 4,579 hectares with a relatively small number of growers making what is generally accepted as some of the finest wine in Germany. Many of the vineyards are on gentle or steep slopes and Riesling occupies the best sites. Wines made in the attractive area between ★Bad Kreuznach and ★Schlossböckelheim can resemble those of the Mosel or Saar. They are elegant, with a wonderfully balanced fruity acidity. The Nahe is very much an agricultural as well as a viticultural region and many vine growers are also involved in farming.

Often the growers are also winemakers and bottle their produce themselves rather than sell their grapes, or their wine in bulk, to others. Among them are a number with great technical expertise and vision. Some 40 percent of a vintage is said to be sold directly to the consumer by estate-bottlers. The best-known on the export market, but not the best wine of the region, is that of the *Grosslage* Rüdesheimer ★Rosengarten. At all quality levels, Nahe wine is normally good value for money.

Nahe-Winzer Kellereien eG Nahe
Central cooperative cellar whose members supply grapes from
1,215 hectares throughout the Nahe, planted with Silvaner,
Müller-Thurgau, Riesling and others. The wines are concentrated
and good value for money. Sales are in Germany and abroad.
Address: Winzenheimerstrasse 30, W-6551 Bretzenheim
Tel: 0671 2232

Narrenkappe Nahe
One of several sloping *Einzellagen* at *Bad Kreuznach producing
essentially racy Riesling wines with fine, fruity acidity. *Grosslage*:
*Kronenberg. Growers: August Anheuser, Paul Anheuser,
Finkenauer, Plettenberg.

Nassverbesserung
Wet-sugaring: the addition of a solution of sugar and water to
wine, to increase the alcohol content and reduce acidity – a practice
forbidden since 1984.

Naturgewächs
Before 1971 a synonym for *Naturrein*.

Naturrein
According to the 1930 German Wine Law, a wine in which the
alcohol content had not been increased by added sugar could be
called *naturrein*. As a result, wines that would have benefited from
more alcohol were sometimes left thin and unbalanced so as to be
able to claim 'purity'. The use of the term was prohibited by the
1971 Wine Law.

Naturwein
A *Naturrein* wine.

Naumburg S-U w
City with a fine cathedral, a remarkable 200-metre relief of
winemaking dating from 1722, carved into rock, and the 120-
hectare Staatsweingut Naumburg.

Neckar

River that rises near the Danube and flows, some 402 kilometres later, into the Rhein at Mannheim. Its Württemberg vineyards are not as continuous as those of the Mosel but are often equally steep and costly to maintain. Many lie well away from the river, diminishing somewhat the river's importance to vine growing.

Neckerauer, Weingut K Rhpf

Old-established 24-hectare estate north of *Bad Dürkheim, selling Weisenheimer wines (40 percent *trocken*) from a wide range of vines suitable to the sandy clay soil (34 percent Riesling).
Address: Ritter von Geisslerstrasse 9, W-6714 Weisenheim am Sand
Tel: 06353 8059

Neef M-S-R w

Small village between *Cochem and *Zell producing positive Riesling wines. Surprisingly for this part of the river, Elbling is also grown. *Grosslage*: Grafschaft.

Neidischer Herbst

Envious autumn. Term used, almost inexplicably, to describe a vintage with a small yield.

Neipperg, Weingüter & Schlosskellerei Graf von Würt VDP

Estate dating back to the 12th century, with the von Neipperg family still in command. Its 31 hectares are planted 26 percent Limberger, 26 percent Riesling and 21 percent Schwarzriesling (Müllerrebe), 60 percent in steep sites. Emphasis in listing and selling the wines is given to the vine variety and *Prädikat* (such as Riesling Spätlese Schwaigerner Ruthe). Annual production is 17,500 cases, of which 98 percent is *trocken*, two percent is exported. The estate also owns Château Canon la Gaffelière and Château La Mondotte in St-Emilion, Bordeaux.
Address: Schloss, W-7103 Schwaigern
Tel: 07138 5081

Nell, Christoph von M-S-R

Estate of 11 hectares planted 100 percent Riesling in steep sites at Kasel. Sole owners of the six-hectare Dominkanerberg *Einzellage*.

Annual production is 6,250 cases, with 55 percent *trocken* – a high percentage for the Mosel-Saar-Ruwer.
Address: W-5501 Kasel
Tel: 0651 5180

Nell, Georg-Fritz von M-S-R VDP

Ten-hectare Trier estate and restaurant, with sole ownership of the Trierer Benediktinerberg and Kurtfürstenhofberg sites as well as holdings at *Wiltingen (*Braunfels), *Ayl (*Kupp) and *Bernkastel (*Graben), 80 percent Riesling. The wines are concentrated in flavour and benefit from bottle-age. Approximate annual production is relatively low (7,500 cases); 45 percent *lieblich*; 20 percent is exported.
Address: Weingut Im Thiergarten 12, W-5500 Trier
Tel: 0651 32397

Nelles, Weingut Toni Ahr

Five-hectare estate at the eastern end of the Ahr valley, planted 40 percent Spätburgunder, 25 percent Portugieser, 20 percent Riesling, and ten percent Ruländer and others. The list is surprisingly long. Fifty percent of the wine is *trocken*, and some of the reds are *lieblich* in the German manner still popular in the Ahr valley.

Barrique-aged Spätburgunder is also offered. Annual production is 5,000 cases; 60 percent is sold to private customers, 30 percent to restaurants, and ten percent is exported.
Address: Göppingerstrasse 13a, W-5483 Heimersheim
Tel: 02641 24349

Nervig
Nervous. A term similar in meaning to *kernig*, or the French *nerveux*. Describes a wine in which the balance of alcohol, extract and acid is very good. Such a wine will be firm, vigorous (not flat and tired), and impress by its style. Not a description that is often used, but could be applied to good Riesling wines.

Neue', 'Der
A *Landwein* from one vintage only (which must appear on the bottle), which may be offered to the consumer between November 10 immediately after the stated vintage, and January 15 of the following year.

Neuer Wein
New wine. The consumer in Germany has as yet no great interest in drinking his own *neuer Wein* within weeks of the vintage. Nevertheless, cheap wines from early-ripening vine varieties are on sale by November, but they are not given great prominence. *See previous entry*.

Neuleiningen Rhpf w
Fine old fortified village perched on a hilltop in the north of the Rheinpfalz, overlooking its sloping vineyards and the Schwarzwald in the distance. The wines (Rieslings and Silvaners) are not great, but characterful and flavoury. *Grosslage*: Höllenpfad.

Neumagen M-S-R w
Ancient wine village linked with *Dhron near *Piesport, producing racy wines, mainly from Riesling. *Grosslage*: *Michelsberg.

Neus, Weingut J Rhh
See Sonnenberg, Weingut

Neustadt Rhpf w (r)
Busy winemaking town in the south of the Bereich ★Mittelhaardt/
Deutsche Weinstrasse. Produces good, meaty wines that are
steadily gaining a reputation in Germany. *Grosslagen*: ★Meerspinne,
Rebstöckel, Pfaffengrund.

**Neustadt-Mussbach/Weinstrasse, Staatsweingut mit
Johannitergut der Landes-Lehr- und Forschungsanstalt**
Rhpf
The 22-hectare estate of a state teaching and research institute,
planted 31 percent Riesling, 12 percent Silvaner. There is also a
plantation of Gänsfüsser, once the star vine for quality wine in the
Rheinpfalz. Its origins are extremely uncertain and it seems to have
been both a red as well as a white grape variety. Many medals have
been won by the estate at competitions. Annual production is
16,700 cases, of which 33 percent is *trocken*, sold mainly to private
customers and restaurants.
Address: Breitenweg 71, W-6730 Neustadt
Tel: 06321 6711

Neutral
Wine term, used mainly within the trade, often applied to QbA or
deutscher Tafelwein with no excesses of flavour or bouquet, made
from grapes such as Elbling, Silvaner and sometimes Riesling. A
neutral flavour is often unrelated to quality, except in a base wine
from which sparkling wine is to be made, in which case it is
normally considered an advantage.

Neuweier Baden w r
Village tucked into the edge of the ★Schwarzwald with an
impressive-looking 100 percent Riesling, 39-hectare, steep Mauer-
berg *Einzellage*, and a 100 percent Spätburgunder *Einzellage*. The
quality wines, which can be sold in the *Bocksbeutel*, seem
overpriced. *Grosslage*: Schloss Rodeck.

Neuzüchtungen
New crossings of one European vine with another, such as
Scheurebe – Silvaner × Riesling. (Crossings of European and
American vines are 'interspecific crossings'. *See* Rebsorte.)

Neveu, Weingut Freiherr von Baden
Estate of some 15 hectares, acquired by the von Neveu family in
1832, on steep vineyards above *Durbach, planted 44 percent
Riesling, and others including Müller-Thurgau, Spätburgunder
and Chardonnay. Sole owners of Durbacher Josephsberg. The full-
bodied, firm white wines and the richly flavoured Spätburgunders
are typical of this leading wine village. The von Neveu wines are
bottled and marketed by the *Badischer Winzerkeller.
Address: W-7601 Durbach
Tel: 0781 41165

Nicolay, Weingut Peter M-S-R
See Pauly-Bergweiler, Weingut Dr

Niederhausen Nahe w
Small village surrounded by steep, game-filled woods and top-
quality vineyards producing some of the most elegant Riesling
wines of the region. Home of the Staatliche Weinbaudomäne (*see
next entry*). *Grosslage*: *Burgweg.

**Niederhausen-Schlossböckelheim, Verwaltung der
Staatlichen Weinbaudomänen** Nahe VDP
Great estate owned by *Rheinland-Pfalz, established in 1902, with
40 hectares in *Schlossböckelheim (*Kupfergrube, *Felsenberg),
*Niederhausen (including *Hermannshöhle, sole owners of *Her-
mannsberg), *Traisen (*Bastei), *Altenbamberg, *Münster-Sarms-
heim and *Dorsheim. Vines are 95 percent Riesling. Cool
fermentation, skilled vinification and maturation in wood, result in
Riesling wines of delicacy and complexity; 50 percent is *lieblich*.
Annual production is 20,000 cases, 15 percent exported.
Address: W-6551 Niederhausen
Tel: 06758 6215

Niederkirchen Rhpf w
Small village with a good cooperative cellar which receives most of
its crop from neighbouring *Deidesheim vineyards. Riesling and
Müller-Thurgau predominate in Niederkirchen. *Grosslage*:
*Hofstück.

Niedermennig M-S-R w
An *Ortsteil* of ★Konz which can produce fine Riesling wine in
good vintages.

Nierstein Rhh w (r)
Small town dedicated to winemaking, 20 kilometres from ★Mainz
in the heart of the ★Rheinterrasse, with many old vaulted cellars and
a wine festival each August. Approximately 1,000-hectare
vineyard, much on the easily recognized '*Rotliegendes*' – reddish
brown slate. The 150 or so growers include some of the best-known
wine names in Germany. *Grosslagen*: ★Spiegelberg, ★Auflangen
and ★Rehbach (and ★Gutes Domtal for one site only, the
Pfaffenkappe).

Nierstein, Bereich Rhh w (r)
Best-known *Bereich* of the Rheinland in export markets, covering
the fine vineyards of the Rheinterrasse north and south of
★Nierstein, as well as those in much of the rolling hinterland away
from the river. A wine sold as Bereich Nierstein will probably not
be of great quality but it will be soft, light, pleasantly fruity and
likely to contain a high proportion of Müller-Thurgau. It will also
be cheap. If it is very cheap, then that is how it will taste.

Niersteiner Winzergenossenschaft eG Rhh
Cooperative cellar with 440 members holding 300 hectares in many
good sites in ★Nierstein (★Ölberg), ★Oppenheim (★Sackträger and
others) and ★Bodenheim (★Laubenheim and ★Dienheim), previously known as the Bezirkswinzergenossenschaft Rheinfront.
Müller-Thurgau and Silvaner predominate. The quality of the
wines reflects the excellent sites from which they come. Annual
production is equivalent to 291,000 cases, 55 percent *lieblich*, 32
percent sold to private customers.
Address: Karolingerstrasse 6, W-6505 Nierstein
Tel: 06133 5115

Nies'chen M-S-R w
Mainly steep, south-southwest-facing *Einzellage* at ★Kasel on the
Ruwer, producing spicy Riesling wines with a positive fruity, crisp
style. Sometimes suffers from frost. *Grosslage*: ★Römerlay.

Growers: Beulwitz, Bischöfliche Weingüter, Karlsmühle, Kesselstatt, Simon, Wegeler-Deinhard.

Nikolai, Weingut Heinz Rhg
An estate of 6·8-hectares, with holdings at ★Erbach (★Michelmark and others), ★Kiedrich (★Sandgrub) and ★Hallgarten, planted 88 percent Riesling and ten percent Spätburgunder. Annual production is 5,000 cases, 40 percent *trocken*; 88 percent is sold to private customers.
Address: Ringstrasse 16, W-6228 Eltville 2
Tel: 06123 62708

Nobling
White grape variety, a Silvaner × Gutedel crossing from the Staatliches Weinbauinstitut ★Freiburg, now covering 145 hectares, almost all in the Bereich ★Markgräflerland where it enjoys the relatively high rainfall. Must weight and acidity are greater than those of Silvaner; the retail price is usually slightly lower. Full-flavoured, characterful wine.

Nordheim Franken w (r)
Village near ★Volkach, east of ★Würzburg, with the largest area under vine in Franken, including the massive 250-hectare Vögelein site. Powerful, soft, long-flavoured Silvaner and Müller-Thurgau wines, many sold directly by the producers. *Grosslage*: Kirchberg.

Nordheim eG, Weingärtnergenossenschaft Würt
Cooperative cellar supplied by 160 hectares south of Heilbronn, planted 30 percent Riesling, 23 percent Müllerreber (Schwarzriesling), Trollinger, Limberger and other varieties. Many prizes have been won over the years, with Limberger *trocken* being particularly successful in the '89 vintage. There is a premium range of wines and some *barrique*-ageing. Annual production is 100,000 cases, 40 percent *halbtrocken*.
Address: Südstrasse 70, W-7107 Nordheim
Tel: 07133 5013

Nordrhein-Westfalen
Federal state within whose southern border lie 21 hectares of

Mittelrhein vineyard near Bonn. The capital is Düsseldorf.

Norheim Nahe w
Village with small *Einzellagen* producing wines with good acidity and flavour. Riesling from the ★Dellchen site can produce great wine in good years. *Grosslage*: ★Burgweg.

Nussbrunnen Rhg w
Small *Einzellage* at ★Hattenheim making full-bodied complex Riesling wines. *Grosslage*: ★Deutelsberg. Growers: Lang, Reinhartshausen, Ress, Schloss Schönborn, Simmern.

Nussdorf Rhpf w r
Village in the Bereich ★Südliche Weinstrasse near ★Landau in der Pfalz, known mainly for inexpensive wines sold under the *Grosslage* name, Bischöfskreuz. Fine wines also produced by a few estates.

Oberbergen Baden w r
Small village offering the usual range of good Bereich ★Kaiserstuhl wine, known for its famous 'Schwarzer Adler' restaurant (*see* Weingut of same name). *Grosslage*: ★Vulkanfelsen.

Oberbergen eG, Winzergenossenschaft Baden
Village cooperative receiving the grapes from 290 hectares, much in the large Bassgeige ('double-bass') *Einzellage*. Planted 46 percent Müller-Thurgau, 24 percent Spätburgunder and 22 percent Ruländer. The latter, harvested in the fresher, crisper Grauburgunder style, is most attractive. Around 40 percent of the production is *trocken*.
Address: Badbergstrasse 2, W-7818 Vogtsburg-Oberbergen
Tel: 07662 788

Oberemmel M-S-R w
Village set in pleasant country near ★Wiltingen in the Saar valley, making finely tuned, racy Riesling wine. *Grosslage*: ★Scharzberg.

Oberhausen Nahe w
Small, rural village across the Nahe from the Staatliche Weinbaudomäne ★Niederhausen, recently come to prominence through

the quality of the wines from Weingut ★Dönnhof. *Grosslage*: ★Burgweg.

Obermosel, Bereich M-S-R
Upper-Mosel *Bereich*, facing the vineyards of Luxembourg across the river. Produces simple, agreeable and refreshing quality wine from Elbling, much of it converted into sparkling wine.

Oberrotweil eG, Kaiserstühler Winzerverein Baden
Cooperative supplied by 360 hectares, all at Oberrotweil, a village known for its wine and as the birthplace of the architect of New York's Grand Central Station. The modernized vineyards are planted 34 percent Spätburgunder, 30 percent Müller-Thurgau, 22 percent Ruländer (Grauburgunder). There is a premium range of wine and some wines are *barrique*-aged. Annual production is 316,700 cases, 55 percent *trocken*.
Address: Bahnhofstrasse 31, W-7818 Vogtsburg-Oberrotweil
Tel: 07662 706

Oberwesel Mrh w
Ancient wine village in the southern Mittelrhein, 40 kilometres from ★Koblenz in the Rhein gorge. All its vineyards are extremely steep, planted almost 100 percent Riesling, and produce racy, firm wines. *Grosslage*: Schloss Schönburg.

Ockfen M-S-R w
Saar village well known for centuries for its ★Bockstein *Einzellage*. Top-quality, flowery, racy Riesling wine. *Grosslage*: ★Scharzberg.

Oechsle, Oechsle scale
Christian Ferdinand Oechsle (1774–1852), a prolific inventor and musician, was born, lived and died in Württemberg. He developed the Oechsle scale, which compares the weight of a must with that of water. The Oechsle figure is the specific gravity of the must, multiplied by 1,000 to give a whole number. Thus 90° Oechsle is equivalent to a specific gravity of 1·090. In other words 1 litre of the must in question would be 90 grams heavier than 1 litre of water at 20°C. *See also* Must, Qualitätswein mit Prädikat.

Oesterreicher
Synonym for Silvaner, a grape variety believed by some to have come to Germany from Austria (Oesterreich).

Oestrich Rhg w (r)
Small Rhein town halfway between *Rüdesheim and the outskirts of *Wiesbaden, making firm, full-bodied Riesling wines that rise to greatness in fine years. *Grosslagen*: *Gottesthal, *Mehrhölzchen.

Oetinger, Weingut Eberhard Ritter und Edler von
Rhg Charta VDP
Estate with eight hectares of vines, 84 percent Riesling, ten percent Spätburgunder, at *Erbach (*Michelmark, *Siegelsberg, *Marcobrunn), *Kiedrich (*Sandgrub) and *Hattenheim.
Address: Rheinallee 2, W-6228 Eltville-Erbach
Tel: 06123 62648

Offenburg, Weingut der Stadt Baden
Ancient charitable estate, founded in 1301, taken over by the town of Offenburg in 1936. Its 30·5 hectares of vines are 35 percent Müller-Thurgau, 17 percent Riesling, 17 percent Spätburgunder, plus a range of other varieties planted, for the most part, in steep sites. The aim is to produce wines with high must weight and therefore there are many QmP.
Address: St Andreas-Hospital-Fonds, Steingrube 7, W-7601 Ortenberg-Käfersberg
Tel: 0781 31111

Offene Weine
See Ausschankwein

OHG
Offene Handelsgesellschaft. General partnership, as in A Gillot & Söhne OHG, a *Sekt* manufacturer at Oppenheim.

Ohnacker, Weingut Rhh
Family-owned, 150-year-old estate of 13·6 hectares, all at *Guntersblum, planted 25 percent Riesling, 25 percent Müller-Thurgau, 20 percent Silvaner and other varieties. The character of

the wines is very much influenced by the varied soil. Most wines spend three to eight months in casks, some of which are 100 years old. Fermentation is controlled and special efforts are made to retain the individuality of each wine. Thirty percent is *trocken*, five percent is exported.

Address: Neustrasse 2, W-6524 Guntersblum

Tel: 06249 1221

Ökologischer Weinbau

Ecological wine production is practised according to German guidelines – which are considerably stronger than those currently discussed in Brussels – by over 80 wine-producing establishments. Only organic manures are used and insecticides and fungicides are avoided as far as possible. Spontaneous fermentation (no added yeast), malolactic fermentation (where desirable), cask maturation and low levels of sulphur dioxide are all recommended and, in part, required. In Germany – the largest market in the world for ecologically produced wines – retail prices reflect the higher labour costs and lower yields involved. It will be difficult for the ecological wine market to develop satisfactorily until rules for its production have been laid down by the EC. Total production of German ecological wine in the early 1990s amounts to about 0·6 percent of the country's grape harvest. However, nearly all grape growers claim to have greatly reduced the use of chemicals in their vineyards in recent years.

Ökonomierat

Agricultural counsellor. Honorary distinction awarded for services to agriculture in its broadest sense. Appears in the title of a number of estates, such as Weingut Ökonomierat August E Anheuser.

Ölberg Rhh w

Einzellage on the ★Rheinterrasse at ★Nierstein producing long-flavoured wines from Riesling, Silvaner and Scheurebe. *Grosslage*: ★Auflangen. Growers: Balbach, Braun, Guntrum, Heyl zu Herrnsheim, Niersteiner Winzergenossenschaft, Rappenhof, St Anthony, H F Schmitt, Schmitt'sches Weingut, G Schneider, Schuch.

Opel, Weingut Irmgard von Rhh VDP

Estate at Schloss Westerhaus with a 13-hectare solely owned *Einzellage* of the same name and 187 hectares of agricultural land. Vines are 51 percent Riesling, 20 percent Spätburgunder, nine percent Müller-Thurgau, plus Chardonnay and others. Over 80 percent of the wine is *halbtrocken* or *trocken*, some is *barrique*-aged. Address: Schloss Westerhaus, W-6507 Ingelheim
Tel: 06130 6674

Oppenheim Rhh w

Town on the *Rheinterrasse, headquarters of a number of important estates and with a well-known viticultural institute (*see next entry*). Wines from the *Sackträger and *Kreuz sites can be superb. Other attractions include the St Katharinen-Kirche and the Deutsches Weinbaumuseum (German Viticultural Museum). *Grosslagen*: *Güldenmorgen, *Krötenbrunnen.

Oppenheim, Staatsweingut mit Weinbaudomäne Rhh VDP

Research and training institute founded in 1895 and owned by the state of Rheinland-Pfalz. The institute has 25 hectares – 70 percent on steep slopes – of vineyards at *Oppenheim (*Sackträger, *Kreuz, Herrenberg, Zuckerberg), *Nackenheim (*Rothenberg), *Dienheim, *Nierstein (*Ölberg and the whole of Glöck) and *Bodenheim (the solely owned Reichsritterstift). Vines are 55 percent Riesling. Because of the estate's experimental role there are also many new crossings. The vineyards are maintained to an exemplary standard and emphasis is laid on retaining the individual grape variety character in the wines. Annual production is 9,600 cases, of which five percent is exported; 34 percent is *trocken*. Address: Mainzerstrasse, W-6504 Oppenheim
Tel: 06133 1434

Optima

White grape variety, a crossing of (Silvaner × Riesling) × Müller-Thurgau from *Geilweilerhof, planted in 471 hectares, mainly in the northern regions of the Mosel-Saar-Ruwer and Rheinhessen. The yield is similar to that of Riesling (about 70 hectolitres per hectare) and wine of *Auslese* quality can be made provided the acidity is not too low. *Edelfäule* is relatively common.

Orbel Rhh w
One of the many excellent *Einzellagen* on the slopes at ★Nierstein, making full-flavoured, weighty wines. *Grosslage*: ★Auflangen. Growers: Braun, Guntrum, Heyl zu Herrnsheim, St Anthony, H F Schmitt, G Schneider, Sittmann, Strub, Wehrheim.

Ordensgut Rhpf w (r)
Grosslage at the northern end of the Bereich ★Südliche Weinstrasse. Many vine varieties and sound, quality wines.

Originalabfüllung
Estate bottling. A term used until 1971 to describe unsugared (*naturrein*) wines that had been produced and bottled by the grower. Cooperative cellars could also sell their wines as *Originalabfüllungen*. The term *Erzeugerabfüllung* has in part superseded *Originalabfüllung*, although it can be applied equally to a sugared or unsugared wine.

Originalabzug
Identical in meaning to *Originalabfüllung*.

Ortega
Early-ripening white grape variety, a crossing of Müller-Thurgau × Siegerrebe from ★Würzburg, planted in 1,266 hectares, mainly in the Rheinhessen, Rheinpfalz and Mosel-Saar-Ruwer regions. It produces good, powerfully scented wine up to *Kabinett* quality, and botrytis-affected *Beerenauslesen*. Insufficient acidity makes it unsuitable for late picking. Benefits from early bottling followed by a period of maturation.

Ortenau, Bereich Baden w (r)
Bereich that stretches south from Baden-Baden at the foot of the ★Schwarzwald. It produces wines of very good quality, especially from Riesling (known locally as Klingelberger). The modern Spätburgunder wines are competitively priced.

Ortenberg Baden w r
Village in the Bereich ★Ortenau known for its wine, half-timbered houses and flowers. It is also the home of the Weingut der Stadt

★Offenburg. Müller-Thurgau, Riesling, Ruländer and Spätburg-under predominate. *Grosslage*: Fürsteneck.

Ortsteil
Part of a larger community, such as the village of ★Erbach in the Rheingau which is an *Ortsteil* of the town of ★Eltville.

Osthofen Rhh w (r)
Small town with many rustic wine bars and cellars, ten kilometres north of ★Worms in the Bereich ★Wonnegau. Very good wines are produced which may become better known during the 1990s as the quality of the wines improves further. *Grosslagen*: ★Pilgerpfad, Gotteshilfe.

Othegraven, Maximilian v M-S-R
See Kanzemer Berg, Weingut

Oxidativ
A wine that shows signs of oxidation, but is not yet fully oxidized, is described as *oxidativ*. Its opposite, a wine from which contact with the air has been kept to a minimum, is *reduktiv*. Most German wines fall into this latter category.

Palatinate
See Rheinpfalz

Pappig
Describes an oversweet, unbalanced wine with low acidity, such as a low-grade *Spätlese* from an overcropped new crossing.

Parfümiert
Disparaging description of a heavily scented, cheap-smelling aroma, as found in poor wines from Morio-Muskat or Siegerrebe.

Parzelle
Plot. For administrative purposes *Einzellagen* are usually sub-divided into smaller parcels of land which are named and numbered. However, the *Einzellage* remains the smallest geographical unit that can be mentioned on a wine label.

Paterberg Rhh w

Largest *Einzellage* (148 hectares) at ★Nierstein, producing stylish, good-quality wine, but not usually the best in the town. *Grosslage*: ★Spiegelberg. Growers: Braun, Gunderloch, Guntrum, St Anthony, H F Schmitt, G Schneider, Sittmann, Strub, Wehrheim.

Paulinshof, Weingut M-S-R

Six-hectare estate with holdings at ★Kesten and ★Brauneberg (sole owners of the ★Kammer *Einzellage*), 92 percent Riesling. Some of the vines are 80 years old. Annual production is approximately 5,800 cases, of which a small amount is matured in Schwaben oak *barriques*, and 35 percent is *trocken*.
Address: W-5561 Kesten bei Bernkastel
Tel: 06535 544

Pauly-Bergweiler, Dr M-S-R

To this well-known estate belongs Weingut Peter Nicolay. Together they have 15 hectares at ★Bernkastel (★Alte Badstube am Doctorberg, ★Lay, ★Schlossberg), ★Graach (★Himmelreich, ★Domprobst), ★Wehlen (★Sonnenuhr), ★Ürzig (sole owners of ★Goldwingert, ★Würzgarten), ★Erden (★Prälat, ★Treppchen), ★Brauneberg (★Juffer-Sonnenuhr). These important holdings are planted 92 percent Riesling, five percent Spätburgunder (in Domprobst) and other varieties. The modern, above-ground cellar is remarkable and probably unique on the Mosel. Temperature-controlled fermentation results in fresh, elegant white wines and, in 1990, a light, true-to-type Spätburgunder. Annual production is 13,600 cases, 40 percent *trocken*; 35 percent is exported.
Address: Gestade 15, W-5550 Bernkastel-Kues
Tel: 06531 3002

Pechstein Rhpf w

Mainly level *Einzellage* at ★Forst making full-bodied, distinguished Riesling wines. *Grosslage*: ★Mariengarten. Growers: Bassermann-Jordan, Bürklin-Wolf, Winzerverein Deidesheim, Forster Winzerverein, Kimich, Mosbacher, Mossbacher-Hof, K Schäfer, Spindler, Wolf.

Perle

White grape variety, a crossing of Gewürztraminer × Müller-Thurgau from *Alzey, with rosé-coloured grapes that produce a light, gentle white wine. It is planted in 246 hectares, mainly in the Rheinhessen and in Franken where much work has been carried out improving the vine at the state viticultural institute at *Würzburg.

Perll, August Mrh

Hundred-year-old estate with six hectares, 80 percent Riesling, on the very steep vineyards of the Bopparder Hamm, overlooking the Rhein upstream from *Koblenz. The slate-grown, racy, lively Riesling wines enjoy remarkable success at national competitions. About 33 percent of production is *trocken*, and 80 percent of the wine is sold to private customers.
Address: Oberstrasse 81, W-5407 Boppard
Tel: 06742 3906

Perll, Weingut Walter Mrh

Five-hectare estate with holdings in the Bopparder Hamm. All are steep, up to an 80 percent (1:2·5) gradient, planted 85 percent Riesling, eight percent Spätburgunder (for rosé), on Devonian slate. Annual production is 5,000 cases, one-third each *trocken*, *halbtrocken* and *lieblich*; 15 percent is exported.
Address: Ablassgasse 11, W-5407 Boppard
Tel: 06742 3671

Perlwein

Semi-sparkling wine, the result of a second fermentation in a pressurized tank or simply of impregnation with carbon dioxide. The bottling and labelling must be such that the wine (which may be a QbA) will not be confused with a sparkling wine. It can be described as *trocken* if it has less than 25 grams per litre of residual sugar. (The equivalent figures are 25–40 grams per litre for *halbtrocken* and over 40 grams per litre for *süss*.) *Trocken* is the most popular style. At best, *Perlwein* is a cheap and pleasant drink but it usually lacks the style and the ability to retain the sparkle once opened that is characteristic of good-quality sparkling wine.

Pettenthal Rhh w
One of the best, mainly steep, *Einzellagen* at ★Nierstein, built by the
Balbach family in the last century. The wine is full of flavour from
the red sandstone and clay soil. *Grosslage*: ★Rehbach. Growers:
Balbach, Baumann, Braun, Guntrum, Heyl zu Herrnsheim,
Rappenhof, St Anthony, H F Schmitt, Schmitt'sches Weingut, G
Schneider, Schuch, Strub, Wehrheim.

Pfalz
Shortened version of ★'Rheinpfalz' which some wish it to replace in
the future on account of the distance of the vineyards from the
Rhein, and to distinguish it from other regions with 'Rhein' in their
name. English speakers used to know the Pfalz as the 'Palatinate', a
name deriving from the Latin *palatium*, meaning a palace, the seat of
a Roman governor. The German equivalent *Palast* has been
corrupted to 'Pfalz'.

Pfeffingen, Weingut Rhpf VDP
Estate near ★Bad Dürkheim with 10·5 hectares of modernized
vineyards in ★Ungstein (Herrenberg and Weilberg). Vines are 70
percent Riesling, 13 percent Scheurebe and others. Family commit-
ment to the estate is total – both the daughter and son-in-law are
qualified *Weinbauingenieure* (vine growers and winemakers) – and
the wines are reasonably priced and highly thought of by other
Rheinpfalz growers. Annual production is 5,800 cases with a high
proportion of QmP; 60 percent is *trocken*, 15 percent *halbtrocken* and
20 percent is exported.
Address: Fuhrmann-Eymael, W-6702 Bad Dürkheim
Tel: 06322 8607

Pfleger, Weingut Jakob Rhpf
Organically manured estate of 7·5 hectares, with holdings at
★Herxheim am Berg, ★Freinsheim and ★Kallstadt (★Steinacker),
planted with 25 percent Scheurebe, 25 percent Riesling, eight
percent Ruländer, ten percent Dornfelder, eight percent Spätburgunder. About 45 percent is *trocken*, showing the grape characteristics well. Many prize-winning wines. Some *barrique*-ageing.
Address: Weinstrasse 38, W-6719 Herxheim am Berg
Tel: 06353 7465

Pfleger, Weingut Werner Rhpf
Nine-hectare estate, established in 1983, with holdings at ★Herx-
heim am Berg, ★Freinsheim and Weisenheim am Berg. Yields are
modest. Practically all the wines are QmP from a range of white
and red vine varieties; 45 percent is *lieblich*. Annual production is
8,300 cases, sold 87 percent to the consumer.
Address: Weinstrasse 34, W-6719 Herxheim am Berg
Tel: 06326 8607

Phylloxera
Known as the *Reblaus* in Germany, where it first appeared in 1874.
Phylloxera (*Phylloxera vastatrix*) is an aphid that causes growths on
the roots of European vines (*Vitis vinifera*) which then rot in winter,
destroying the root system. To avoid this, vinifera vines are grafted
onto phylloxera-resistant non-vinifera rootstocks.

Piedmont, Weingut Max-G M-S-R VDP
Fourth-generation family estate near the confluence of the Saar and
Mosel. Six hectares of vineyards, all in ★Filzen. Vines are 90 percent
Riesling and ten percent Weissburgunder, producing excellent
spicy wines in good years (30 percent is *lieblich*). No *Süssreserve* is
used. Annual production is 3,750 cases; 40 percent is *trocken*, 15
percent exported.
Address: Saartal 1, W-5503 Filzen
Tel: 06501 16806

Piesport M-S-R w
One of the best-known village names on the Mosel, particularly
when linked to its *Grosslage* ★Michelsberg or its *Einzellage*
★Goldtröpfchen. While the high quality of the best Piesporter
Rieslings cannot be disputed, equally good wines at lesser prices can
often be found elsewhere on the Mosel.

Pikant
Describes a wine with much fruity *Weinsäure*, such as well-made
Riesling *Kabinett* wines.

Pilgerpfad Rhh w (r)
Grosslage of over 1,000 hectares in sandy, clay soil, producing

pleasant, agreeable wines without the flair of the best from the ★Rheinterrasse.

Pittermännchen Nahe w
Steep, south-facing Riesling *Einzellage* at ★Dorsheim. *Grosslage*: ★Schlosskapelle. Growers: Diel, M Schäfer.

Pittersberg Nahe w
Sloping *Einzellage* at ★Münster-Sarmsheim producing fruity wines with good body but usually less finesse than those made up-river at ★Schlossböckelheim. *Grosslage*: ★Schlosskapelle. Growers include Adelseck, Kruger-Rumpf, Niederhausen-Schlossböckelheim Staatliche Weinbaudomäne.

Plettenberg, Weingut Reichsgraf von Nahe VDP
Estate of 40 hectares with 18th-century origins. Holdings are at ★Bad Kreuznach (★Brückes, ★Narrenkappe), ★Schlossböckelheim (★Kupfergrube and ★Felsenberg), ★Bretzenheim, ★Winzenheim, ★Roxheim and ★Norheim, planted 66 percent Riesling, 20 percent Müller-Thurgau and other varieties. Around 75 percent is *lieblich*. Sales are international.
Address: Winzenheimerstrasse, W-6550 Bad Kreuznach
Tel: 0671 2254

Plump
Describes a wine with high extract, possibly an excessive alcohol content and certainly too little acid. With modern winemaking methods, in which acidity and freshness are retained, plump wines are not so common as they were 20 years ago. The Rheinpfalz, Rheinhessen, Franken and Baden are potentially more likely to produce wines that are plump than regions further north.

Pokal
Glass with a coloured stem and a content of 200 or 250 milli-litres in which 'open wine' (*Ausschankwein*) is served. *See* Römer.

Pommern M-S-R w (r)
Known by the Romans as Pomaria on account of its apple orchards, the village of Pommern is appreciated today for its fruity, stylish

Riesling wines from approximately 66 hectares of vineyard. *Grosslage*: ★Goldbäumchen.

Popp KG, Weingut Ernst Franken

Wine merchants with 14 hectares, receiving grapes from growers in a further 20 hectares at Iphofen and Rödelsee. Vines are 35 percent Müller-Thurgau, 35 percent Silvaner, plus Scheurebe, Riesling and others. *Trocken* wines account for 65 percent of total production. Sales are abroad and in Germany, much via the company's two wine bars.

Address: Rödelseer Strasse 14–15, W-8715 Iphofen

Tel: 09323 3371

Portugieser, Blauer

After Spätburgunder, the most widely planted red vine variety in Germany, covering 3,508 hectares, of which more than half lie in the Rheinpfalz. The yield is large, the must weight is low and the acidity high. It is suggested that the Portugieser is often picked too early in the season, and that if it were gathered after the Müller-Thurgau a more satisfactory wine would result. As red wine, the colour seems light to non-Germans, but the Portugieser makes an attractive *Weissherbst* in the Rheinpfalz. Like Müller-Thurgau, Portugieser is considerably improved on the rare occasions when the yield is restricted.

Prädikat

A quality distinction. *See* Qualitatswein mit Prädikat (QmP).

Prälat M-S-R w

Very small, 2·2-hectare, top-quality *Einzellage* at ★Erden, planted exclusively in Riesling. Great wines in the best years, among the finest on the Mosel. *Grosslage*: ★Schwarzlay. Growers: Christoffel, Loosen, Mönchof, Nicolay (Pauly-Bergweiler), Weins-Prüm.

Prämierung

See Bundesweinprämierung

Probe

Tasting. For a guide to tasting wine in Germany, *see* pages 35–36.

Probsthof, Weingut Rhpf VDP
Nine-hectare award-winning estate with holdings at *Wachenheim (*Gerümpel, *Fuchsmantel), *Haardt, *Forst and *Neustadt, planted 60 percent Riesling. Annual sales of 6,250 cases (40 percent *trocken*, 40 percent *lieblich*), sold 85 percent to private customers.
Address: Probstgasse 7, W-6730 Neustadt-Haardt
Tel: 06321 6315

Prüfungsnummer
See Amtliche Prüfung

Prüm, Weingut Joh Jos M-S-R VDP
One of the most prestigious estates on the Mosel, best known for the five-hectare holding in the Wehlener *Sonnenuhr, which the estate has done so much to make famous. A further nine hectares are in other sites at *Wehlen and at *Graach (*Himmelreich), *Zeltingen-Rachtig (*Sonnenuhr) and *Bernkastel. The grapes (mainly Riesling) are usually gathered as late as possible. The wines are made with immense care and attention to detail to ensure they reach their full potential. Although the *Kabinett* wines in off-vintages can surprise by their style and positive *spritzig* flavour, the estate is best known for its incredibly luscious *Auslesen*.
Address: Uferallee 19, W-5550 Bernkastel-Wehlen
Tel: 06531 3091

Prüm Erben, Weingut S A M-S-R VDP
Estate of 6·5 hectares, established in 1911 when the original Prüm family property was divided among the heirs (*Erben*), S A Prüm owns holdings at *Wehlen (including *Sonnenuhr), *Bernkastel, *Graach (*Himmelreich, *Domprobst) and *Zeltingen-Rachtig (*Schlossberg). Vines are 100 percent Riesling, all on steep slopes, 90 percent ungrafted. The aim is to make racy, elegant wines; 30 percent is dry and all are cask-matured. Only QmP from the top sites are sold with an *Einzellage* name. No *Süssreserve* is used. Approximate annual production is 4,400 cases and 45–50 percent of this is exported.
Address: Uferallee 25–26, W-5550 Bernkastel-Wehlen
Tel: 06531 3110

Pünderich M-S-R w

Small, picturesque wine village, just inside the boundaries of the Bereich ★Bernkastel near ★Zell. Much good, sound wine is sold under the *Grosslage* name, vom ★heissen Stein. Elegant, fruity Riesling wines appear under the various *Einzellage* names.

Qualitätsschaumwein

Quality sparkling wine. A sparkling wine may only be described as Qualitätsschaumwein in the EC if it has fulfilled the conditions of production laid down in its country of origin. In Germany most quality sparkling wine (more widely known as *Sekt*) is sold under a brand name (*Markensekt*). Sales are increasing of *Sekt* from a specified region (*Sekt* bA) bearing a vintage, and made from a single vine (usually Riesling – *Rieslingsekt*), but as yet they are a small fraction of total *Sekt* production. A *Sekt* bA can bear a site, a village or a district (*Bereich*) name, if 85 percent of the base wine was grown in the place stated. The remaining 15 percent must come from the same region (*Anbaugebiet*). The best Qualitätsschaumwein is stylish, crisp and clean in flavour.

Qualitätswein eines bestimmten Anbaugebietes (QbA)

Quality wine from a specified region (*bestimmtes Anbaugebiet*). In the eyes of the law, the category of a quality wine is only established once it has passed the official examination (★Amtliche Prüfung). To qualify for consideration it will have been made from legally recommended or authorized vine varieties and its must weight will have reached certain minimum levels, depending on the vine variety and region of origin. It will not have been blended with wine from another region. Some 95 percent of German wine is classified as quality wine. In contrast, 87 percent of Italian and 64 percent of French wines are table wines. *See* The Quality Categories, pages 12–13.

Qualitätswein mit Prädikat (QmP)

'Quality wine with distinction': wine made from grapes with sufficient natural sweetness to need no sugar added during vinification. The six levels of *Prädikat* are *Kabinett, Spätlese, Auslese, Beerenauslese, Eiswein* and *Trockenbeerenauslese*. Any of these distinctions may be won by a wine from must of a certain minimum weight, provided it achieves the necessary 'marks' at an official control (*Amtliche Prüfung*) centre. The grapes will also have been harvested according to a procedure, established in law, appropriate to the particular *Prädikat*.

The minimum must weights – and therefore potential alcohol – for each *Prädikat* vary depending on the region and the variety. Those for Riesling in the Mosel-Saar-Ruwer, for example, are:

M-S-R Riesling	Minimum must weight in degrees Oechsle	Potential alcohol content by volume
Kabinett	67	8·6
Spätlese	76	10·0
Auslese	83	11·1
Beerenauslese/Eiswein	110	15·3
Trockenbeerenauslese	150	21·5

A *Beerenauslese*, *Eiswein* or *Trockenbeerenauslese* from the Mosel-Saar-Ruwer is traditionally sweet, but the acidity prevents it from becoming cloying. Normally, a Mosel *Auslese* is also sweet or *lieblich*, but the amount of residual sugar in a *Spätlese* or *Kabinett* wine can vary from very little to more than 30 grams per litre. In top-quality estates the sweetness in wines below *Auslese* level may not be very noticeable: just sufficient to balance the acidity.

Querbach, Weingut Wilfried Rhg Charta
Estate of 8·5 hectares with holdings at *Oestrich (*Lenchen, *Doosberg), *Winkel (*Hasensprung), *Hallgarten (*Schönhell) and *Mittelheim, planted 88 percent Riesling, 12 percent Spätburgunder. Vineyard management and winemaking are modern and 'green', and much has been invested in vineyard and cellar. Annual production is 6,700 cases, 75 percent *trocken*, 89 percent sold directly to the consumer.
Address: Dr-Rody-Strasse 2, W-6227 Oestrich-Winkel
Tel: 06723 3887

Radebeul S w (r)
Almost a suburb of Dresden, best known for the Staatsweingut Radebeul at Schloss Wackerbarth.

Randersacker Franken w (r)
Village a few kilometres from ★Würzburg, with buildings that date
back to the 14th century. Its steep sites produce fine, powerfully
flavoured Silvaner wine and elegant Rieslings. Like all Franken
wine, relatively expensive. *Grosslagen*: ★Ewig Leben, Teufelstor.

Randersacker eG, Winzergenossenschaft Franken
Cooperative cellar supplied by 130 hectares of vineyards in
★Randersacker (★Teufelskeller and others), ★Sommerhausen and
★Würzburg. Vines are 40 percent Müller-Thurgau, 30 percent
Silvaner, the balance made up with other varieties. Malolactic
fermentation (*see* Apfelsäure) is allowed for some wines, and 75
percent is *halbtrocken*.
Address: Maingasse 33, W-8701 Randersacker
Tel: 0931 709001

Rappenhof, Weingut Rhh VDP
Estate dating from the 17th century: 45 hectares of Riesling (45
percent), Weissburgunder (20 percent), Spätburgunder (ten percent) and others, including Chardonnay. Some vines are 60 years
old and ungrafted. Trials are being held with ★interspecific
crossings. A fascinating list of wines from ★Alsheim (★Frühmesse,

*Fischerpfad), *Guntersblum, *Oppenheim (*Sackträger) and *Nierstein (*Pettenthal, *Ölberg). Annual production is 33,300 cases, of which 20 percent is exported, and 60 percent is *trocken* – the Weissburgunder is especially attractive. Some wines are *barrique*-aged.

Address: Bachstrasse 47, W-6526 Alsheim

Tel: 06249 4015

Rassig

Racy. Describes a wine with pronounced but pleasant acidity and style, as is often found in the Mosel-Saar-Ruwer region.

Ratzenberger, Weingut J Mrh VDP

Six-hectare estate with holdings at *Bacharach and *Steeg planted 80 percent Riesling and 12 percent Spätburgunder, producing top-quality wine, including an elegant, balanced Riesling *Auslese trocken* in 1990. Annual production is 3,300 cases, 50 percent *trocken*, 60 percent sold to private customers.

Address: Blücherstrasse 167, W-6533 Bacharach-Steeg

Tel: 06743 1337

Rauenthal Rhg w

Important wine village on the slopes above *Eltville, not far from *Wiesbaden. Its best-known *Einzellage* is *Baiken. Typical Rauenthaler wines have excellent acidity and need bottle-age. *Grosslage*: *Steinmächer.

Rausch M-S-R w

Steep Riesling *Einzellage* at *Saarburg. The decomposed slate helps to produce splendidly long-lasting wines with a strong backbone of tartaric acid. *Grosslage*: *Scharzberg. Growers: Hausen-Mabilon, Zilliken.

Rautenstrauch'sche Weingutsverwaltung M-S-R VDP

Ruwer estate, established in the 14th century, with 19 hectares, 90 percent Riesling, on the *Karthäuserhofberg. The wines are beautifully made, and are among the finest in the region.

Address: W-5500 Trier-Eitelsbach

Tel: 0651 5121

Rebe
Vine, such as Huxelrebe, Scheurebe. *See* Rebsorte.

Rebholz, Weingut Ökonomierat Rhpf VDP
Nine-hectare estate owned by a family involved in vine growing for some 300 years. Holdings, 25 percent terraced, are at ★Siebeldingen, now starting to be recognized as a source of some of the best wines in the Rheinpfalz. Vines are 33 percent Riesling, 14 percent Müller-Thurgau, 23 percent Spätburgunder and others. The estate was the first to produce a *Trockenbeerenauslese* from Müller-Thurgau (in 1949). *Süssreserve* is not used and much *trocken* wine is made. None of the wine is enriched – *see* Anreicherung.
Address: Weinstrasse 54, W-6741 Siebeldingen
Tel: 06345 3439

Reblaus
See Phylloxera

Rebsorte
Vine variety. At present all commercially grown vines in Germany are of the genus *vitis vinifera*. It is likely that eventually the latest interspecific crossings of vinifera with non-vinifera varieties (previously known as 'hybrids') will also be allowed for quality wine production in parts of the EC, including Germany. Their resistance to disease and therefore their need for virtually no chemical spraying commends them.

Reduktiv
Describes a wine that after fermentation has been protected as far as possible from contact with the atmosphere. Many Riesling wines in the northern regions are produced in this way, which encourages their natural tendency to taste fresh and fruity. The opposite of *reduktiv* is *oxidativ*.

Refractometer
Small hand-held instrument, widely used during the harvest, that measures the refraction of light passing through a sample of grape juice, giving a quick measurement of must weight.

Regner

White grape variety, a crossing of Luglienca bianca (a table grape) × Gamay früh (a red grape), planted in 170 hectares, mostly in the Rheinhessen. The main harvest is usually shortly before that of Müller-Thurgau but the grapes can be left on the vine to produce *Spätlese* wine. Acidity is low but the quality is good. The wine is described as 'traditional' (it has no extreme flavours) with a gentle Muskat bouquet.

Reh GmbH & Co KG, Carl

A wine merchant's business and export house founded in 1920 – part of the much enlarged group, Günther Reh AG.

Reh & Sohn GmbH & Co KG, Franz M-S-R

Family business of wine merchants, now re-united with Carl Reh GmbH & Co KG and Günther Reh AG. The family owns the Weingut Josefinengrund with holdings at ★Leiwen and ★Trittenheim (★Apotheke, ★Altärchen) and the Weingut Marienhof at ★Piesport (★Goldtröpfchen, ★Treppchen, ★Günterslay and all of the steep little Gärtchen site) and at ★Dhron. Sales are mainly outside Germany.

Address: Römerstrasse 27, W-5559 Leiwen
Tel: 06507 3031

Rehbach Rhh w

Small *Grosslage* of some 65 hectares overlooking the Rhein above ★Nierstein – one of the best in Germany. Its *Einzellagen* include the distinguished ★Hipping and ★Pettenthal and also one of the smallest individual sites in Germany, the 0·6-hectare Goldene Luft.

Reichensteiner

White grape variety, a crossing of Müller-Thurgau × (Madeleine Angevine × Calabreser-Fröhlich) from the state viticultural institute at ★Geisenheim. Planting increased from five hectares in 1970 to 334 hectares in 1988. The yield is similar to that of Müller-Thurgau, the must weight heavier by 5–10° Oechsle and acidity is also greater. The flavour of the wine is neutral and pleasant. Given the right weather conditions, a late harvest is possible.

Reichsfreiherr
Title received from the Kaiser; appears in the name of various estates, such as Weingut des Reichsfreiherrn von Ritter zu Groenesteyn.

Reichsgraf
Count, appointed by the Kaiser. The inheritor of the title would be a Graf but not a Reichsgraf.

Reichsrat
A state representative, at national level, in the formation of national law. Found in the title of, for example, the Rheinpfalz wine grower Weingut Reichsrat von Buhl.

Reif
Ripe. Describes a wine that is full, mature. *See also* Flaschenreife (bottle ripeness).

Reil M–S–R w
One of the best-known Mosel villages, downstream from ★Traben-Trabach, making very good Riesling wine. The original home of the exporting house and estate owner Rudolf ★Müller. *Grosslage*: vom ★heissen Stein.

Reinhartshausen
See Schloss Reinhartshausen

Reintonig
Describes a wine that smells and tastes absolutely clean.

Reiterpfad Rhpf w
Sloping Riesling *Einzellage* at ★Ruppertsberg producing some good-quality, elegant wines. *Grosslage*: ★Hofstück. Growers: Bassermann-Jordan, Biffar, Buhl, Bürklin-Wolf, Winzerverein Deidesheim, Dr Deinhard, Giessen, Kern, Kimich, Ruppertsberg Winzerverein, Spindler.

Rentamt
Originally the local authority for financial administration within a

state, later used to describe a similar office on a large country estate. Appears, for example, in the title of Fürst von Metternich-Winneburg'sches Domäne Rentamt at Schloss Johannisberg.

Repperndorf Franken w
Wine village near *Kitzingen. Its vineyards are alleged to have been planted by Charlemagne. Now known mainly as the site of the large regional cooperative cellar that handles a third of the Franken grape harvest. *Grosslage*: Hofrat.

Ress, Weingut Balthasar Rhg Charta VDP
Important family estate of 28 hectares, founded more than 100 years ago. Leaseholders since 1978 of the vineyards of *Schloss Reichartshausen, plus holdings in many well-known sites including *Berg Schlossberg, *Berg Rottland and others at *Rüdesheim; *Kläuserweg at *Geisenheim; *Hasensprung and *Jesuitengarten at *Winkel; *Doosberg and *Lenchen at *Oestrich; *Nussbrunnen and *Wisselbrunnen at *Hattenheim; *Sandgrub at *Kiedrich; *Domdechaney, *Hölle and others at *Hochheim; Höllenberg at *Assmannshausen. Vines are 90 percent Riesling, seven percent Spätburgunder. Annual production is 18,300 cases, 40 percent *trocken*, 40 percent exported.
Address: Rheinallee 7, W-6228 Eltville 3
Tel: 06723 3011

Restsüsse
Residual sugar in a wine, the result of an incomplete fermentation or the addition of *Süssreserve*. A certain amount of unfermented, or residual, sugar was characteristic of most German wines until the 1980s. It is the fine balance of acid, alcohol and restrained sweetness that gives this style of wine charm and delicacy.

Restzucker
Unfermented sugar in a wine which provides the residual sweetness (*Restsüsse*) for which it is, in practice, a synonym.

Reverchon, Weingut Edmund M-S-R
Estate with 26 hectares at Filzen (sole owner of Herrenberg), *Ockfen (*Bockstein), *Kanzem, *Wiltingen (*Gottesfuss) and

*Konz; 92 percent Riesling. Low yields produce concentrated, light, lively Saar wines, 40 percent *trocken*. Annual production is 16,700 cases, five percent exported.
Address: Saartalstrasse 3, W-5503 Konz-Filzen
Tel: 06501 16909

Rhein

The great river that rises in the Swiss Alps, flows through the heart of the German vine-growing regions and on to the North Sea, some 1,300 kilometres from its source. Along the way it is fed by the Neckar, Main, Nahe, Lahn, Mosel and Ahr. For centuries the river served as the best route for moving wine from the regions where it was produced to customers in Germany and, via Rotterdam, abroad. Thirty years ago the uncertainties of river transport put this traffic into the motorway system, but the Rhein remains important to wine for climatic reasons, as a tourist attraction and as a factor, directly or indirectly, linking many of the vineyards of Germany.

Rheinblick Rhh w

Grosslage that includes within its boundaries the Alsheimer *Fischerpfad and *Frühmesse *Einzellagen*. Many of the vineyards are on steep or sloping sites and the quality of wine is often higher than that sold under other *Grosslage* names from the region.

Rheinfront

See Rheinterrasse

Rheingau w (r)

Compact region of 2,904 hectares, including some of the best vineyards in Germany. Vines are 82 percent Riesling. There are 380 growers who bottle their own wine, but only 24 estates with more than ten hectares of vineyards. However, it is from their winemaking over the centuries that the reputation of Rheingau Riesling derives. The Rheingau climate and soil produce Rieslings that have the elegance of a Mosel or a fine Nahe wine but with more body and depth of flavour. They vary from straightforward, simple quality wines to complex *Auslesen* and they can be bone dry or lusciously sweet. Rheingauer wines are not the cheapest in

Riesling vines growing at Mäuseturm in the Rheingau

Germany but they are often less expensive than wines of similar standing from Baden, Württemberg or Franken, and are seldom overpriced. In Germany the modern *halbtrocken* Rheingau Riesling is much appreciated.

The circuitous Rheingauer Riesling Route that runs the length of the region makes it easy to visit the widely known wine villages by road, and for those with more time and an inclination to walk there is a signposted path through the vineyards.

Rheingrafenberg eG, Winzergenossenschaft Nahe
Relatively small cooperative cellar with grapes supplied from 150 hectares, 60 percent Riesling, plus Müller-Thurgau, Bacchus, Kerner and others. The quality of the wines is generally good and the *trocken* versions (about 24 percent of production) are particularly well known.
Address: Naheweinstrasse 63, W-6553 Meddersheim
Tel: 06751 2667

Rheinhell Rhg w
Einzellage on an island in the Rhein called the Mariannenau after Princess Marianne of Prussia who bought the nearby ★Schloss

Reinhartshausen in 1855. The site benefits from a mild micro-climate and the humidity from the Rhein encourages *Edelfäule*. It is planted with Riesling, Chardonnay, Weissburgunder and others. *Grosslage*: ★Honigberg.

'Rheinhess', der

A *halbtrocken* QbA based on Müller-Thurgau supplied by a number of Rheinhessen producers.

Rheinhessen w (r)

Largest of the wine regions with 24,871 hectares of vines, including many new crossings – for example, Scheurebe, Faberrebe, Huxel-rebe – from the viticultural institute at ★Alzey in the heart of the region. For consistently the best Rheinhessen Riesling or Silvaner wines one must look to the ★Rheinterrasse near ★Nierstein, with its fine sites overlooking the river, or possibly to the vineyards at ★Bingen, where the Rhein meets the Nahe, and at ★Ingelheim. Away from the Rheinterrasse the vineyards often occupy slightly sloping ground adjacent to farmland. The wines from such sites tend to be softer than those from the Nahe or the Mosel-Saar-Ruwer but have a useful ability to combine the flavour from the soil with that of the new vine varieties. Some 70 percent of Rheinhessen wine is sold in bulk by the growers to the wine trade for bottling. Approximately 3,000 growers bottle their own wine, and among these will be found some of the best estates in Germany. At the other extreme, Rheinhessen also produces very cheap wine, which should be agreeable as a light drink but will probably have very little character.

Rheinhessen Silvaner Trocken

A good QbA produced individually by about 80 growers and sold under a common black and orange label, mainly via wine merchants or directly to the consumer.

Rheinland–Pfalz

Federal state with 67 percent of Germany's planted viticultural area, covering the Rheinpfalz, Rheinhessen, Nahe, Ahr and most of the Mosel-Saar-Ruwer and Mittelrhein. The capital is ★Mainz.

Rheinpfalz w r
Region of 22,625 hectares, also known as the Palatinate, which
stretches from the frontier with France to the Rheinhessen border.
The northern part, the Bereich *Mittelhaardt/Deutsche Weinstrasse, has a dry, warm climate, and the success and reputation of its
wine, judged by the prosperity of the region's villages, has been
noted by writers over the centuries. There are many leading estates,
situated mainly between *Kallstadt and *Ruppertsberg, with a
high proportion of Riesling in their vineyards, making wine to the
very finest standard. The supremacy of the famous estates has
declined a little, as others in outlying villages can now rival them. In
a great year magnificent meaty wines are produced, that only begin
to be at their best eight years or so after the vintage. 'Off' years
produce slimmer wines, with attractive acidity and fruit, that show
the characteristics of the vine variety well.

The wines from the southern Rheinpfalz, the Bereich *Südliche
Weinstrasse, are improving rapidly and the best estates are
comparable to those further north. The countryside is rural and
vine growing is clearly the most important type of farming. The
vineyards lie mainly on level land or on gentle slopes, overlooked
by wooded hills rising to 600 metres or more. Visitors to the region
will find living inexpensive, comfortable and unsophisticated. *See
also* Pfalz.

Rheinpfalz Riesling Trocken
Form of regional branded QbA with a minimum of 7·5 grams per
litre total acid and a minimum must weight of 70° Oechsle, sold
under a common label by a number of producers.

Rheinterrasse Rhh w (r)
Name given to the vineyards alongside the Rhein from the village
of *Bodenheim in the north to *Mettenheim in the south. With the
possible exception of those at *Bingen, all the best Rheinhessen sites
are on the slopes of the Rheinterrasse, with its two particularly
famous small towns of *Oppenheim and *Nierstein. The proportion of Riesling and Silvaner planted is greater than elsewhere in the
region, and the wines can have much weight and depth of flavour.
The Rheinterrasse is an enlargement of the area previously known
as the Rheinfront.

Rhodt unter Rietburg Rhpf w

Picturesque wine village near *Edenkoben, below Schloss Ludwigshöhe, summer residence of Ludwig I of Bavaria. Produces
interesting, good–value–for–money wines from many vine varieties. A number of long-established growers and the large *Rietburg
Gebietswinzergenossenschaft, also the vineyard with the
oldest vines in Germany – 300-year-old Traminers. *Grosslage*:
*Ordensgut.

Richter, Weingut Max Ferd M-S-R

Family-owned estate dating from 1680 with 15 hectares at
*Traben-Trabach, *Wehlen (*Sonnenuhr), *Graach (*Himmelreich, *Domprobst, which the estate spells 'Dompropst'), *Bernkastel (*Schlossberg), *Mülheim (sole owners of *Helenenkloster),
*Erden, *Veldenz, *Brauneberg (*Juffer). Vines are 85 percent
Riesling. Annual production is 12,500 cases, of which no less than 60
percent is exported. The top-quality wines are cask-matured, and
25 percent is *trocken*. *Eiswein* is a speciality. The estate's *Rieslingsekt*
receives widespread acclaim.

Address: Hauptstrasse 37/85, W-5556 Mülheim
Tel: 06534 704

Richter, Weingut Richard M-S-R

Seven-hectare estate with steep holdings at *Winningen (including
*Uhlen) soon to be planted 100 percent Riesling. Good, serious,

typical Mosels with the expected acidity and the necessary body to fill out the flavour.
Address: Marktstrasse 19, W-5406 Winningen
Tel: 02606 311

Richtershof, Weingut M-S-R
Estate of ten hectares, 85 percent on steep slopes at *Mülheim and *Veldenz. Vines are 90 percent Riesling (the oldest dating from about 1911), and Müller-Thurgau has been grown since 1924. Yield is restricted and quality is good. Elegant, simplified labels. Annual sales of 8,300 cases, plus a spirit, Marc vom Riesling.
Address: Hauptstrasse 81–83, W-5556 Mülheim
Tel: 06534 702

Riedel, Weingut Jakob Rhg
Small estate with 17th-century origins. Its 3·5 hectares at *Hallgarten (*Schönhell and others) are 100 percent Riesling. Bottling is early to retain freshness; 70 percent is *trocken*.
Address: Taunusstrasse 1, W-6227 Hallgarten
Tel: 06723 3511

Rieslaner
White grape variety, a crossing of Silvaner × Riesling from *Würzburg grown over 44 hectares, mainly in Franken, its region of origin. With a must weight of less than 90° Oechsle (12 percent alcohol) the wine tastes thin. Acidity is high, and the grapes ripen late in the season. At its best the wine is very stylish and fairly neutral in flavour. Other vines perform more consistently and produce better wine more easily – not a vine for a small estate.

Riesling, Weisser
White grape variety that produces the finest German wine. It is planted over 20,716 hectares – 20 percent of the total area under vine. Where the best vineyards are to be found, in the Mittelhaardt in the Rheinpfalz, in the Rheingau, in the middle Nahe and on the Mosel, the percentage of Riesling grown will be high, for the Riesling in Germany demands a top-quality site. Depending on location the harvest will take place in October, November or even December for certain speciality wines. One of the main characteris-

tics of Riesling is the elegant acidity that makes the flavour of the wine last in the mouth, and gives it the ability to develop over many years in bottle. Riesling flavour is positive and yet restrained, unlike that of a full-blown Traminer. It is therefore able to transmit the taste that comes from the soil, without imposing any strong additional flavour upon it. As a result the variations between a Riesling from one region and those from another are clearly differentiated. All qualities of Riesling wine can be produced, depending on the vintage and the site, from table wine to the richest *Trockenbeerenauslese*. *Trocken* and *halbtrocken* versions are much in demand in Germany, and increasingly so abroad.

Rieslingsekt

Quality sparkling wine from the Riesling grape. Although the number of German sparkling wines that indicate a vine variety on the label is still small, *Rieslingsekt* has a niche of its own. It shows well the qualities of freshness and style enjoyed in German still wine. *See also* Lagensekt, Markensekt.

Riesling-Hochgewächs

A QbA still wine in the Ahr, Mosel-Saar-Ruwer, Mittelrhein, Nahe, Rheinhessen and Rheinpfalz regions may be described as 'Riesling-Hochgewächs' if the original must weight reached the equivalent of $1 \cdot 5°$ alcohol by volume more than the minimum laid down for standard Riesling QbA. In addition, the wine must reach the enhanced level of quality required by the control (*Amtliche Prüfung) authorities.

Rietburg eG, Gebietswinzergenossenschaft Rhpf

Large cooperative cellar of 1,160 members founded in 1958, covering 1,050 hectares in villages between *Neustadt and *Landau. The choice of vines is wide, including Müller-Thurgau, Silvaner, Riesling, Ruländer, Kerner. Interesting range of superior quality single-vine wines, and a huge list of wines typical of the region from some 220 different bottlings each year. A popular source of sound wine for many of the large buyers from abroad. Sixty-eight percent of the wine is *lieblich*.
Address: Edesheimerstrasse 50, W-6741 Rhodt unter Rietburg
Tel: 06323 2061

Rivaner
Synonym for Müller-Thurgau originally used mainly in Luxembourg but now common in the Mosel-Saar-Ruwer, Baden and elsewhere. It was intended that Rivaner should always be a fresh wine with relatively little alcohol but some producers are confusingly ignoring this understanding.

Rödelsee Franken w r
Village near ★Kitzingen producing top-quality wines that are spicy, powerful and long-flavoured. In recent years many of the vineyards, known to have been in production in the 13th century, have been reconstructed, modernized and replanted, mainly in Silvaner and Müller-Thurgau. *Grosslage*: Schlossberg.

Römer
Wine glass or rummer of ancient origin. The standard *Römer* used for the sale of wine by the glass contains 200 or 250 millilitres. The stem is usually green or amber and the bowl is clear but sometimes engraved. The liquid content is, by law, always marked. Finer *Römer* of varying sizes are produced for private use.

Römerlay M-S-R w
Grosslage covering the vineyards on the Mosel around ★Trier and those of the little Ruwer valley, including ★Eitelsbach and ★Kasel. Very high proportion of Riesling.

Rosengarten Nahe w (r)
Best-known *Grosslage* in the Nahe valley, covering more than 600 hectares. None of the individual sites is among the best of the region and much use is made of the *Grosslage* name, combined with that of the village of ★Rüdesheim – not to be confused with the town of the same name in the Rheingau. A Rüdesheimer Rosengarten will usually be a blend of Silvaner and Müller-Thurgau, similar to a wine from the Bereich ★Bingen in the Rheinhessen across the river Nahe, but with more acidity.

Roséwein, Roseewein
Pale pink wine made from red grapes, closer in style to white wine than to red. *See* Weissherbst.

Rotberger
A high-yielding crossing of Trollinger × Riesling from ★Geisen-heim planted in 25 hectares. Its red grapes are particularly suitable for rosé and sparkling red wine production.

Rotenfels Nahe w (r)
Einzellage at ★Traisen that takes its name from the nearby rock face, the Rotenfels (at 214 metres, the highest cliff in Europe north of the Alps). Produces strongly flavoured Riesling wines of great character. *Grosslage*: ★Burgweg. Growers include Crusius.

Rothenberg Rhh w
Twenty-hectare *Einzellage* adjacent to Niersteiner ★Pettenthal on the slopes of the ★Rheinterrasse at ★Nackenheim. The red slate and sandstone soil can produce wines of real elegance, charm and style. *Grosslage*: ★Spiegelberg. Growers: Gunderloch, Guntrum, Staats-weingut Oppenheim.

Rothenberg Rhg w
Sloping, modernized *Einzellage* at ★Geisenheim that produces big, balanced Riesling wines with a slight, attractive taste of the soil. *Grosslage*: ★Burgweg. Growers: Erbslöh, Forschungsanstalt Gei-senheim, Schloss Schönborn, Wegeler-Deinhard, Zwierlein.

Rotling
A rosé-coloured wine produced by blending red and white grapes or their pulp – not a blend of wine or musts. Not widely produced.

Rotwein
Red wine.

Roxheim Nahe w (r)
Village a few kilometres northwest of ★Bad Kreuznach producing Riesling and Silvaner wines well regarded in the region for their style. Cannot be compared to the best from the Nahe. Usually appropriately priced. *Grosslage*: ★Rosengarten.

Ruck, Weingut Johann Franken VDP
Ten-hectare, respected estate, with holdings in ★Julius-Echter-Berg

and other sites at ★Iphofen, half on steep slopes. Thirty-five percent
Silvaner, 30 percent Müller-Thurgau, 15 percent Riesling. Spätburgunder will be offered in the future. Storage is in stainless steel,
producing wines typical of vine variety and site. Of the annual
production equalling 7,200 cases, 75 percent is *trocken*. Sales are
principally to private customers but five percent is exported.
Address: Marktplatz 19, W-8715 Iphofen
Tel: 09323 3316

Rüdesheim Nahe w

Village near ★Bad Kreuznach often linked with the *Grosslage*
★Rosengarten, a Nahe answer to Niersteiner ★Gutes Domtal. The
sites at Rüdesheim itself are planted in Müller-Thurgau and
Silvaner. Not to be confused with Rüdesheim in the Rheingau.

Rüdesheim Rhg w

Town 25 kilometres southwest of ★Wiesbaden, a major target for
tourists and widely known for its street of wine bars, the
Drosselgasse – tolerable only to the most gregarious. Its vineyards,
protected from the north by the Niederwald (wood) and facing
south across the Rhein to ★Bingen, enjoy a good microclimate but
can suffer in drought years. Full-flavoured, splendid, positive
wines. *Grosslage*: ★Burgweg.

Ruländer

Vine variety planted over 2,811 hectares, produces good, full-
bodied, soft white wines from blue grapes. Known also as
★Grauburgunder and as Pinot Gris in France. In Baden and the
Rheinpfalz, where the wines are fuller than those made further
north, the Ruländer seems to reflect the regional character
particularly well. It should be planted on a good site where must
levels can reach at least 80° Oechsle to avoid being thin and
uninteresting. Ruländers sometimes have a 'barnyard' bouquet.
They lack the elegance of the paler-coloured Riesling, but as a
Spätlese or *Auslese* they can impress by their power and fullness.

Rumpel & Cie, Riesling-Weingut M-S-R

Long-established three-hectare estate at ★Traben-Trabach with
holdings that are all steep and planted exclusively in Riesling.

Annual production is 3,300 cases, of which 50 percent is *trocken*, and ten percent is exported.
Address: Am Bahnhof 20, W-5580 Traben-Trabach
Tel: 06541 6427

Rund
Describes a wine in which a full flavour is balanced by adequate but not pronounced acidity, and possibly by a little residual sugar. Good examples could be found in some Riesling wines from Württemberg or Baden.

Ruppertsberg Rhpf w (r)
Village near ★Deidesheim producing attractive Riesling and Silvaner wines and very stylish Scheurebe. The best are fine and powerful. *Grosslage*: ★Hofstück.

Ruppertsberger Winzerverein 'Hoheburg' eG Rhpf
Cooperative cellar supplied by grapes from 215 hectares, mainly at ★Ruppertsberg (including ★Reiterpfad, ★Linsenbusch). Vines are 50 percent Riesling, plus Müller-Thurgau, Silvaner and others. Thirty percent of the wine is *trocken*. Efficient modern winemaking in a top-quality part of the Rheinpfalz.
Address: Hauptstrasse 23, W-6701 Ruppertsberg
Tel: 06326 6035

Ruwer
River that rises in the high ground of the Hunsrück and flows some 40 kilometres later into the Mosel near the village of Ruwer close to ★Trier. In good years the Ruwer vineyards can produce great Riesling wines, positive and firm in flavour, similar in weight to those of the other important river in their shared *Bereich*, the Saar, although the flavour is less distinct. The little Ruwer valley is characterized by a handful of villages of ancient origin, famous wine estates overlooked by woods and walnut trees, and some of the most interesting wines of the Mosel-Saar-Ruwer region.

Saale-Unstrut w (r)
Attractive rural region whose widespread vineyards (400 hectares) follow the course of the Saale and Unstrut rivers. They are planted

37 percent Müller-Thurgau, 28 percent Silvaner, six percent each Bacchus and Gutedel, plus others including Portugieser and Spätburgunder. The economic circumstances are identical to those of ★Sachsen. Outside the region it is often said Saale-Unstrut wines resemble those of Franken, but their elegant, light structure from chalky soil makes this seem doubtful.

Saar

Tributary of the Mosel that rises in the Vosges mountains and enters the Bereich ★Saar-Ruwer upstream from ★Saarburg. On either side of the river, beyond the vineyards, the landscape is wooded and attractive and has been an area for relaxation for the people of ★Trier since the time of the Roman occupation. The hard slate soil is natural – none being added as happened in many Mosel vineyards – and gives the wine a strong, steely flavour. Great wines from a number of fine estates are made in good years.

Saar-Mosel-Winzersekt GmbH

An association established in 1983 and now comprising some 120 grape growers in the Mosel-Saar-Ruwer region. It produces bottle-fermented *Sekt* exclusively from the members' Riesling and Elbling wines. Annual production is the equivalent of 20,800 cases.
Address: Gilbertstrasse 34, W-5500 Trier
Tel: 0651 42627

Saar-Ruwer, Bereich w

The *Bereich* that covers the Saar and Ruwer vineyards.

Saarburg M-S-R w

Ancient town known for its old buildings and half-timbered houses, its bell foundry and its wine. It lies on the river Saar at the upstream end of the vine-growing area. Many of the sites are owned, in part or in whole, by well-known estates. Saarburger Riesling wines in good years are among the best on the Saar. They have a strong slaty Riesling flavour, with a bouquet to match. Prices are comparable to those from Mosel villages such as ★Wehlen, ★Bernkastel and ★Brauneberg. *Grosslage*: ★Scharzberg.

Saarland

Federal state with 98 hectares of vineyards, including those of the Bereich Moseltor near the German-Luxembourg-French frontier. (The rest of the Mosel-Saar-Ruwer is in the state of ★Rheinland-Pfalz.) The capital is Saarbrücken.

Sachsen

Federal state which includes the vine-growing region of the same name. Dresden is the capital.

Sachsen w (r)

The most easterly vine-growing region of Germany, covering about 300 hectares in the Elbe valley, with a long tradition of winemaking. The climate is continental and frost damage is frequent in winter and late spring. The vineyards, many on dilapidated terraces, are planted 38 percent Müller-Thurgau, 15 percent Weissburgunder, 15 percent Traminer, 11 percent Gutedel, seven percent Riesling – the rest includes Portugieser and St Laurent. Sachsen and ★Saale-Unstrut have enormous economic problems left over from their communist past, but the growth of their trade in wine is likely to be helped by an increase in local tourism. The vineyards' high production costs and low yields will probably not allow Sachsen wines to become internationally competitive for some years.

Sachsen Anhalt

Federal state which includes the ★Saale-Unstrut vine-growing region. Magdeburg is the capital.

Sächsische Winzergenossenschaft Meissen eG S

Cooperative receiving grapes from 490 members covering 120 hectares spread throughout the Sachsen wine-producing region. Planted 40 percent Müller-Thurgau, 18 percent Weissburgunder, eight percent Traminer, and eight percent each Ruländer and Riesling. All the wines are *trocken* and sold as QbA or *Tafelwein* – no QmP. The annual production (among the most variable in Germany) was 33,300 cases in 1988, 100,000 cases in 1989, and 83,300 cases in 1990. At present 50 percent is sold to hotels and restaurants and 20 percent to private customers.

Schloß
Seußlitz
1990
TRAMINER
Seußlitzer Heinrichsburg
QUALITÄTSWEIN b.A. · SACHSEN
12,0% vol   TROCKEN   ℮ 0,75ℓ
SÄCHSISCHE WINZERGENOSSENSCHAFT MEISSEN E.G.
8250 MEISSEN

Address: Bennoweg 9, O-8250 Meissen
Tel: 53 3293

Sackträger Rhh w
Sloping *Einzellage* on the outskirts of ★Oppenheim producing
refined wines, which can be outstanding in good years. *Grosslage*:
★Güldenmorgen. Growers: Baumann, Dahlem, Guntrum, Koch,
Niersteiner Winzer, Staatsweingut Oppenheim, Rappenhof,
Schuch, Sittmann.

Saftig
Juicy. Describes a wine with good acidity and a fruity flavour that
lasts in the mouth. Might apply to a well-made Riesling *Spätlese*
from the ★Rheinterrasse.

St Alban Rhh w (r)
Grosslage of just under 1,000 hectares between ★Mainz and
★Nackenheim that takes its name from the St Alban monastery at
Mainz, once a large landowner in the district. Makes sound, easy-
to-drink Rheinhessen wines.

St Anthony, Weingut Rhh VDP
Estate of 23 hectares with holdings among the best sites at
★Nierstein (★Findling, ★Hipping, ★Ölberg, ★Orbel, ★Paterberg,
★Pettenthal), planted 60 percent Riesling, 15 percent Silvaner, and

other grapes, including Spätburgunder. A small amount is aged in *barrique* and 71 percent is *trocken*. Annual production is 10,800 cases, sold exclusively to private customers.
Address: Wörrstädterstrasse 22, W-6505 Nierstein
Tel: 06133 5482

St Johann Rhh w (r)
A village name mainly met in conjunction with that of the *Grosslage* Abtey on bottles of inexpensive wine.

St Laurent
Vine variety with Alsatian origins grown on a small scale in the Rheinpfalz. Needs a good site if the wine is to be balanced. The retail price in the region is similar to that of Spätburgunder.

St Michael M-S-R w
Large *Grosslage* of more than 2,200 hectares. The best-known sites are around the villages of ★Klüsserath and ★Leiwen, where the vines are mainly Riesling. There are also significant plantations of Müller-Thurgau.

St-Nikolaus Hospital M-S-R
An old people's home dating from 1465 with 7·5 hectares at ★Brauneberg (★Juffer), ★Bernkastel (★Graben, ★Lay, ★Bratenhöfchen), ★Wehlen (★Sonnenuhr) and elsewhere. Cask-matured wines. Forty percent is *lieblich*.
Address: Cusanusstrasse, W-5550 Bernkastel-Kues
Tel: 06531 2101

St Rochuskapelle Rhh w (r)
Grosslage of more than 2,400 hectares in the northeast corner of the Rheinhessen. Some of the vineyards lie alongside the river Nahe and the wines often have more acidity than those made further south in the region. Best-known individual site within the *Grosslage* is the ★Scharlachberg at ★Bingen.

St Ursula Weingut & Weinkellerei GmbH
Wine merchants, probably best known outside Germany for the excellent Goldener Oktober range of QbA.

Address: Mainzerstrasse 184, W-6530 Bingen
Tel: 06721 70225

Salem, Markgräfliche Landwirtschaftsverwaltung, Weingüter Max von Markgraf von Baden Baden

With 44 hectares by the *Bodensee, the largest wine estate of the Markgraf von Baden, planted with 60 percent Müller-Thurgau, 30 percent Spätburgunder. Sixty percent of the wine is *trocken*.
Address: W-7777 Salem
Tel: 07553 81272

Salm-Dalberg'sches Weingut, Prinz zu Nahe VDP

Oldest wine-producing cellar in Germany dating from 1200 with 8·5 hectares planted in *Wallhausen, *Roxheim and Sommerloch (70 percent Riesling). From 1990, *Einzellage* names are used only for the best wines. The style is elegant and fruity; 50 percent of the wine is *trocken*. Annual sales of 5,000 cases, with 25 percent exported.
Address: Schloss Wallhausen, W-6511 Wallhausen
Tel: 06706 289

Salwey, Weingut Baden VDP

Much-respected 15-hectare estate with holdings in the Bereich *Kaiserstuhl, and in the Glottertal which climbs into the Schwarzwald.

Vine varieties are 44 percent Spätburgunder, 15 percent Ruländer (Grauburgunder), 13 percent Riesling, ten percent Müller-Thurgau, and others. Some of the Burgunder (Pinot) wines are aged in *barrique* and sold as *Tafelwein*. Annual production is 10,000 cases, 98 percent *trocken*, two percent *halbtrocken*.
Address: Hauptstrasse 2, W-7818 Vogtsburg-Oberrotweil
Tel: 07662 384

Samtig

Velvety. Good quality, full-bodied red wines with relatively little tannin (perhaps through ageing) are said to be 'smooth as velvet'.

Samtrot

Red grape variety, a mutation of Müllerrebe, planted on 73 hectares, almost entirely in Württemberg.

Sandgrub Rhg w
Einzellage in two clearly defined and separate sections south of
*Kiedrich, planted mainly in Riesling. Produces stylish, good-
quality wine that improves with bottle-age. *Grosslage*: *Heiligen-
stock. Growers: Groenesteyn, von Hessen, Knyphausen, Lang,
Nikolai, Oetinger, Reinhartshausen, Ress, Simmern, Tillmanns,
Weil.

Sanitätsrat
Award given to medical practitioners up to 1918 nationally, and
thereafter by some individual states. Appears, for example, in the
title of Weingutsverwaltung Sanitätsrat Dr Dahlem KG.

Sasbachwalden Baden r w
*Schwarzwald wine village best known for its Spätburgunder and
Riesling. *Grosslage*: Schloss Rodeck.

Sasbachwalden eG, Winzergenossenschaft Baden
Cooperative cellar supplied by 400 growers with 230 hectares,
planted 55 percent Spätburgunder, 20 percent Riesling, 18 percent
Müller-Thurgau. Good distribution throughout Germany of
approximately 170,000 cases annually. Stylish, serious wines, some
matured in Allier oak *barriques*.
Address: Talstrasse 2, W-7595 Sasbachwalden
Tel: 07841 4033

Saumagen Rhpf w r
Once a *Grosslage*, now an *Einzellage* at *Kallstadt producing wine
from the ordinary to the outstanding, but particularly known for its
Silvaners. Translated, Saumagen means 'sow's stomach' – the name
of a well-known local sausage dish – a Pfälzer alternative to haggis.
Grosslage: *Kobnert. Growers: Koehler-Ruprecht, Winzer-
genossenschaft Herrenberg-Honigsäckel, Winzergenossenschaft
Kallstadt.

Säure
Acidity. Because of the cool nights when the grapes are ripening,
the acid level of German wine, at between five and nine grams per
litre, is higher than that of most wines produced in a warmer

climate. As a result the wine has a unique freshness that is carefully retained during vinification and maturation. The main acids in German wine are tartaric (*Weinsäure*) and malic (*Apfelsäure*). The amount present depends on the ripeness and variety of grape. Top-quality wines such as a *Beerenauslese* or an *Eiswein* often have particularly high acidity, balanced by a large amount of residual sugar. Such wines need years of maturation in bottle to reach their peak and for the acidity to soften. Wines with relatively low acidity (for example Müller-Thurgau) are usually best drunk young. The addition of acids to German wine is illegal, but ★deacidification is allowed. Many young growers in Germany (and Austria) in the 1980s have sought a higher than usual acidity. In the 1990s, the trend may be towards wines with a higher alcohol content.

Schäfer, Weingut Karl Rhpf VDP

Estate dating from 1843 with 17 hectares of holdings (some terraced) at ★Bad Dürkheim (★Spielberg and others), ★Forst (★Pechstein), ★Wachenheim (★Fuchsmantel) and ★Ungstein. Vines are 71 percent Riesling. All qualities of wine are matured in cask in the old vaulted cellar and are expected to develop in bottle. Seventy percent of the Riesling is *trocken*. In recent years the Dürkheimer wines have been particularly successful, both at national competitions and in commercial terms.
Address: Weinstrasse Süd 30, W-6702 Bad Dürkheim
Tel: 06322 2138

Schäfer, Weingut Michael Nahe

Thirteen-hectare estate with holdings at ★Burg Layen, ★Dorsheim (★Pittermännchen, ★Goldloch), ★Münster-Sarmsheim and elsewhere. Site names will be used for the best wines only in future and the *trocken* wines are often enriched (*see* Anreicherung) *Spätlesen*. Annual production is 10,000 cases, roughly one-third each *trocken*, *halbtrocken* and *lieblich*. A high 55 percent is exported.
Address: W-6531 Burg Layen
Tel: 06721 43097

Schaffer, Weingut Egon Franken VDP

Small 3·2-hectare estate. Two-thirds of the holdings at ★Escherndorf (★Lump and others) are on steep slopes. Vines are 48 percent

Müller-Thurgau, 28 percent Silvaner, 15 percent Riesling. Annual production is 2,500 cases of *trocken* wine, sold almost exclusively to private customers.

Address: Astheimerstrasse 17, W-8712 Escherndorf

Tel: 09381 9350

Schales, Weingut Rhh

Market-orientated estate of 36 hectares founded in 1783 in the south of the Rheinhessen. Planted 30 percent Riesling, 17 percent Müller-Thurgau, 14 percent Weissburgunder. Annual production is 29,200 cases including 'Germany's best' brand wine, 'Trullo'. Around 40 percent is *trocken*, and 30 percent is exported.

Address: Alzeyerstrasse 160, W-6523 Flörsheim-Dalsheim

Tel: 06243 7003

Scharlachberg Rhh w

Well-known *Einzellage* at *Bingen on mainly sloping ground overlooking the river Nahe. The wines are close in style to those of the Lower Nahe, or even the Rheingau, with attractive acidity and charm. *Grosslage*: *St Rochuskapelle. Grower: Villa Sachsen.

Scharzberg M-S-R w

Grosslage of about 1,600 hectares covering the whole viticultural area of the Saar, where many may feel that the archetypal German wine is produced. A light, elegant, fruity acidity is its main characteristic – more positive and less subtle than a wine from the *Mittelmosel. Wines using the Scharzberg name are not the cheapest but are usually of much better quality than those sold at rock-bottom prices from the *Grosslage* Bernkasteler *Kurfürstlay.

Scharzhofberg M-S-R w

Mainly steep, 27-hectare vineyard near *Wiltingen with the status of a village or community, so that its wine is sold under the single name 'Scharzhofberg'. Elegant Riesling wine, full of character in good years from the decomposed slate soil. Often one of the great wines of Germany. The Scharzhofberg wines of *Müller-Scharz-hofberg are *primus inter pares* on the Saar. *Grosslage*: *Scharzberg. Growers: Bischöfliche Weingüter, Hövel, Kesselstatt, Müller-Scharzhofberg, Vereinigte Hospitien, Volxem.

Schatzkammer

Literally 'treasure room'. A part of a cellar set aside for storing the finest, and by implication the oldest, wines. Some estates list a number of rare wines from their *Schatzkammer*.

Schaumwein

Sparkling wine that meets certain technical standards but is basically cheap and cheerful. Approximately ten percent of sparkling wine produced in Germany is classified simply as Schaumwein. The balance is ★Qualitätsschaumwein. *See also* Sekt.

Schenkenböhl Rhpf w (r)

Grosslage of about 600 hectares on either side of the ★Deutsche Weinstrasse between ★Bad Dürkheim and ★Wachenheim. The individual sites are mainly flat or gently sloping with a good proportion of Riesling. They form some of the finest vineyards of the Rheinpfalz, so that a wine sold under the *Grosslage* name is still likely to be very stylish and full of quality.

Scheurebe

White grape variety, a very successful crossing of Silvaner × Riesling, named after its developer Dr Georg Scheu. It now covers 4,159 hectares, spread throughout all the vine-growing regions. Planted in a good site, suitable for Silvaner, the Scheurebe can produce *Spätlese* wine of absolute top quality. Lesser wines have a pronounced flowering-currant bouquet, but this is not so marked in fine *Auslese* wines for which Scheurebe also has a considerable reputation. The acidity in unripe Scheurebe grapes is so pronounced that the resulting wine is best used for blending with ★neutral, soft wines.

Schielerwein

A *Schillerwein* (*see next entry*) produced in ★Sachsen.

Schillerwein

★Rotling QbA and QmP (including *Eiswein*) produced in Württemberg may be called *Schillerwein*. The name has nothing to do with the poet Friedrich Schiller, a Württemberger by birth, but arises from the wine's varying shades of rosé colour. (*Schillern* means to change colour.) In the past, red and white vine varieties were intermingled in the vineyards (★'Gemischter Satz') and both were harvested and vinified together.

Schlangengraben M-S-R w

Einzellage at ★Wiltingen planted in Riesling and Müller-Thurgau, producing fruity, stylish wines. Well known, but not the best site on the Saar. *Grosslage*: ★Scharzberg. Growers include Volxem.

Schleinitz'sche Weingutsverwaltung, Freiherr von M-S-R

Family-owned 6·5 hectare estate at the still underrated wine-producing end of the Mosel near ★Koblenz. Holdings are all at ★Kobern (including ★Uhlen) and Niederfell, one of the prettiest parts of the river. Vines are 99 percent Riesling, one percent Spätburgunder. Stylish wines, including *trocken Auslesen*. Many have won awards at national competitions. Annual production is 4,200 cases, of which ten percent is exported.
Address: Kirchstrasse 17, W-5401 Kobern-Gondorf
Tel: 02607 268

Schloss

Castle or palace. Wine that bears the name of a Schloss (for example Schloss Johannisberg, Schloss Vollrads) must have been made entirely from grapes grown in the castle's vineyards. It may then be called a *Schlossabfüllung* (castle-bottling) as opposed to the usual *Erzeugerabfüllung* (estate- or producer-bottled). The word Schloss also often forms part of an *Einzellage* name (Serriger Schloss Saarfelser Schlossberg) or a district name (Bereich Schloss Böckelheim), so 'Schloss' on a label does not necessarily mean that the wine comes from an individual castle or estate.

Schloss Böckelheim, Bereich Nahe w (r)

District covering the Nahe region upstream from ★Bad Kreuznach, including the well-known sites at ★Niederhausen and the village of ★Schlossböckelheim. Many of the vineyards are widely separated. The quality of wine sold under the *Bereich* name is generally good and will not be as cheap as a Bereich ★Nierstein, especially when made from Riesling.

Schloss Deidesheim Rhpf
See Kern, Weingut Dr

Schloss Groenesteyn, Weingut des Reichsfreiherrn von Ritter zu Groenesteyn Rhg VDP
Important estate dating from the 14th century and owned by the Groenesteyn family since 1640. Thirty-two hectares, 92 percent Riesling, concentrated in ★Rüdesheim (★Berg Rottland, ★Berg Roseneck, ★Berg Schlossberg, ★Bischofsberg) and ★Kiedrich (★Gräfenberg, ★Wasseros, ★Sandgrub). Wines are matured in wood and are among the best in the region. Fifty percent is *lieblich* – a high proportion. Fifty percent is exported. All are offered as Schloss Groenesteyn followed by the wine name.
Address: W-6229 Kiedrich
Tel: 06123 2492

Schloss Hallburg Franken
See Schönborn, Weingut Graf von

Schloss Johannisberg, Fürst von Metternich-Winneburg'sches Domäne Rentamt Rhg VDP
Great estate of 35 hectares, planted 100 percent in Riesling. The estate was recorded as the first (in 1716) to plant Riesling on its own, unmixed with other vine varieties. Maturation in wood in the cool cellars helps to produce the fine, weighty wines for which the Schloss is famous. Different-coloured capsules are used for the various quality categories. The estate is particularly proud of the quality of its QbA – full-bodied, serious wine. *Spätlese* wines are made only in outstanding years and, in common with other Rheingau estates, an *Auslese* is a rarity. Most of the buildings, restored after serious damage in World War II, date from the 17th century. Schloss Johannisberg is legally an *Ortsteil* and the wine is sold without any individual site names. Around 70 percent is exported.
Address: W-6222 Geisenheim-Johannisberg
Tel: 06722 8012

Schloss Kirchberg, Markgräflich Badisches Weingut Baden
Seventeen-hectare estate at Kirchberg and Hagnau on the

*Bodensee with vineyards 400–500 metres above sea level, planted 70 percent Müller-Thurgau and 26 percent Spätburgunder. In addition to *interspecific crossings on trial, there are also plantations of Zweigelt (Blaufränkisch (Limberger [Limberger Blauer]) × St Laurent) from Austria, Comtessa (Madeleine Angevine × Traminer) from *Geilweilerhof. Annual production is 13,300 cases, 70 percent *trocken*, and sold 90 percent to private customers. Address: Schloss Kirchberg, W-7997 Immenstaad
Tel: 07545 6156

Schloss Kosakenberg Rhg
See Zwierlein, Weingut Freiherr von

Schloss Ortenberg, Weinbauversuchsgut Baden
Estate founded in 1950 as an experimental institute. Its 7·5 hectares of vineyards on steep granite slopes are planted with 25 percent Riesling, 15 percent Müller-Thurgau, 11 percent Traminer and Gewürztraminer, plus a range of varieties, reflecting the estate's research work. The wines are matured in cask or stainless steel, according to their individual needs. Some *barrique*-ageing. Annual production is 3,300 cases; 75 percent *trocken*, 90 percent sold to private customers.
Address: Burgweg 19a, W-7601 Ortenberg
Tel: 0781 34848

Schloss Reichartshausen Rhg w
A much-restored castle, originating in the 12th century, now regarded as an *Ortsteil*, with three hectares of vineyard owned entirely by Balthasar *Ress.

Schloss Reinhartshausen, Administration Prinz Friedrich von Preussen Rhg VDP
Seventy-hectare estate with origins believed to date back to Charlemagne. Holdings are at *Erbach (including *Marcobrunn, *Siegelsberg and sole ownership of Schlossberg), on Mariannenau island in the Rhein including sole ownership of Erbacher *Rheinhell, and at *Hattenheim (*Wisselbrunnen, *Nussbrunnen and others), *Kiedrich (*Sandgrub), *Rauenthal and *Rüdesheim (*Bischofsberg). Vines are 86 percent Riesling plus Weissburg-

under, Spätburgunder, Chardonnay and others. Apart from the fine traditional wines expected of a great Rheingau estate, the Schloss also makes a powerful Weissburgunder and Chardonnay *trocken*. Some ★Burgunder wines are *barrique*-aged. Annual production is 50,000 cases, 65 percent *trocken*, 20 percent exported.
Address: Hauptstrasse 35, W-6228 Eltville 2
Tel: 06123 4009

Schloss Saaleck Franken

In 1964 the town of ★Hammelburg bought the ancient steep vineyards around Schloss Saaleck, now covering 30 hectares. Vines are 30 percent Müller-Thurgau, 20 percent Silvaner, ten percent Bacchus. ★Interspecific crossings are on trial. Fifty percent of the wine is *fränkisch trocken* and 70 percent is sold to private customers. Sales are mainly in Germany.
Address: Städtlicher Weingut, W-8783 Hammelburg
Tel: 09732 802–28

Schloss Saarfels Sektkellerei GmbH & Co KG M-S-R

A small producer (6,700 cases per year) of steely *Rieslingsekt* from the Saar valley – 50 percent is *brut*, 50 percent *trocken*. High-quality Saar estate-bottled Riesling wines are also offered under the Schloss Saarfels name.
Address: W-5512 Serrig
Tel: 06581 2827

Schloss Saarfelser Schlossberg M-S-R w
Mainly steep *Einzellage* at ★Serrig near the upper end of the Saar vine-growing area. Sole owner is the ★Vereinigte Hospitien at ★Trier. Produces scented, positive, light, stylish Riesling wines that can be superb in good years. *Grosslage*: ★Scharzberg.

Schloss Saarstein, Weingut M-S-R VDP
Eleven-hectare estate planted 96 percent in Riesling, with a commanding position overlooking the Saar. The *Einzellage* at ★Serrig, Schloss Saarstein, and the estate share the same name. All the holdings, including that at ★Wawern, are steep. The wines are classics, characterized by wonderful fruity acidity. Seventy-five percent is *trocken*. Annual production is 5,400 cases.
Address: W-5512 Serrig
Tel: 06581 2324

Schloss Schönborn, Domänenweingut Rhg VDP
Estate of 63 hectares owned by the distinguished church and political von Schönborn family, which acquired its first Rheingau vineyards in 1349. The Weingut's present holdings, based on ★Hattenheim (★Nussbrunnen, ★Wisselbrunnen, and sole owner-ship of Pfaffenberg), are at ★Oestrich (★Doosberg), ★Rüdesheim (★Berg Schlossberg, ★Berg Rottland, ★Bischöfsberg), ★Geisenheim (★Rothenberg, ★Mäuerchen), ★Winkel (★Hasensprung), ★Hoch-heim (★Hölle, ★Domdechaney, ★Kirchenstück), ★Johannisberg, ★Erbach (★Marcobrunn), ★Rauenthal (★Baiken) and ★Assmanns-hausen (★Höllenberg). Vines are 88 percent Riesling, six percent Spätburgunder. Maturation is in wood, producing full, big-scale Riesling wines, with good, pronounced varietal characteristics. Sales are worldwide.
Address: Hauptstrasse 53, W-6228 Eltville-Hattenheim
Tel: 06723 2007

Schloss Sommerhausen, Weingut Franken VDP
Estate of 20 hectares with holdings at ★Sommerhausen, ★Rander-sacker, Eibelstadt, and in the *Grosslage* Iphöfer Burgweg, nearer the Steigerwald. Traditional Franken vines are grown plus Auxerrois (a relative of Weissburgunder) and Chardonnay. Spätburgunder is aged in *barrique*. Annual production is 16,400 cases, 75 percent

trocken. Fifty percent is sold to restaurants, five percent is exported. Address: Ochsenfurterstrasse 17–19, W-8701 Sommerhausen Tel: 09333 260.

Schloss Staufenberg, Markgräflich Badisches Weingut
Baden
The Margrave of Baden (the title corresponds in rank to an English marquess) owns four wine estates, one of which, based on the 11th-century Schloss Staufenberg, is set in splendid hilly wooded country overlooking the village of ★Durbach. The 27 hectares of steep vineyards are planted mainly in Riesling (40 percent), Müller-Thurgau (15 percent) and Spätburgunder (30 percent). The Rieslings are firm but rounded; 75 percent of the wine is *trocken*. The estate's wine bar has distant but spectacular views of the Vosges mountains.
Address: Staufenberg 1, W-7601 Durbach
Tel: 0781 42778

Schloss Thorn M-S-R
An impressive castle, owned by Freiherr von Hobe's family since 1534, looking across the Mosel to Luxembourg. Twenty hectares of vineyard, 80 percent on steep slopes, planted 30 percent each Riesling and Weisser Elbling and with Müller-Thurgau and the rare Roter Elbling, used for rosé production. Good characterful wines. Annual production is 12,500 cases, 25 percent *trocken* and 50 percent *halbtrocken*. Thirty percent is exported.
Address: W-5510 Schloss Thorn
Tel: 06583 433

Schloss Vollrads, Graf Matuschka-Greiffenclau'sche Güterverwaltung Rhg Charta VDP
Remarkable and possibly most famous private estate in Germany, its 50 hectares protected by the woods that shelter the Rheingau above ★Winkel. The Greiffenclau family is known to have been selling wine in the 12th century and built Schloss Vollrads at the start of the 14th century. Today, Schloss Vollrads is an *Ortsteil*, regarded in law as a 'community'. Like ★Scharzhofberg and ★Steinberg it sells its annual production of approximately 33,750 cases (28 percent abroad) with no additional village or vineyard

name. Planted 98 percent in Riesling, the Schloss, with its vineyards somewhat higher than many in the Rheingau, produces wines with pronounced acidity and fine fruit. The estate uses different-coloured capsules to indicate variations in the style and quality of its wines. Sixty-two percent is *trocken*, 25 percent is ★Charta wine.

Schloss Vollrads

As well as its Weingut, Schloss Vollrads also owns the Graues Haus restaurant in Winkel, where a range of wines from many different Rheingau growers is served. In 1979 Graf Matuschka-Greiffenclau leased the Weingut Fürst ★Löwenstein in Hallgarten. Wines that do not reach the estate's high standards are sold in bulk to the wine trade and are not allowed to bear the Löwenstein or Vollrads name.

Address: W-6227 Oestrich-Winkel
Tel: 06723 660

Schloss Wallhausen Nahe
See Salm-Dalberg'sches Weingut

Schloss Westerhaus Rhh
See Opel, Weingut Irmgard von

Schlossabfüllung
Castle-bottled. *See* Schloss.

Schlossberg M–S–R w
Schlossberg is a common site name in Germany. The *Einzellage* at
★Bernkastel on the Mosel, half steep, half sloping, is not in the
town's first division but produces stylish wines, mainly from
Riesling. *Grosslage*: ★Kurfürstlay. Growers: Heidemanns-Berg-
weiler, Pauly-Bergweiler, M F Richter, Selbach-Oster,
Wegeler-Deinhard.

Schlossberg M–S–R w
Steep *Einzellage* at ★Zeltingen-Rachtig, next to the ★Sonnenuhr,
producing elegant Riesling wines. *Grosslage*: ★Münzlay. Growers:
Friedrich-Wilhelm-Gymnasium, Kesselstatt, Prüm, Selbach-
Oster, Vereinigte Hospitien.

Schlossböckelheim Nahe w
Small but important winemaking community producing elegant,
fresh Riesling wines to the highest standards. Set in rural
surroundings, upstream from ★Bad Münster am Stein-Ebernburg,
it is still largely undiscovered by tourists. The Schloss (castle) is now
a ruin. *Grosslage*: ★Burgweg.

Schlosskapelle Nahe w
Grosslage on the left bank of the river Nahe south of ★Bingen. Best-
known sites are at ★Münster-Sarmsheim and ★Dorsheim, where
full-bodied, meaty Riesling wines with much style are made.

Schlossmühle, Weingut Nahe
Family-owned 27-hectare estate established in 1775 with holdings
at ★Burg Layen, ★Dorsheim, ★Münster-Sarmsheim, planted 53
percent Riesling, 20 percent Müller-Thurgau, and others. Sole
owners of Winzenheimer in den siebzehn Morgen. Fifty-two
percent of the wine is *lieblich*. Some wines are aged in *barrique* and
there is a range of carefully selected wines of superior quality.
Address: Dr Josef Höfer, Naheweinstrasse 2, W-6531 Burg Layen
Tel: 06721 45000

Schlumberger Privat-Weingut H Baden
Seven-hectare estate in the Bereich ★Markgräflerland planted
40 percent Gutedel, 25 percent Spätburgunder, 15 percent

Weissburgunder, and other varieties. In a restricted list, most of the wines are offered without an *Einzellage* name, the emphasis being on the wine variety. Some *barrique*-aged Spätburgunder, and *Sekt* from relatives in Austria, the well-known Schlumberger Wein- und Sektkellerei of Vienna. Annual production is 5,000 cases, 95 percent *trocken*, sold 85 percent to private customers.
Address: Weinstrasse 19, W-7811 Sulzburg-Laufen
Tel: 07634 8992

Schmitt, Weingut Hermann Franz Rhh

Estate of 27 hectares established in 1549 by the direct ancestors of the present owners. Among the well-situated holdings at *Nierstein are parts of *Ölberg, *Hipping, *Pettenthal, and sole ownership of the 2·5-hectare Zehnmorgen site. Vines are 40 percent Riesling, 11 percent Silvaner, 15 percent Müller-Thurgau, etc. Style, body and good acidity are the hallmarks of the estate wines, and they are matured in wood. Forty percent is *trocken*, 20 percent is exported.
Address: Hermannshof, Kiliansweg 2, W-6505 Nierstein
Tel: 06133 59796

Schmitt, Weingut Robert Franken VDP

Family estate of seven hectares dating back 300 years, with holdings at *Randersacker (including *Teufelskeller) and *Würzburg, producing mainly fully fermented wines (*fränkisch trocken*). There is no *Anreicherung*. Annual production is 3,750 cases, 100 percent *trocken*.
Address: Maingasse 13, W-8701 Randersacker
Tel: 0931 708351

Schmitt's Kinder, Weingut Franken VDP

Thirteen-hectare estate at *Randersacker (including *Teufels- keller), planted 25 percent Silvaner, 20 percent Müller-Thurgau, 15 percent Bacchus, Domina, and others. Some *barrique*-aged wines. Annual production is 10,000 cases, 50 percent *trocken*, 70 percent sold to private customers.
Address: Am Sonnenstuhl, W-8701 Randersacker
Tel: 0931 708303

Schmitt'sches Weingut, Gustav Adolf Rhh

Estate owners, established in 1618, with 61 hectares of holdings in ★Nierstein (★Pettenthal, ★Ölberg, ★Hipping, ★Kranzberg), ★Oppenheim (including ★Kreuz), ★Dienheim and ★Dexheim. Planted 65 percent in traditional vines (such as Riesling, Silvaner). Ninety percent of the wine is exported. Twenty-five percent is *trocken*, 35 percent is *lieblich*.

Address: Wilhelmstrasse 2–4, W-6505 Nierstein

Tel: 06133 5708–0

Schneider, Weingut Georg Albrecht Rhh

Family-owned estate with origins reaching back over seven generations. Fifteen hectares of holdings at ★Nierstein, including ★Paterberg, ★Bildstock, ★Findling, ★Orbel, ★Ölberg, ★Pettenthal and ★Hipping – all top-quality sites. Vines are 40 percent Riesling, 25 percent Müller-Thurgau, eight percent Silvaner. Approximate annual production is equivalent to 10,000 cases. Only the better-quality wines are bottled; the rest is sold in bulk. The reputation of the estate is for fine, *nervig*, fruity wines. Fifty percent is *lieblich*.

Address: Oberdorfstrasse 11, W-6505 Nierstein

Tel: 06133 5655

Schneider, Weingut Jakob Nahe

Estate owned by the Schneider family, who are livestock farmers as well as vine growers, for more than 400 years. Nine hectares in fine sites at ★Niederhausen (★Hermannshöhle and others) and ★Norheim are planted 88 percent in Riesling. Organic manuring, late picking and individual cask maturation after a temperature-controlled fermentation produce spicy, elegant wines. Forty percent is *trocken*. Sales are mainly to private customers.

Address: Winzerstrasse 15, W-6551 Niederhausen

Tel: 06758 6701

Schnepfenflug an der Weinstrasse Rhpf w (r)

Grosslage of more than 500 hectares on level land near the well-known wine villages ★Wachenheim and ★Forst, growing many different vine varieties. Not to be confused with Schnepfenflug vom Zellertal, also in the northern Rheinpfalz.

Scholl & Hillebrand GmbH Rhg

Exporting house established in 1880 selling estate- and non-estate-bottled wines.

Address: Geisenheimerstrasse 9, W-6220 Rüdesheim

Tel: 06722 1028

Schönborn, Weingut Graf von Franken VDP

Estate of 27 hectares, the old hunting and summer residence of the von Schönborn family (*see* Schloss Schönborn, Domänenweingut), near to *Volkach, planted 25 percent each Silvaner and Müller-Thurgau. The wines from low yields are splendidly concentrated in flavour. Eighty-seven percent is *trocken*. Annual production is 16,700 cases, of which half is sold to private customers.

Address: Schloss Hallburg, W-8712 Volkach

Tel: 09381 2415

Schönburger

Grape variety, a crossing of Spätburgunder × an Italian table grape grown at present on 63 hectares, mainly in the Rheinhessen and Rheinpfalz. The grapes, which are luscious to taste and a marvellously delicate pink in colour, produce a white wine with a bouquet reminiscent of Traminer, a high must weight (15° Oechsle more than Riesling) and a dangerously low acidity. *Auslese* wine can be made from grapes affected by *Edelfäule* (noble rot).

Schönhell Rhg w

Riesling *Einzellage* at *Hallgarten making full-bodied, balanced wines. *Grosslage*: *Mehrhölzchen. Growers: Eser, Winzergenossenschaft Hallgarten, Löwenstein, Ress, Riedel, Wegeler-Deinhard.

Schoppenwein

Synonym for *Ausschankwein*.

Schubert'sche Gutsverwaltung, Carl von M-S-R

Fine estate of 33 hectares with origins dating back to 966, bought by the von Schubert family in 1882. The holdings are three solely owned *Einzellagen* at *Maximin-Grünhaus – Bruderberg, Herrenberg and Abtsberg – planted 98 percent Riesling. As well as the

modernized vineyards there is land for cattle raising, fruit farming and hunting. Very distinguished, *spritzig*, racy wines are made – they are superb and well worth their relatively high price. Annual production is 20,000 cases; 65 percent is *trocken*.
Address: W-5501 Grünhaus-Trier
Tel: 0651 5111

Schuch, Weingut Geschwister Rhh VDP

Family-owned estate of 15 hectares, dating from 1817. Holdings are at ★Nierstein (such as ★Ölberg, ★Pettenthal, ★Findling), ★Oppenheim (★Sackträger) and ★Dienheim, planted with 70 percent Riesling. Annual production is 8,300 cases. Sixty percent is *lieblich*. Ten percent is exported, but private customers take 60 percent.
Address: Oberdorfstrasse 22, W-6505 Nierstein 1
Tel: 06133 5652

Schultz-Werner, Weingut Oberst Rhh VDP

Family-owned 13-hectare estate dating from 1833, with holdings at ★Gau-Bischofsheim near ★Mainz. Vines are 50 percent Riesling, 19 percent Müller-Thurgau, 12 percent Silvaner. The wines receive individual attention, appropriate to the vine variety; all are fairly full-bodied, well structured and retain a lively acidity. Thirty percent is *lieblich*.
Address: Bahnhofstrasse 10, W-6501 Gau-Bischofsheim
Tel: 06135 2222

Schuster, Weingut Eduard Rhpf

A 15-hectare estate founded by the Schuster family in 1840. Holdings are at ★Kallstadt (★Steinacker), ★Ungstein and ★Bad Dürkheim (★Spielberg). Planted 57 percent in Riesling, 14 percent Silvaner, six percent Müller-Thurgau. The aim is to maintain the wine's individuality, grape and vintage characteristics. Maturation is in 100–120-year-old casks. Annual production is 12,500 cases; 40 percent is *trocken*.
Address: Neugasse 21, W-6701 Kallstadt
Tel: 06322 8011

Schwarze Katz M-S-R w

Best-known *Grosslage* of the lower Mosel, near ★Zell, covering some 630 hectares. A very high proportion of Riesling is grown on the steep slopes, except in the north-northeast-facing Kaimter Marienburger site. None of the individual sites is so well known as the *Grosslage* name Schwarze Katz (black cat). The wine is usually sound and often sold with a label showing a large black cat, arching its back, making Schwarze Katz almost a brand name.

'Schwarzer Adler', Weingut Baden

Estate of 14 hectares with a further 24 hectares attached to it in the form of an *Erzeugergemeinschaft*. The holdings are planted 35 percent Ruländer (Grauburgunder), 25 percent Müller-Thurgau, ten percent Silvaner. All the wines are dry with the exception of *Beerenauslesen*. No *Süssreserve* has ever been used at this estate. Of the annual production (25,000 cases including the *Erzeugergemeinschaft* wines) 15 percent is exported. The estate owns a two-star Michelin restaurant and has a merchant business in top-quality imported wines (ten vintages of Château Cheval Blanc are listed). Most of the wines are fully fermented, made to accompany food, particularly in leading German restaurants. Owner Franz Keller is a well-known publicist for German *trocken* wines.
Address: Badbergstrasse 23, W-7818 Vogtsburg-Oberbergen
Tel: 07662 715

Schwarzerde Rhpf w

Grosslage of more than 1,100 hectares in the northern Rheinpfalz, with no well-known vine-growing villages. Wines sold under the *Grosslage* name will be pleasant, agreeable and easy to drink.

Schwarzlay M-S-R w

Grosslage of more than 1,200 hectares in the *Mittelmosel, including the villages *Ürzig, *Erden, *Kinheim, *Traben-Trabach and *Enkirch. Many of the sites are planted with 100 percent Riesling. A good-quality Mosel *Grosslage*.

Schwarzriesling

See Müllerrebe

Schwarzwald

Probably the best-known forest in Europe. It protects many of the

Black Forest Baden vineyards, especially those of the Bereich
★Ortenau. The sites extend up to the edge of the forest, sharing the
steep slopes with orchards. Wonderfully rural and pretty, with
mini Alpine scenery.

Schweich M–S–R w

Village near ★Trier, at the head of the steep-sided Mosel gorge that
follows an almost uninterrupted but erratic course down to
★Koblenz. Produces fresh and fruity wines. *Grosslage*: ★Probstberg.

Schweinhardt Nachf, Weingut Bürgermeister Willi Nahe

A large estate for the Nahe (35 hectares) which has been trading
under the Schweinhardt name since 1859, with holdings at
★Langenlonsheim, ★Laubenheim and ★Guldental. Vines are 30
percent Riesling plus a range of other varieties including Müller-
Thurgau, Scheurebe, Ruländer. Annual production is 20,800 cases,
sold mainly to the consumer. Five percent is exported.
Address: Heddesheimerstrasse 1, W-6536 Langenlonsheim
Tel: 06704 1276

Seal

See Siegel

Sekt

Short German word for *Qualitätsschaumwein*, originating in the
early 19th century. Since 1975 the word *Sekt* has no longer been
reserved for quality sparkling wine produced in Germany. In
German-speaking countries one therefore finds *französischer*
(French) *Sekt*, *italienischer* (Italian) *Sekt*, and so on. Sparkling-wine
production in Germany amounts to about 42 million cases a year
and is increasing.

Sekt bA

Quality sparkling wine made solely from grapes grown in the
region stated on the label.

Selbach-Oster, Weingut M–S–R

Seven-hectare estate, owned by the Selbach family – involved in
vine growing since 1661. The 100 percent Riesling holdings (many

ungrafted and a few hundred years old) are at *Zeltingen-Rachtig (*Himmelreich, *Schlossberg and *Sonnenuhr), *Wehlen, *Graach (*Domprobst) and *Bernkastel (*Schlossberg). Wines are matured in oak and are typical of the Mosel – crisp, racy, fruity. Annual production is 6,000 cases, sold in Germany and abroad.
Address: Uferallee 23, W-5553 Zeltingen
Tel: 06532 2081

Septimer

A crossing of Gewürztraminer × Müller-Thurgau, grown in 24 hectares, mainly in the Rheinhessen. The dark pink grapes make white, full-bodied and very soft wine. Yield and acid content are low and must weight is high.

Serrig M-S-R w

Village, almost at the furthest extremity of the vineyards, upstream on the Saar. Steely Riesling wines are made on a number of top-quality estates. Often a source of excellent base wine for sparkling wine production. *Grosslage*: *Scharzberg.

Sichel Söhne GmbH, H Rhh

Important exporter of good-quality German wine, founded in 1857 and now best known for the leading and long-established brand Blue Nun Liebfraumilch. Sichel Novum, another brand, is a carefully crafted dry wine to suit the international taste. There are also close connections with a number of estates.
Address: Werner von Siemensstrasse 14–18, W-6508 Alzey
Tel: 6731 4060

Siebeldingen Rhpf w (r)

Village tucked below the foothills of the Haardt range west of *Landau in der Pfalz. Home of some excellent producers of intense wines, often with a high alcohol content. Good value for money. Little known abroad. *Grosslage*: Königsgarten.

Siegel

Seal. Now used to indicate the awards, sometimes in the form of a seal but also through strip labels, granted by the *Deutsche Landwirtschaft Gesellschaft and other organizations.

Siegelsberg Rhg w
Einzellage near the Rhein at *Erbach producing racy Riesling
wines. *Grosslage*: *Deutelsberg. Growers: Staatsweingut Eltville,
Knyphausen, Oetinger, Reinhartshausen.

Siegerrebe
White grape variety, a crossing of Madeleine Angevine × Gewürztraminer from *Alzey in the Rheinhessen, planted over 236
hectares. Bees and wasps can totally destroy the crop, but if the
grapes escape attack they produce a must of considerable weight,
some 15–20° Oechsle greater than that of Müller-Thurgau. Yield
and acidity are low and the wine has an extremely strong bouquet.
Siegerrebe is sometimes bottled as a single-vine wine of high
quality but is more often used by producers to add interest to
commercial blends.

Siegrist, Weingut Rhpf
An estate that has helped in the last decade to place the Süd Pfalz
among the best wine-producing districts of Germany. An area of 12
hectares is planted 26 percent Müller-Thurgau, 20 percent Riesling,
17 percent Spätburgunder, and Weissburgunder and Dornfelder.
Siegrist wines have flavour, depth, concentration, and body.
Barriques are used in a serious, well-considered manner. Annual
production is 6,250 cases, 90 percent *trocken*, 70 percent sold to
private customers.
Address: Südliche Weinstrasse, W-6741 Leinsweiler
Tel: 06345 1309

Silvaner, Grüner
Once the most widely grown vine in Germany, now found in 7,562
hectares (7·5 percent of the vineyard area), being steadily replaced
by Müller-Thurgau and other vines. The wine is neutral in flavour
and does not hide the character that comes from the soil and site. As
a dry wine from a restricted yield, Silvaner has much flavour and
style. It can make top-quality *Spätlese* wine, especially on the
*Rheinterrasse around *Nierstein and in Franken. Simple Silvaner
wine is often blended with Riesling, Morio-Muskat and Scheurebe.
Silvaner has many synonyms and is usually spelt Sylvaner outside
Germany – including Austria. It is often said that the search for

increased yield in the postwar period has resulted in poor clones being planted, and therefore the quality of wine has deteriorated, leading, in turn, to its current fall from favour.

Simmern'sches Rentamt, Freiherrlich Langwerth von
Rhg VDP
Important, 43-hectare estate, owned by the von Simmern family since 1464, with fine old cellars and administrative buildings. Holdings are at ★Erbach (★Marcobrunn), ★Hattenheim (including ★Nussbrunnen), ★Rauenthal (including ★Baiken) and ★Eltville, planted 93 percent Riesling. Well-structured, cask-matured, long-lived wines. Approximate annual production is 20,000 cases, 40 percent *trocken*, 30 percent exported.
Address: Kirchgasse, W-6228 Eltville
Tel: 06123 3007

Simon, Bert M-S-R VDP
Estate of 24 hectares, 90 percent steep vineyards. Sole owner of the Herrenberg, Würtzberg, Antoniusberg and König Johann Berg sites at ★Serrig and of the Staadter Maximiner Prälat at the

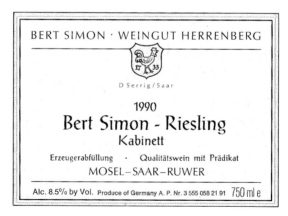

BERT SIMON · WEINGUT HERRENBERG

D Serrig / Saar

1990
Bert Simon - Riesling
Kabinett

Erzeugerabfüllung   ·   Qualitätswein mit Prädikat
MOSEL–SAAR–RUWER

Alc. 8.5% by Vol. Produce of Germany A. P. Nr. 3 555 058 21 91 750 ml e

upstream edge of the Saar vine-growing region. Further holdings are at ★Eitelsbach (Marienholz), ★Mertesdorf and ★Kasel (★Kehrnagel, ★Nies'chen and Herrenberg). Vines are 86 percent Riesling, seven percent Weissburgunder and six percent Müller-Thurgau.

The Weissburgunder in particular produces interesting *Kabinett* wine. Excellent wines, light and well structured. The use of site names is being reduced. Annual production is 16,670 cases, of which 50 percent is exported.
Address: Weingut Serriger Herrenberg, Romerstrasse, W-5512 Serrig
Tel: 06581 2208

Singen Baden w r
Here is the Olgaberg, the highest vineyard in Germany (up to 530 metres) on the Hohentwiel hill, solely owned by the Staatsweingut ★Meersburg. It is planted mainly with Müller-Thurgau and Spätburgunder. *Grosslage*: Sonnenufer.

Sittmann GmbH, Weingut–Weinkellerei Carl Rhh
The largest privately owned estate in the Rheinhessen, established in 1879, with some 86 hectares at ★Oppenheim (including ★Sackträger), ★Dienheim, ★Alsheim (including ★Frühmesse) and ★Nierstein. The estate produces a full range of typically regional wines; 75 percent *lieblich*. The Sittmanns are wine merchants and exporters as well as vineyard owners. Weingut Ernst Jungkenn is a subsidiary estate.
Address: Wormserstrasse 61, W-6504 Oppenheim
Tel: 06133 4909–0

Slaty
The soils of the Mosel-Saar-Ruwer, Ahr and Mittelrhein are varied, but many of their vineyards contain slate, much of which has been added by hand over the centuries. Its pervading greyness, both in the soil and on the house roofs, combined with the similarly coloured basalt from the nearby Eifel hills, can make the Mosel a sombre place when the sun does not shine. However, Riesling wines from slate sites have elegance and finesse, and a particular flavour that by association has become known as slaty.

Sobernheim Nahe w
Village upstream from ★Schlossböckelheim making good, lively Riesling and flowery Müller-Thurgau wines. *Grosslage*: Paradiesgarten.

Sommerach Franken w (r)
Village downstream from *Volkach with some 250 hectares of vineyards. Known for its asparagus and its strongly flavoured Müller-Thurgau and Silvaner wine. *Grosslage*: Kirchberg.

Sommerach eG, Winzerkeller Franken
Oldest cooperative cellar in Franken founded in 1901, with 170 hectares of vines, planted 45 percent Müller-Thurgau, 25 percent Silvaner. Of the wines produced 45 percent is dry and there is also a range of wines from low yields.
Address: Zum Katzenkopf 1, W-8711 Sommerach
Tel: 09381 3066

Sommerhausen Franken w (r)
Small village upstream from *Würzburg, with sweeping, modernized vineyards reaching down to the Main. Produces good-quality Müller-Thurgau and Silvaner wines. *Grosslage*: Ölspiel.

Sonnenberg, Weingut Rhh VDP
Mainly red-wine-producing estate founded in 1881, with ten hectares of vines in the long-established enclave of Spätburgunder around *Ingelheim, facing *Mittelheim and *Oestrich across the Rhein. The vines are 60 percent Spätburgunder, plus others including Portugieser. The soft wines are *trocken* and much admired in Germany.
Address: J Neus, Bahnhofstrasse 96, W-6507 Ingelheim
Tel: 06132 7003

Sonnenhof, Weingut Würt
Estate of 28 hectares northwest of *Stuttgart, with holdings at Gündelbach, Rosswag and elsewhere; 60 percent of production is of soft red wine from Trollinger, and the more powerful Spätburgunder and Limberger. Whites are mainly from Riesling. Some red and white wines are aged in *barrique*. *Trocken* wines make up 55 percent of production. A large list includes Limberger and Trollinger *Eisweine*. Sales are mainly in Germany.
Address: Bezner-Fischer, W-7143 Vaihingen-Gündelbach
Tel: 07042 21038

Sonnenuhr M-S-R w

Two *Einzellagen* of this name lie side by side above the Mosel. One forms part of the vineyards of ★Zeltingen-Rachtig, the other comes within the boundaries of ★Wehlen. Both are well situated, 100 percent steep, 100 percent Riesling and make top-quality wine. The better parts of the Wehlener Sonnenuhr in particular have a reputation for wines of great finesse and fruit, more gentle than those from neighbouring ★Bernkastel sites but with a wonderfully luscious flavour, that can reach the peak of winemaking on the river. *Grosslage*: ★Münzlay.

Growers in Zeltingen-Rachtig: Friedrich-Wilhelm-Gymnasium, Kesselstatt, Selbach-Oster, Vereinigte Hospitien, Weins-Prüm.

Growers in Wehlen: Christoffel, Heidemanns-Bergweiler, Lauerburg, Loosen, Pauly-Bergweiler, J J Prüm, S A Prüm, M F Richter, St-Nikolaus, Studert-Prüm, Vereinigte Hospitien, Wegeler-Deinhard, Weins-Prüm.

Sorte

Variety, species. (*See next entry and* Rebsorte.)

Sortencharakter

Character of the vine variety. The style of a wine from any one vineyard will change each year to a greater or lesser extent, depending on the vintage. Within these variations those qualities that originate in the soil and the variety of grape will normally remain more or less constant. If the character of the vine variety is pronounced, this is usually considered a good thing. With the richest wines of *Auslese* quality and upwards the vine character is sometimes replaced by that of noble rot (*Edelfäule*).

Sparkling Hock

Sparkling wine from the Rhein. In the 1840s as the German sparkling-wine industry was expanding, both ★Kupferberg and ★Deinhard sold sparkling wines with names the British could easily understand, among which were 'Sparkling Hock' and 'Sparkling Moselle'. Sparkling Hock as a description is now rare.

Sparkling wine

See Qualitätsschaumwein, Schaumwein, Sekt

Spätburgunder, Blauer

Red grape variety, more commonly known elsewhere as Pinot Noir. In Germany it needs a good site where its wine can reach over 13 percent of natural alcohol (without sugar being added). Blauer Spätburgunder usually has less tannin than a French Pinot Noir and non-serious versions with residual sugar are offered in Germany. However, the amount available of good, dry tannic Spätburgunder is increasing, with those from Baden being the cheapest. Of Germany's 5,003 hectares of Spätburgunder, 70 percent is in Baden. As a *Beerenauslese* from the Rheingau with a great amount of residual sugar, it is a unique and fascinating wine.

Spätlese

Late-picked. Grapes intended for a *Spätlese* wine cannot be picked earlier than seven days after the start of the main harvest of the vine variety in question. Often the *Spätlese* harvest of an early-ripening vine, such as Müller-Thurgau, will have been gathered before the main harvest of the late-ripening Riesling or Trollinger has begun. By delaying picking, the grapes develop more sugar. The difference in must weight between a *Spätlese* and a QbA varies depending on vine variety and region, but it can be as much as the equivalent of 4·4 percent alcohol (the figure in Württemberg). No sugar enrichment (*Anreicherung*) is allowed. Some of the best German *trocken* wines are *Spätlesen*.

Spiegelberg Rhh w (r)

Grosslage of more than 600 hectares covering some excellent individual sites on the ★Rheinterrasse at ★Nierstein, including ★Findling, ★Bildstock and ★Paterberg.

Spielberg Rhpf w

Good *Einzellage* on the outskirts of ★Bad Dürkheim making stylish, fruity Riesling wines. *Grosslage*: ★Hochmess. Growers: Bart, Bassermann-Jordan, Fitz-Ritter, Karst, K Schäfer.

Spindler, Weingut Eugen Rhpf

Estate of 13·5 hectares, with cellars and administrative buildings on the southern edge of ★Forst. Holdings are at ★Deidesheim (★Grainhübel, ★Leinhöhle, ★Kieselberg, ★Herrgottsacker),

*Ruppertsberg (including *Reiterpfad and *Linsenbusch) and Forst itself (*Pechstein, *Ungeheuer and notably *Jesuitengarten). Address: Weinstrasse 55, W-6701 Forst
Tel: 06326 338

Spritzig

Slightly sparkling. Term used to describe a wine that gives a gentle prickling sensation on the tongue produced by carbon dioxide. It can be found in Mosel-Saar-Ruwer wine of all qualities up to and including *Auslesen* and adds to their freshness and charm. If an ordinary wine from elsewhere is *spritzig* it may well be the result of carbon dioxide being used as a part of cellar technique, rather than through the natural gas formed in fermentation. In Germany, whereas white and rosé wines are sometimes expected to be *spritzig*, red wine should have no noticeable carbon dioxide.

Stahlig

Steely. Describes a wine in which the acidity is high and the flavour is very direct and clean. It is unlikely to be subtle and certainly not delicate. Wonderfully steely Riesling wines, especially at top-quality QbA and *Kabinett* levels from good estates, come from the Saar and from the river Nahe near *Traisen. Other wines, such as Weissburgunder, from the northern regions, can also be described as *stahlig* on occasions.

Stallmann–Hiestand, Weingut Rhh

A 17-hectare estate, partly on the famous *Rheinterrasse, planted 26 percent Riesling, 20 percent Silvaner, 12 percent Müller-Thurgau plus other varieties, including new crossings, to be replaced by traditional vines where possible. There is an unusually high proportion for the region of *trocken* wines (80 percent). They are serious, clean, and fresh and the prices reflect the current undervaluing of good Rheinhessen wine. Annual production is 10,000 cases of which five percent is exported.
Address: Eisgasse 15, W-6501 Uelversheim
Tel: 06249 8463

Stapf'sches Weingut, von Würt VDP

Eight-hectare estate with all its holdings in the large Erlenbacher

Kayberg *Einzellage*; 68 percent is on steep slopes. Of the wines produced 45 percent is *trocken*.

Address: Lerchenstrasse 1, W-7101 Erlenbach bei Heilbronn

Tel: 07132 2988

Steeg Mrh w

If Mittelrhein wines received the recognition the best of them deserve, Steeg, in a side valley of the Rhein gorge near ★Bacharach, would be well known. The steep Riesling sites yield steely, strongly flavoured wines, and have great potential for producing *halbtrocken* wine, cheaper than the equivalent Rheingau wine. Also excellent for *Sekt*. *Grosslage*: Schloss Stahleck.

Steffensberg M-S-R w

Einzellage in a steep side valley of the Mosel at ★Enkirch, producing firm, stylish Riesling wines. *Grosslage*: ★Schwarzlay. Growers include Immich-Batterieberg.

Steigerwald, Bereich w (r)

A district of about 1,000 hectares on the western slopes of the Steigerwald with the greatest concentration of top-quality Franken vineyards and estates outside ★Würzburg, centred on ★Castell and ★Iphöfen. Among a range of successful wines, including Rieslaner and Scheurebe, Silvaner does particularly well.

Steil Rhg r w

Grosslage of about 140 hectares at ★Assmannshausen, between ★Rüdesheim and ★Lorch, planted with Spätburgunder and Riesling. The true-to-type red Spätburgunder wines are much respected locally. Expensive when drunk abroad.

Steillagen

Steep sites. The *Flurbereinigung* authorities define a steep site as having an inclination greater than 50 percent. Although running costs of such vineyards can be greater than those of vineyards on the flat by as much as 200 percent, and the yield is always less, they do produce some of the best wines in Germany. To emphasize their origin, wines from steep sites may be referred to as *Steillagenweine* or *Bergweine* but the terms are not legally established.

Stein Franken w

Most famous *Einzellage* in Franken, at ★Würzburg. The steep slopes produce outstanding Riesling wines, powerful and with lasting flavour, as well as more gentle wines from Silvaner (*see also* Steinwein) and other varieties. *Grosslage*: Marienberg. Growers: Bürgerspital, Juliusspital, Würzburg Staatlicher Hofkeller.

Steinacker Rhpf w (r)

Large, mainly sloping *Einzellage* at ★Kallstadt, producing very good quality white wines from a variety of grapes and some less distinguished red wine from Portugieser. *Grosslage*: ★Kobnert. Growers: Bonnet, Winzergenossenschaft Kallstadt, Koehler-Ruprecht, J Pfleger, Schuster.

Steinberg Rhg w

Classified as an *Ortsteil*, the 32·1-hectare vineyard, near ★Kloster Eberbach, is enclosed by a high stone wall. Cistercian monks from Kloster Eberbach planted the first vines in the Steinberg in the 12th century. Today it is owned by the Staatsweingut ★Eltville. Vines are 95 percent Riesling and the wines have 'size', breeding and finesse. They are sold simply under the name Steinberger – no village name.

Steinkopf Hess Berg w

Top-quality *Einzellage* on sloping or steep terrain at ★Heppenheim, producing well-structured wines from Riesling and Ruländer. *Grosslage*: Schlossberg. Growers: Bergsträsser Gebiets-Winzer-genossenschaft, Staatsweingut Bergstrasse.

Steinmächer Rhg w

Grosslage of some 600 hectares almost in the suburbs of ★Wiesbaden. The best-known wine village in the *Grosslage* is ★Rauenthal. Standard, good-quality wines that benefit from bottle-age (especially those made from Riesling) are sold under the Steinmächer name.

Steinwein

For at least 250 years, wine in ★Bocksbeutel from ★Würzburg in Franken was often sold simply as 'Steinwein'. In this century the definition has become more precise, and since 1971 only wine from the *Stein *Einzellage* on the outskirts of Würzburg can be sold as Würzburger Stein.

Stetten Franken w
Village with steep *Muschelkalk* (fossiliferous limestone) vineyards high above the Main, with one *Einzellage* called Stein – not to be confused with the famous Würzburger *Stein. Good, full-flavoured Silvaner and Müller-Thurgau wines. *Grosslage*: Rosstal.

Stift
Religious foundation. A *Stift* must have religious connections whereas a *Stiftung* need not.

Stiftung
An endowed institution. Some of the finest wine-producing estates are endowed institutions, often with religious origins (such as the Stiftung Staatliches Friedrich-Wilhelm-Gymnasium in Trier). Many landowners hoped that by leaving their good farming land and their best vineyards to the church while in this world they would have an easier time in the next.

Stigler, Weingut Rudolf Baden VDP
Five-hectare estate famous in Germany for its wines from the *Winklerberg site at Ihringen, planted 35 percent Riesling, 21 percent Spätburgunder, 11 percent each Müller-Thurgau and Silvaner. The Rieslings from vines from the Mosel are most impressive, full and steely. Yields are low.
Address: Bachenstrasse 29, W-7817 Ihringen
Tel: 07668 297

Stillwein
Wine with little or no carbon dioxide, in contrast to *Perlwein* or *Schaumwein*, is classified as *Stillwein*.

Stoffig
Describes a full-bodied wine with much extract, such as a dry *Auslese* from Grauburgunder or Gewürztraminer.

Strausswirtschaft

'Bush Inn'. Those for whom vine growing is their principal occupation are allowed for a period totalling not more than four months each year to sell their wine, accompanied by simple food, on their own premises. This ancient practice is advertised by a bush (*Strauss*) hung outside wherever the wine is being offered. Theoretically a good wine will sell without this publicity, for 'a good wine needs no bush'. Also known as *Besenwirtschaft* (in Württemberg), where a *Besen* (broom) replaces the *Strauss*, as *Heckenwirtschaft* (*Hecke*, hedge) in parts of Franken, and as *Buschenschank* in Austria and the Süd Tirol. Other regional synonyms have included *Stubenwirtschaft, Kranzwirtschaft, Strohwirtschaft* and *Reifwirtschaft*.

Strohwein

'Straw wine', made for centuries from grapes that had been dried on straw to concentrate their juice and increase their sugar content. Its production has been illegal in Germany since 1971. In style *Strohwein* was similar to a *Beerenauslese* but even more of a rarity. *Strohwein* is still made outside Germany, and in particular in the Jura in France where it is known as *vin de paille*.

Strub, Weingut J & H A Rhh

Family-owned estate dating from 1864, with 18 hectares of holdings at ★Dienheim and ★Nierstein (★Hipping, ★Ölberg, ★Orbel, ★Paterberg, ★Findling, ★Pettenthal). Vines are 50 percent Riesling, Silvaner and Müller-Thurgau. A serious estate producing top-quality ★Rheinterrasse wine. Sixty percent is *lieblich*. Annual production is 8,300 cases, of which 35 percent is exported.
Address: Rheinstrasse 42, W-6505 Nierstein 1
Tel: 06133 5649

Stück

Wooden cask, twice as large as the more common *Halbstück*, used mainly for storage. *See* Fass.

Studert-Prüm, Stephan M-S-R VDP

Estate of five hectares, with holdings at ★Wehlen (including ★Sonnenuhr), ★Graach (★Himmelreich, ★Domprobst) and

★Bernkastel (★Graben) – all top-quality sites. Vines are 90 percent Riesling; 65 percent of the *Fuder*-matured wine is *lieblich* and 40 percent is exported. The estate awards stars to its bottlings to differentiate between what it feels are the various qualities of *Auslese* wines: two stars indicate fine *Auslese*, and three stars indicate finest *Auslese*. Annual production is 4,200 cases.
Address: Maximinhof, W-5550 Bernkastel-Wehlen
Tel: 06531 2487

Stumpf
Blunt or dull. Describes a wine that has aged too quickly and has lost its character and life.

Stuttgart Würt r w
Large industrial city and capital of the state of Baden-Württemberg, heavily damaged in World War II. Wooded hills and vineyards reach almost to the centre of the city, and Trollinger and sound Riesling wines are made. The Rotenberg *Einzellage* to the east of the city is a fine example of a modernized, reconstructed vineyard. Stuttgart is the site of the Intervitis viticultural and wine-related exhibition.

Süd Pfalz
Popular name for the Bereich ★Südliche Weinstrasse.

Südliche Bergstrasse/Kraichgau eG, Winzerkeller Baden
See Wiesloch eG, Winzerkeller

Südliche Weinstrasse, Bereich Rhpf w (r)
District covering the whole of the Rheinpfalz, known in the past for a high yield of undistinguished wine. The quality today is much better, and the best wines nowadays are comparable to those of the Bereich ★Mittelhaardt/Deutsche Weinstrasse.

Süffig
Tasty. Describes a light wine, probably not of very high quality, with balanced sweetness, pleasant to drink in large quantities. Just what a good glass of 'Hock' should be.

Sugaring
See Anreicherung

Süss
Sweet. EC description, applicable to a *Stillwein* containing more than 45 grams per litre of residual sugar. In the case of good, estate-bottled wines, only *Auslesen* and wines of a higher quality category are likely to be sweet.

Süssreserve
Sweet reserve: unfermented grape juice that is added to wine shortly before bottling to arrive at the required level of sweetness. Complicated regulations govern the quality and geographical origin of a *Süssreserve* but in principle both must be similar to that of the wine to which the *Süssreserve* is added. The use of *Süssreserve* has simplified the problems of bulk storage and has enabled sulphur dioxide levels to be reduced. It has also made it possible to supply medium-sweet wines at the low price for which the consumer asks – its use in fine wines is probably declining.

Sylvaner
See Silvaner, Grüner

Tafelwein
Table wine. This term has been precisely defined by EC regulations to describe the category below quality wine. It can only be produced from prescribed vines growing within the EC, and must reach certain analytical standards. ★*Deutscher Tafelwein* is subject to additional national legislation. It is now incorrect to use the description table wine as a synonym for 'dinner wine', or wine to accompany a meal. Some good producers sell their experimental or unusual wines (such as *barrique*-aged wines) as *Tafelweine*, to avoid their rejection by conservative ★Amtliche Prüfung authorities.

Tafelwein, Deutscher (DTW)
See Deutscher Tafelwein

Tannin
See Gerbstoff

Tartaric acid
See Weinsäure

Tasting
See Probe

Taunus
A range of hills, rising at its highest point to 880 metres, defining the northern limits of the Rheingau and protecting the region from the worst extremes of the weather.

TBA, TbA
See Trockenbeerenauslese

Tesch, Weingut Erbhof Nahe VDP
Estate established in 1723, technically advanced, committed to quality-wine production. The vines cover 27 hectares in ★Laubenheim, ★Dorsheim and ★Langenlonsheim, 75 percent of which is Riesling – a high proportion for the Nahe. A third of the wine is *trocken*, and all is stored in vat with minimum use of sulphur.
Address: An den Naheweisen, W-6536 Langenlonsheim
Tel: 06704 20404

Teufelskeller Franken w
Einzellage on the slopes at ★Randersacker overlooking the Main, planted mainly in Silvaner and Müller-Thurgau. Broad-flavoured wines. *Grosslage*: ★Ewig Leben. Growers: Bürgerspital, Gebhardt, Juliusspital, Winzergenossenschaft Randersacker, R Schmitt, Schmitt's Kinder, Würzburg Staatlicher Hofkeller.

Thanisch, Weingut Wwe Dr H M-S-R VDP
Until 1988 part of a larger estate; this section, known as Thanisch-Knabben, has 6·5 hectares at ★Bernkastel (★Doctor, ★Graben, ★Lay, ★Schlossberg), ★Graach (★Domprobst, ★Himmelreich), and ★Brauneberg (★Juffer-Sonnenuhr), planted 100 percent Riesling. High-quality wines. Annual production is 4,200 cases, 90 percent *lieblich*, 75 percent exported.
Address: Saarallee 31, W-5550 Bernkastel-Kues
Tel: 06531 2282

Thanisch, Weingut Wwe Dr H M-S-R

This, the Müller-Burggraef part of the Thanisch estate (*see previous entry*), has 7·5 hectares at ★Bernkastel (★Doctor and ★Graben), ★Brauneberger (★Juffer-Sonnenuhr), ★Graach (★Himmelreich), and ★Lieser. It also administers the holdings of Weingut ★Müller-Burggraef at ★Reil. The Thanisch-Müller-Burggraef estate is planted 95 percent Riesling; 80 percent of the wine made is *lieblich*, and no less than 80 percent is exported. Annual production is some 7,100 cases.
Address: W-5586 Reil
Tel: 06532 610

Thiergarten, Weingut M-S-R

See Nell, Georg-Fritz von

Thüngersheim eG, Winzergenossenschaft Franken

Highly successful cooperative cellar that produces award-winning wines. The 350 members own 250 hectares of vineyards on the river Main downstream from ★Würzburg. Annual production is 292,000 cases, including *Trockenbeerenauslesen*, individually produced from eight different vine varieties.
Address: Untere Hauptstrasse 1, W-8702 Thüngersheim
Tel: 09364 5009–0

Tillmanns Erben Weingut, H Rhg VDP

Estate with 15 hectares of holdings at ★Erbach (including ★Michelmark) and ★Kiedrich (★Sandgrub) administered by ★Schloss Reinhartshausen. Vines cultivated are 92 percent Riesling, eight percent Spätburgunder. The 500-year-old cask cellar provides a marvellous atmosphere for tastings. Annual production is 12,500 cases, 45 percent *trocken*.
Address: Hauptstrasse 41, W-6228 Eltville 2
Tel: 06123 4000

Tischwein

Literally, table wine. Not a legal definition but used to describe a wine, probably not of high quality, that would accompany food well. *See* Tafelwein.

Ton

Has two quite separate meanings: it is a type of clay and also a characteristic style or accent. Thus wines from cellars that always follow one individual type of cellar procedure may be said to have a *Betriebston*, a sort of signature tune associated with the *Betrieb* or 'works'. A *Kellerton* usually indicates a slightly dirty 'cellar flavour' in a wine.

Traben-Trabach M-S-R w

Health resort and tourist attraction divided by the river Mosel, surrounded by the game-filled woods of the Hunsrück and the Eifel, and since the 16th century a centre for the wine trade. A number of wine export houses that include the name Languth in their title are based in the town. Their names are better known internationally than the wines from the local vineyards, many of which, nevertheless, are very steep and planted 100 percent in Riesling. Among the best sites is the Trabener Würzgarten, producing full-bodied, fruity wines at a somewhat lower price than those from the nearby villages of ★Erden or ★Ürzig. *Grosslage*: ★Schwarzlay.

Traditionelle Rebsorten

Traditional vine varieties, or vine varieties that were growing in Germany before the *Neuzüchtungen* became popular in the 1960s. The good structure, unexaggerated flavour and aroma of their wines allows many to be successful when dry – in the modern German manner.

Traisen Nahe w (r)

Village close to ★Bad Münster am Stein-Ebernburg with top-quality Riesling sites, including the ★Bastei, by the Rotenfels cliff. The rhyolite rock is believed to give the wine its particular background flavour, which combined with a firm, lively Riesling acidity, is most impressive and positive. *Grosslage*: ★Burgweg.

Traminer, Roter

Red grape variety producing stylish, spicy white wine. Yield is low and the vine requires a good site. With the Gewürztraminer it is planted in 832 hectares, mainly in the Rheinpfalz and Baden. Given the right weather conditions, estate bottlers will produce small quantities of single-vine wine from Traminer, regarded very much as a 'speciality' by their customers. The Traminer seems to show unusually pronounced variations in character from one vineyard to another, making controlled improvement of the vine difficult on a national scale. A German Traminer wine does not have quite the pungency of a Traminer from Alsace. In the Bereich ★Ortenau the Traminer is known as Clevner. *See also* Gewürztraminer.

Transvasierverfahren
A little-used method for making sparkling wine, pioneered by the ★Kupferberg Sektkellerei in the 1950s. Wine which has gained its sparkle in bottle, is transferred under pressure to a vat, filtered and then bottled.

Trappenberg Rhpf w (r)
Grosslage of more than 1,600 hectares in the southern Rheinpfalz. A high proportion of Müller-Thurgau is grown on the level sites, as well as Silvaner, Morio-Muskat and a variety of other new crossings. Some Riesling is grown in vineyards near the old cathedral city of Speyer. Wines sold under the *Grosslage* name Trappenberg are unlikely to be distinguished, but will be sound and agreeable.

Traube
Grape or bunch of grapes. Most German grapes are white, some are red and others, such as Ruländer and Traminer are in-between. They are grown mainly for winemaking although varieties such as Gutedel, Portugieser, Müller-Thurgau, Huxelrebe, Bacchus and Ortega also serve as table grapes.

Traubenvollernter
Mechanical grape-harvesting machine, which gathers the crop from a hectare in two to three hours, thus saving the usual 250–300 man or woman hours and reducing costs per hectare considerably. Some 830 harvesting machines were available for use in the flat or less steep vineyards of the state of ★Rheinland-Pfalz in 1991.

Treppchen M–S–R w
Very much a steep Riesling *Einzellage* at ★Erden, recognized as one
of the best Mosel sites. Produces top-quality, stylish wines.
Grosslage: ★Schwarzlay. Growers: Bischöfliche Weingüter, Christ-
offel, Loosen, Mönchof, Nicolay (Pauly-Bergweiler), Weins-
Prüm, M F Richter.

Treppchen M–S–R w
Large, 250-hectare *Einzellage* at ★Piesport, on the right-hand bank
of the Mosel looking across the river and up to the famous
★Goldtröpfchen site. Vines are mainly Müller-Thurgau and
Riesling producing sound, good-quality wines, normally of no
very great distinction. *Grosslage*: ★Michelsberg.

Tresterwein
A rather unhealthy wine made by adding water to the pulp left
behind when the grapes have been pressed. It cannot be sold
commercially and is used mainly as *Haustrunk*.

Trier M–S–R w
The oldest city in West Germany, established before the birth of
Christ. In spite of considerable damage in World War II there are
many old buildings, including the second-century Roman
gateway, the Porta Nigra, and the cathedral, part of which dates
back to the fourth century. Trier has been involved with viticulture
for centuries and there are more than 370 hectares of vineyards
within the city boundaries. The *Einzellage* names are not widely
known outside Germany but the city is the base for a number of
important wine estates (including ★Bischöfliche Weingüter,
★Friedrich-Wilhelm-Gymnasium, ★Kesselstatt, ★Vereinigte Hospitien) with holdings in most of the best sites of the Mosel-Saar-
Ruwer. Trier is also the home of many wine-related institutions,
and the birthplace of Karl Marx. *Grosslage*: ★Römerlay.

Trier, Verwaltung der Staatlichen Weinbaudomänen M–S–R
Established in 1896, this 42-hectare estate is owned by the state of
★Rheinland-Pfalz, and planted with 83 percent Riesling. Like many
state cellars it operates as a testing station for new vine varieties and
viticultural methods. The fully modernized vineyards are

controlled from three *Domäne*, with holdings at ★Ockfen (★Bockstein), Avelsbach, between Trier and the river Ruwer, and at ★Trier itself. The wines from this estate are light in alcohol, wonderfully refreshing and often slightly *spritzig*. Approximate annual production is 33,300 cases.
Address: Deworastrasse 1, W-5500 Trier
Tel: 0651 48068

Trittenheim M-S-R w
Small village near ★Piesport, set in a great half-circle of vineyards, already known for its wine in the ninth century. Said to be the site of the first planting of Riesling on the Mosel in the 16th century. Today the vineyards lie on both banks of the river. Best known sites are ★Apotheke and ★Altärchen. *Grosslage*: ★Michelsberg.

Trocken
Dry. A wine may be called *trocken* if the residual sugar content is not greater than four grams per litre, or nine if the total acidity is less than the residual sugar content by no more than two grams per litre (for example: residual sugar eight grams per litre, total acidity not less than six grams per litre). The swing to producing *trocken* wines that began in the 1990s continues. *See* chart, page 29.

Exports are relatively small, but all enterprising wine lists now include German *trocken* wines. *Trocken* (EC definition for sparkling wine, 17–35 grams per litre of residual sugar) is the preferred style of many medium-price branded *Sekte* made in Germany.

Trockenbeerenauslese
An immensely rich wine with a minimum potential alcohol content of 21·5 percent (22·1 percent in certain districts of Baden), made from overripe grapes, usually heavily infected with *Botrytis cinerea* (*Edelfäule*). The most shrivelled and therefore the sweetest grapes are selected either at the moment of picking in the vineyard or in the press house. The must will not ferment easily and therefore, by law, the actual alcohol content need not be more than 5·5 percent, leaving the wine enormously sweet. However, the tendency since the mid-1980s has been to encourage the sweetest wines to ferment to a higher alcoholic level (say 12 percent) than in the past. Experiments have also been made in fermenting

Trockenbeerenauslesen to 16 percent alcohol or more and ageing them in *barrique*.

A *Trockenbeerenauslese* can only be harvested in fine vintages with good autumn weather. It is the ultimate in German winemaking and a high price has to be paid for it, often eight times greater than that for a 'simple' *Auslese*. Production costs are also high and the yield is usually minute. It is not a commercial proposition but an act of faith. *See* Hauptlese.

Trollinger, Blauer
Red grape variety, planted in 2,154 hectares – all but seven of which are in Württemberg, where its popularity as a symbol of regional identity remains well established. Trollinger ripens late, even later than Riesling, producing a light insubstantial wine, often vinified as *Schillerwein*. Yield is high (100–150 hectolitres per hectare), and in parts of Württemberg averaged 222 hectolitres per hectare in the large 1989 vintage.

Tuniberg, Bereich Baden w r
District, once part of a larger Bereich Kaisterstuhl-Tuniberg, delivering most of its grapes to the ★Badischer Winzerkeller.

Uelversheim Rhh w
Small village a few kilometres south of ★Oppenheim. Its distinguished wines would probably be better known abroad if its name was more easily spoken. *Grosslagen*: ★Krötenbrunnen and ★Güldenmorgen.

Uhlen M-S-R w
Steep Riesling *Einzellage* at ★Winningen and ★Kobern with some of the highest average must weights in the region. The powerful, elegant wines need bottle-age. *Grosslage*: ★Weinhex. Growers: Heddesdorff, Heymann-Löwenstein, Knebel, R Richter, Schleinitz.

Ungeheuer Rhpf w
Einzellage at ★Forst, south of ★Bad Dürkheim. All the vineyards at Forst are capable of producing excellent Riesling wines. Those from the Ungeheuer are powerful, full-flavoured and show earthy

regional characteristics. *Grosslage*: ★Mariengarten. Growers: Bassermann-Jordan, Buhl, Bürklin-Wolf, Winzerverein Deides-heim, Forster Winzerverein, Giessen, Kern, Mosbacher, Moss-bacher-Hof, Spindler, Wegeler-Deinhard, J L Wolf.

Ungstein Rhpf w

Village adjacent to ★Bad Dürkheim producing excellent, rich and fruity wine. The Scheureben from Weingut ★Pfeffingen are particularly good. *Grosslagen*: ★Honigsäckel, ★Hochmess and ★Kobnert.

Untergebiet

Subdistrict. *Deutscher Tafelwein* (DTW) may take its name from the four *Weinbaugebiete* or their eight subdistricts (*see* chart, pages 12–13). In some instances the *Untergebiet* name is better known than that of the *Weinbaugebiet*, so that whereas *deutscher Tafelwein* Rhein-Mosel is not often met, DTW Rhein and DTW Mosel are relatively common.

Urban

Old Württemberg red vine variety, related to Trollinger, growing in 1·3 hectares at Weingut Graf ★Adelmann. Three different holy men called Urban have been regarded as patrons of wine.

Ürzig M-S-R w

Village of half-timbered houses and old wine cellars. It lies at the foot of a sweep of steep vineyard on the opposite bank of the Mosel to ★Erden, a few kilometres upstream from ★Traben-Trabach. The Ürziger ★Würzgarten is one of the best-known *Einzellagen* of the Bereich ★Bernkastel. *Grosslage*: ★Schwarzlay.

Valckenberg GmbH, P J Rhh

A 200-year-old firm of wine merchants and vineyard owners, with the largest holding in the ★Liebfrauenstift-Kirchenstück *Einzellage*. As merchants their best-known brand is 'Madonna' Liebfraumilch, which is exported all over the world.
Address: Valckenbergstrasse und Weckerlingplatz, W-6520 Worms
Tel: 06241 6871

Varnhalt Baden w (r)
Village in the Bereich ★Ortenau close to Baden-Baden, allowed to
sell its quality wine in the *Bocksbeutel*. High proportion of Riesling
on steep sites with soils from flavour-imparting porphyritic rock.
Grosslage: Schloss Rodeck.

VDP
See Verband Deutscher Prädikats- und Qualitätsweingüter eV

Veldenz M-S-R w
Village in a pretty side valley of the Mosel near ★Bernkastel,
looking across the river to the ★Brauneberg vineyards. Produces
pleasant, stylish Riesling wines. *Grosslage*: ★Kurfürstlay.

Verband Deutscher Prädikats- und Qualitätsweingüter eV
An association currently of some 165 estates, originating in 1910
and now known generally as the 'VDP'. From 1991 the rules of the
association have been further tightened, so that the best bottles of
German wine are increasingly likely to bear the association's
spread-eagle symbol. Annual sales of VDP wine are 2·3 million
cases or about two percent of an average German harvest.

Vereinigte Hospitien, Güterverwaltung M-S-R VDP
Ancient charitable organization in ★Trier endowed over the
centuries with vineyards, forestry and farming land. There are 55
hectares of vineyards including sole ownership of four sites:
★Schloss Saarfelser Schlossberg at ★Serrig, ★Hölle at ★Wiltingen on
the Saar, Schubertslay at ★Piesport, and Augenscheiner at ★Trier on
the Mosel. The estate also has holdings on other sites at Serrig,
Wiltingen (including ★Braunfels, ★Braune Kupp), ★Kanzem
(★Altenberg), Trier, Piesport (★Goldtröpfchen), ★Graach, ★Zelt-
ingen-Rachtig, ★Bernkastel, ★Wehlen and in the ★Scharzhofberg.
Vines are 91 percent Riesling, four percent Müller-Thurgau, five
percent Kerner. Maturation is in oak and care is taken to allow the
wines to show the character of the vine variety and site. The
Vereinigte Hospitien maintains a friendly contact with its opposite
number in Beaune, the 'Hôtel Dieu'.
Address: Krahnenufer 19, W-5500 Trier
Tel: 0651 468210

Vereinigte Winzergenossenschaft Hallgarten/Rhg eG Rhg
See Hallgarten/Rhg eG, Vereinigte Winzergenossenschaft

Vereinigte Weingüter, J Dötsch-H Haupt M-S-R
High-quality (9·6-hectare) estate at *Kobern, planted 82 percent Riesling and 18 percent Spätburgunder. Owner Franz Dötsch, president of the important *Erzeugergemeinschaft* *Deutsches Eck, restricts yields to 50 hectolitres per hectare, which results in concentrated, flavoury wines. Annual production is 4,600 cases; 74 percent is *trocken*.
Address: Lenningstrasse 38, W-5401 Kobern-Gondorf
Tel: 02607 383

Verschlossen
Closed up. Until they have sufficiently matured, many good wines can taste 'closed up' and do not show their true quality for a year or more. Generally speaking, the best wines need the greatest bottle-age.

Verschnitt
A blend of two or more wines or musts, that should normally be better in quality than the individual parts from which the blend has been made. At its simplest, a soft Müller-Thurgau, for example, may be blended with a Riesling high in acidity to produce a better-balanced wine with an enhanced commercial value. The laws that govern blending are complex and include geographical origin, vine variety, vintage and quality category.

   Blending plays a vital role in the making of champagne, sherry, port and often in red-wine production. In Germany its traditional purpose is to provide adequate quantities of one style of medium-priced or cheap wine to meet the expectations of the consumer. In the 1990s blends of high-quality wine are also being offered, such as Cuvée Victor of Schlossgut *Diel.

Versteigerung
Auction. A number of wine auctions are held in spring and autumn every year in different parts of the vine-growing area. It is usual for a group of growers to put up parcels of wine for sale in lots of not more than about 600 bottles, for which all bidding must be made

through brokers. Before each lot is auctioned a tasting sample is poured for all those attending the auction. Among the most famous groups who auction their wines are the *Grosser Ring*, based at Trier, and the Messe & Versteigerungsring of *Kloster Eberbach.

Versuchsanstalt

Experimental institute. The Federal Republic and its states own a number of viticultural institutes carrying out research and experimental work, for example the Staatsweingut der Landes-Lehr-und Versuchsanstalt Oppenheim, owned by the federal state of Rheinland-Pfalz. *See also* Lehranstalt.

Verwalter, Verwaltung

Verwaltung, meaning administration, appears in titles of certain estates, such as the Verwaltung der Staatsweingüter Eltville. (The Schloss Reinhartshausen estate, on the other hand, actually uses the word 'Administration' in its title.) The manager of an estate is known as the *Verwalter*.

Vier Jahreszeiten-Kloster Limburg eG, Winzergenossenschaft Rhpf

Excellent cooperative cellar founded in 1900. Its 242 members own 330 hectares of holdings in the immediate vicinity of *Bad Dürkheim. Vines are Riesling (38 percent), Müller-Thurgau (15 percent) and Portugieser, with some Traminer, Muskateller and Spätburgunder. Some wines are matured in *barrique*; 20 percent only is *trocken*.

Address: Limburgerstrasse 8, W-6702 Bad Dürkheim
Tel: 06322 8107

Villa Sachsen, Weingut Rhh VDP

An estate of 23 hectares. All the holdings are at *Bingen, including 12 hectares in the well-known *Scharlachberg site. Vines are 55 percent Riesling, eight percent Müller-Thurgau, eight percent Kerner. The annual production of 13,300 cases is carefully vinified, yielding fresh, elegant wines, of which 20 percent is exported and 65 percent is *trocken*, with some *barrique*-aged *Tafelweine*.

Address: Mainzerstrasse 184, W-6530 Bingen
Tel: 07621 13001

Vintage
See Jahrgang

Volkach Franken w (r)
Small historic town 25 kilometres east of *Würzburg, making wine from one large 150-hectare *Einzellage*, the Ratsherr. The principal vine varieties grown here are Silvaner and Müller-Thurgau. *Grosslage*: Kirchberg.

Vollernter
See Traubenvollernter

Volxem, Weingut Bernd van M-S-R VDP
Family-owned Saar estate dating from 1866, with nine hectares at *Wiltingen (including *Braunfels, *Schlangengraben, *Gottesfuss and Schlossberg), *Oberemmel (Rosenberg) and part of the famous *Scharzhofberg. Vines are principally Riesling (80 percent) and Weissburgunder (15 percent); some are over 100 years old. The style of the wines stresses acidity and fruitiness. Many of the wines are *spritzig*; 50 percent is *trocken*. Annual production is 6,700 cases, 30 percent exported.
Address: Dehenstrasse 2, W-5516 Wiltingen
Tel: 06501 16510

Vorlese
The picking of grapes in advance of the main harvest; a practice that may be allowed as a result of poor weather conditions. The aim will be to rescue a damaged crop or to eliminate unsound grapes (which can include those enriched by *Edelfäule*) and thereby improve the standard of the rest of the harvest.

Vulkanfelsen Baden r w
Grosslage covering much of *Kaiserstuhl, the district in Baden with the warmest climate in Germany, well known for its red and white wines from Spätburgunder and Ruländer. Where the soil is volcanic, the white wines have a stronger flavour.

Wachenheim Rhpf w (r)
Village just south of *Bad Dürkheim, with some of the best

Einzellagen of the Bereich ★Mittelhaardt/Deutsche Weinstrasse. A top-quality, old-style Wachenheimer is fine, rich, fat and full-bodied, or slimmer and more acidic in the currently preferred way. Riesling and other vine varieties are grown. *Grosslagen*: ★Schenken-böhl, ★Schnepfenflug an der Weinstrasse, ★Mariengarten.

Wachtenburg-Luginsland eG, Winzergenossenschaft Rhpf
Cooperative cellar supplied by 313 hectares at Gönnheim and ★Wachenheim, including part of ★Gerümpel. As usual in the best part of the Bereich ★Mittelhaardt/Deutsche Weinstrasse, the proportion of Riesling is quite high for the Rheinpfalz. Portugieser is the next most widely grown vine.
Address: W-6706 Wachenheim
Tel: 06322 8101

Wagner, Weingut-Weinhaus Mrh
A 6·1-hectare estate set in the idyllic and secluded Mühlental valley, five minutes' drive from the centre of ★Koblenz. The very steep vineyards are planted 60 percent in Riesling, ten percent Müller-Thurgau, five percent Spätburgunder. The estate is a member of the *Erzeugergemeinschaft* ★Deutsches Eck and sells most of its annual production of approximately 6,200 cases through its wine bar and wine garden. *Lieblich* wine makes up 65 percent of production and 15 percent is *trocken*.
Address: Mühlental 23, W-5400 Koblenz-Ehrenbreitstein
Tel: 0261 73614

Waldrach M-S-R w
Village on the Ruwer upstream from ★Kasel, surrounded by hills. Its vineyards, planted with a high proportion of Riesling, include no absolutely top-flight sites but produce elegant, fresh wines that can step right out of their class in good years. *Grosslage*: ★Römerlay.

Waldulm Baden r (w)
A village, well known in Germany, which makes its living from steep vineyards of Spätburgunder and from ★Schwarzwald fruit brandies. *Grosslage*: Schloss Rodeck.

Wallhausen Nahe w

Village with one of the largest areas under vine, 400 hectares, part of it on unsuitable land. The best wines from the *Salm-Dalberg'sches estate are likely to become better known in the 1990s. *Grosslage*: Pfarrgarten.

Walluf Rhg w (r)

Village near *Wiesbaden, split into Ober- and Niederwalluf by the little river Walluf. Makes Riesling wine that is typical of the region and seldom found elsewhere, plus fine Spätburgunder on Weingut J B *Becker. *Grosslage*: *Steinmächer.

Walporzheim Ahr r (w)

Small village, much visited by tourists, producing light, red wine from Spätburgunder that can usually only be sampled locally. *Grosslage*: Klosterberg.

Walthari

Process of winemaking, particularly without the use of sulphur dioxide, developed by Werner Walter of *Edenkoben.

Wasseros Rhg w

Sloping *Einzellage* at *Kiedrich, sometimes showing that average-quality Rheingau vineyards can be as good as the best elsewhere. Planted 100 percent Riesling. *Grosslage*: *Heiligenstock. Owners: Groenesteyn, Weil.

Wawern M-S-R w

Small Saar village overlooked by its hill, the Herrenberg, from which almost the whole length of the Saar vineyard area can be seen. (The Wawerner Herrenberger *Einzellage* is solely owned by Weingüter Dr *Fischer.) A high proportion of Riesling on steep sites guarantees outstanding wines in good years. If they lack the elegance and breeding of a fine wine from the neighbouring *Ayl, they generally make up for it by their sheer 'zip' and life. *Grosslage*: *Scharzberg.

Wegeler-Deinhard, Gutsverwaltung Bernkastel, M-S-R

Estate of 31 hectares dating from 1900 and owned by *Deinhard &

Co in Koblenz, with holdings in ★Kasel (including ★Nies'chen, ★Kehrnagel, ★Hitzlay), ★Graach (★Himmelreich, ★Domprobst), ★Wehlen (★Sonnenuhr), ★Bernkastel (★Doctor, ★Graben, ★Bratenhöfchen), ★Kesten and ★Lieser. Vines are 97 percent Riesling, grown mainly on steep or very steep (greater than 60 percent incline) sites. The grapes are pressed in Bernkastel-Kues and the must is vinified in Koblenz. The aim is for fresh, balanced wines, showing the true character of the vine variety, with restrained amounts of residual sugar. Deinhard has an important holding in the Doctor, probably the finest site on the Mosel. Site names are used for the best wines only. Annual production is 21,700 cases, 70 percent *trocken*, sold 60 percent to hotels and restaurants. No wine is sold to private customers.
Address: Martertal 2, W-5550 Bernkastel-Kues
Tel: 06531 2493

Wegeler-Deinhard, Gutsverwaltung Deidesheim,
Rhpf VDP
Estate acquired by ★Deinhard & Co, Koblenz in 1973, with 19 hectares in ★Forst (★Ungeheuer), ★Deidesheim (★Herrgottsacker) and ★Ruppertsberg (★Linsenbusch). Vines are 91 percent Riesling, eight percent Müller-Thurgau. The *trocken* wines from the Ungeheuer site are powerful in flavour. Riesling style is well to the fore. There are no direct sales to the consumer.
Address: Weinstrasse 10, W-6705 Deidesheim
Tel: 06326 221

Wegeler-Deinhard, Gutsverwaltung Oestrich
Rhg Charta VDP
Important Rheingau estate. The 56 hectares, planted 98 percent Riesling, are in villages such as ★Rüdesheim, ★Geisenheim, ★Johannisberg, ★Oestrich and ★Winkel. Under a new marketing policy only the best wines bear a site name. Dry wines make up 76 percent of production – 38,300 cases annually – many of which are sold to better-quality restaurants in Germany, where the estate has gained a high reputation.
Address: Friedensplatz 9, W-6227 Oestrich-Winkel
Tel: 06723 7031

RHEINGAU

ESTATE BOTTLED

Wegeler-Deinhard
Riesling

CHARTA

1990 KABINETT

Qualitätswein mit Prädikat · L/A. P. Nr. 2902403291
Erzeugerabfüllung Gutsverwaltung Geheimrat Wegeler-Deinhard
Oestrich · Germany

750 ml e   10 % vol

VIN BLANC RIESLING·WHITE RIESLING WINE·PRODUIT D'ALLEMAGNE·PRODUCT OF
GERMANY EXPORTE PAR/SHIPPED BY DEINHARD & CO.,WEINEXPORT·D-5400 KOBLENZ

Wehlen M-S-R w
Pleasant village, backed by a hillside dotted with fruit trees, facing
its most important sites across the Mosel. All are a little
overshadowed by the worldwide reputation of the Wehlener
★Sonnenuhr site that forms part of the continuous sweep of
vineyards from ★Bernkastel to ★Zeltingen-Rachtig. *Grosslage*:
★Münzlay.

Wehrheim, Weingut Eugen Rhh
Eleven-hectare estate owned by the Wehrheim family, involved in
vine growing since 1693. Holdings are all at ★Nierstein in
★Findling, ★Bildstock, ★Paterberg, ★Orbel and ★Pettenthal, and
planted 44 percent Riesling, 23 percent Silvaner, 12 percent Müller-
Thurgau. The estate produces long-lasting, well-differentiated

wines of character, which win many awards. Annual production is 6,700 cases, 70 percent *lieblich*, ten percent exported.
Address: Mühlgasse 30, W-6505 Nierstein
Tel: 06133 58125

Weich
Soft to the point of flabbiness.

Weil, Weingut Dr R Rhg Charta VDP
Probably the best-known ★Kiedrich estate, established in 1867, with 35 hectares of holdings planted 96 percent Riesling. The holdings include ★Sandgrub, ★Wasseros and ★Gräfenberg sites, although their names are now used for wines of *Auslese* quality and upwards only. Yields are restricted, and the aim is to produce wines to accompany food. Annual production is 20,800 cases, 50 percent *trocken*, 30 percent *halbtrocken*.
Address: Mühlberg 5, W-6229 Kiedrich
Tel: 06123 2308

Weiler, Weingut Heinrich Mrh
Estate of 6·5 hectares owned by a family involved in vine growing since 1607. Holdings are on steep, slaty sites at ★Oberwesel, Engelhöll and Kaub, on either side of the Rhein, and include sole ownership of the 1·1-hectare Kauber Rosstein site. Vines are 70 percent Riesling, 20 percent Müller-Thurgau, producing balanced, slightly earthy wine.
Address: Mainzerstrasse 2–3, W-6532 Oberwesel
Tel: 06744 323

Weinbau
Vine growing. *See* pages 20–23.

Weinbaudomäne
See Domäne

Weinbaugebiet
The area from which a table wine is drawn. It is subdivided into *Untergebiete* and *Gebiete für Landwein* (areas for country wine). There are no separate areas for making table wine and quality wine,

as in France, and the name chosen to describe the wine will depend mainly on its quality and the marketing policy of the bottler. *See also* pages 12–13.

Weinbauingenieur
A graduate in viticulture and cellar technique. In Germany the degree course is currently available at the viticultural institute at ★Geisenheim only.

Weinberg
Vineyard.

Weinbrand
Brandy made from wine. Much sound brandy is produced in Germany, usually from imported wine, fortified up to 20 percent alcohol. It is unfortunately often served in restaurants and cafés in small glasses more suited to a mini-cocktail than to the appreciation of brandy. Producers such as Asbach, Dujardin and Chantré are household names in Germany.

Weinbruderschaften
Wine brotherhoods. Societies whose main aim is to develop and encourage interest in wine in a spirit of altruism. Wine brotherhoods are found all over Germany and not solely in the wine-producing regions.

Weinessig
Wine vinegar, which in Germany may contain a certain amount of vinegar of non-vinous origin.

Weingarten
Term used in Württemberg for 'vineyard' – in other regions the term *Weinberg* is usually used. There are also two wine-producing villages, in Baden and the Rheinpfalz, called Weingarten.

Weingärtnergenossenschaft
Name used in Württemberg for a *Winzergenossenschaft*.

Weingrosskellerei

Wholesale cellar that buys must and wine, much of it in bulk, from all over the world and supplies the wine trade, hotels and restaurants in Germany and abroad.

Weingut

Wine-producing estate. A term that can only appear on a wine label if the wine and any *Süssreserve* have been made exclusively from grapes grown on the estate mentioned.

Weinhex M-S-R w

Grosslage of about 500 hectares on the Mosel upstream from *Koblenz. Many of the individual sites are immensely steep and planted 100 percent in Riesling. The wines are steely and somewhat earthy compared to those from the well-known sites of the *Mittelmosel. In this respect they resemble those of the neighbouring Mittelrhein.

Weinkellerei

Commercial wine cellar that buys grapes, must or wine but does not necessarily own vineyards. Often used in the form *Weingut-Weinkellerei*. This indicates that the company named owns vineyards from which it makes its own wine and also buys from other growers or merchants – a practice more common in Alsace.

Weinlehrpfad

'Instructional wine path' through the vineyards, especially in Baden but also at Schweigen and *Edenkoben in the Rheinpfalz, *Würzburg in Franken, *Winningen and *Reil on the Mosel and elsewhere. Notices alongside the paths give details about the sites, vine varieties and other relevant information. Such paths make it possible to combine study with a little exercise and often include a wine bar en route, offering a range of local wines.

Weinprobe

Wine tasting. *See* pages 35–36.

Weinsäure

Tartaric or 'wine acid', the acid that gives wine its backbone and grip. Unfortunately it can also appear in bottled wine as one of the causes of a white crystalline deposit (*Weinstein*) that ideally should have been discarded while the wine was still in bulk. The deposit is harmless, natural, falls quickly to the lowest part of the bottle and is not evidence of a sickness, but its appearance in white wine often worries the consumer. (In red wine it is usually accepted as a natural result of ageing.) The likelihood of the formation of a 'tartrate deposit', as it is commonly called, cannot always be both satisfactorily and totally eliminated, but objections to it are understandable if misplaced.

Weinsberg Würt w r
Town seven kilometres east of ★Heilbronn, home of the important state viticultural institute (*see next entry*) where the Kerner vine was developed. Riesling and Trollinger produce wines typical of the region. *Grosslagen*: Staufenberg and Salzberg.

Weinsberg, Staatliche Lehr- und Versuchsanstalt für Wein & Obstbau Würt VDP
Oldest viticultural institute in Germany, established by King Charles of ★Württemberg in 1868 to improve the economic position of viticulture. A large variety of vines is grown by the institute for experimental and also commercial purposes. (Kerner, Dornfelder and Helfensteiner were developed at Weinsberg.) Forty-five hectares of holdings are all in the northern part of Württemberg near ★Heilbronn.

Although the institute is the largest *Weingut* in Württemberg, its major contribution lies in the skill of the students it trains and the benefits that result from its experimental work. Annual production is 29,200 cases, of which 90 percent is *trocken* – a high percentage for Württemberg.

Address: Traubenplatz 5, W-7102 Weinsberg
Tel: 07134 5040

Weinschorle
A mixture of wine and mineral water, making a pleasant summer drink when served well chilled.

Weinsiegel
See Siegel

Weins–Prüm (Selbach), Weingut Dr M–S–R VDP
Four-hectare estate with small holdings at famous sites including Wehlener ★Sonnenuhr, Graacher ★Domprobst and ★Himmelreich, Ürziger ★Würzgarten, Erdener ★Treppchen and ★Prälat, and on the Ruwer at ★Waldrach, planted with 100 percent Riesling. Annual production is 4,000 cases of fine, crisp, cask-matured wine; 60 percent is *lieblich* and 60 percent exported.
Address: Uferallee 20, W-5550 Bernkastel-Wehlen
Tel: 06531 2270

Weinstein
See Weinsäure

Weinstrasse
Wine road, often met in France as *route du vin*. There are several *Weinstrassen* that follow a well-signposted, if rambling, course through the vineyards. The oldest (established in 1935) and best known is the Deutsche Weinstrasse which runs 80 kilometres through the Rheinpfalz and gives its name to the Bereich ★Mittelhaardt/Deutsche Weinstrasse.

Weissburgunder
White grape variety, also known as Weisser Burgunder, and more widely outside Germany as Pinot Blanc. It is said to be the result of a mutation of Ruländer. There are 1,009 hectares, mainly in Baden and Rheinpfalz, but also in the northern regions of Sachsen, Ahr and Mosel-Saar-Ruwer on a smaller scale. The dry wine is crisp and attractive and the heavier versions age well in *barrique*. A vine with good prospects in Germany.

Weisser Elbling
See Elbling, Weisser

Weisser Gutedel
See Gutedel, Weisser

Weisser Riesling

See Riesling, Weisser

Weissherbst

Rosé QbA and QmP produced, with their *Süssreserve*, from a single grape variety in the regions of Ahr, Baden, Franken, Rheingau, Rheinhessen, Rheinpfalz and Württemberg. Originally *Weissherbst* was made from red grapes that had lost colour through *Botrytis cinerea* (*Edelfäule*). In Baden, Spätburgunder Weissherbst is very popular for its fresh, clean, fruity flavour and low tannin content.

Werner'sches Weingut, Domdechant Rhg VDP

Award-winning family estate established in 1780, now into its seventh generation. The 12 hectares of holdings at *Hochheim include *Domdechaney, *Kirchenstück and *Hölle, and are planted 98 percent Riesling, two percent Spätburgunder. Maturation in cask in the vaulted cellar reveals a traditional approach to winemaking, balanced with sensible use of modern techniques. The result is elegant, fruity wine. Even in poor vintages the classy style remains. Annual production is 7,500 cases; 40 percent is *trocken* and 40 percent is exported.
Address: Rathausstrasse 30, W-6203 Hochheim
Tel: 06146 2008

Westhofen Rhh w (r)

Vine-growing village in the Bereich *Wonnegau with a reputation for good-quality wines. Not widely known outside Germany. The home of Fritz Huxel, a local grower after whom the Huxelrebe was named. *Grosslage*: Bergkloster.

Wiesbaden Rhg w

Capital of the state of Hessen, at the eastern end of the Rheingau; an elegant and modern business city, and the home of the sparkling-wine producers *Henkell & Söhnlein. In a region of much fine wine, the Wiesbaden wines from its only *Einzellage* (the Neroberg) are not well known.

Wiesloch eG, Winzerkeller Baden

A central cellar for 21 cooperatives covering 1,260 hectares – over

half of the Bereich ★Südliche Bergstrasse/Kraichgau. Vines are 35 percent Müller-Thurgau, 25 percent Riesling, 12 percent Weissburgunder. Annual production is 500,000 cases (35 percent *trocken*), sold exclusively in Germany. A top-quality series is named after the 19th-century vineyard expert and writer, Johann Philipp Bronner. Address: Bögnerweg 3, W-6908 Wiesloch
Tel: 06222 4331

Wilhelmshof, Weingut Rhpf
Ten-hectare estate, planted 30 percent Riesling, Müller-Thurgau, Spätburgunder and Weissburgunder. Eighty percent of the wine is *trocken*. They are sold primarily under the name of the vine variety and quality category – site names are not so prominent. Good, interesting wines in a village offering excellent value for money. Twenty percent of the harvest is made into *Sekt*. Annual production is 5,800 cases.
Address: Queichstrasse 1, W-6741 Siebeldingen
Tel: 06345 1817

Wiltingen M-S-R w
Well-known Saar wine village, much damaged in the past by feuds between Luxembourg and the archbishops of nearby ★Trier. A high proportion of Riesling is grown at sites on both sides of the river, producing wine of a quality and price similar to that of the best ★Mittelmosel villages such as ★Bernkastel and ★Brauneberg. *Grosslage*: ★Scharzberg.

Wincheringen M-S-R w
Village in the Bereich ★Obermosel, becoming better known
outside Germany through the sales of its Elbling wine by
★Moselland eG. *Grosslage*: Gipfel.

Wine festivals
See Visiting the Vineyards, pages 35–36.

Wine museums
See Visiting the Vineyards, pages 35–36.

Wingert
Rather a rustic word for 'vineyard', found in a number of site
names, such as Ürziger Goldwingert, Wachenheimer Königs-
wingert, Piesporter Kreuzwingert.

Winkel Rhg w (r)
Small village, close to the Rhein, known for Riesling wines of
finesse, the best of which in a good vintage will develop over many
years in bottle. The straight Riesling flavour is powerful without
pronounced overtones from the soil. Wines from most of the
leading, and many lesser-known, estates can be enjoyed in the
Graues Haus restaurant (the oldest stone house in Germany) owned
by ★Schloss Vollrads. *Grosslagen*: ★Honigberg and ★Erntebringer.

Winklerberg Baden w r
Einzellage at Ihringen. One of the warmest sites in Germany,
enlarged threefold in 1971 to its present 150 hectares. The varied soil
is planted in Spätburgunder, Ruländer, Riesling, Traminer, Muskateller and other varieties. *Grosslage*: ★Vulkanfelsen. Growers:
Winzergenossenschaft Ihringen, Gebr Müller, Stigler.

Winningen M-S-R w
Attractive riverside wine village, almost in the suburbs of
★Koblenz, much visited by tourists from Köln and the Ruhr
district, and the scene of Germany's oldest wine festival. The
vineyards are excessively steep and planted mainly in Riesling. The
steely wines have gained in reputation in recent years. The quality
of the best is outstanding. *Grosslage*: ★Weinhex.

Wintrich M-S-R w

Typical Mosel village, set back from the right-hand bank of the river upstream from *Brauneberg. Some sites are planted 100 percent Riesling; others contain much Müller-Thurgau. Good wines, though not generally felt to be among the finest of the river. *Grosslage*: *Kurfürstlay.

Winzenheim Nahe w

A part of *Bad Kreuznach. Its best-known *Einzellage*, Rosenheck, produces excellent long-lasting Riesling wines from vineyards on steep slopes. *Grosslage*: *Kronenberg.

Winzergenossenschaft

Cooperative cellar. The first cooperative cellar in Germany was established in the Ahr valley in 1868 to improve the low income of its members. Today the aim remains similar, and the contribution made by the cooperatives to the economics of vine growing can hardly be overestimated. More than 75 percent of the growers in Germany (approximately 70,000) deliver their grapes to cooperative cellars, from about 39 percent of the total viticultural area. Eighty percent of the wine is sold in bottle; the rest is taken in bulk by the wine trade.

Although cooperatives can sell the wine from their members' grapes as producer-bottled (*Erzeugerabfüllung*), they are only directly involved in the winemaking and selling – not in the vine growing. They have most support where growers' holdings are very small (for example, Baden-Württemberg) but cooperatives in the Mosel-Saar-Ruwer, Rheinhessen and Rheinpfalz have been the most active in the export markets.

The most elegant German wines come from the well-known private or state-owned estates in the northern regions, but wines from the best cooperatives of the Rheinpfalz and the village cooperatives of Baden can be almost as good, in a different, more alcoholic way. *See also* Zentralkellerei.

Winzersekt

Term describing a quality sparkling wine from a single German *Anbaugebiet*, the growing and harvesting of the grapes and the vinification and production of the sparkling wine having taken place in the same establishment. *Erzeugergemeinschaften* may also produce *Winzersekt* from their members' must or wine. A small but rapidly growing part of the German *Sekt* industry.

Winzersekt GmbH, Erzeugergemeinschaft Rhh

An *Erzeugergemeinschaft* making *Sekt* bA, 95 percent bottle-fermented (*see* Flaschengärung), from Rheinhessen, Nahe and Rheingau base wines. Annual production is the equivalent of some 2·2 million bottles, of which 60 percent is sold under the customers' label.
Address: Michel-Mort-Strasse 3, W-6555 Sprendlingen
Tel: 06701 1686

Winzerverein, Winzervereinigung

Alternative names for *Winzergenossenschaften* (cooperative cellars).

Wirsching, Weingut Hans Franken VDP

Great estate established by the Wirsching family in 1630, with 56 hectares mainly at *Iphofen (including *Julius-Echter-Berg, *Kalb). Vines include the traditional Silvaner, Müller-Thurgau, Riesling, and Scheurebe. The cellars date from the 17th century, but in 1970 a modern press house and machinery park were built outside Iphofen. The wines are exciting, concentrated (low yields) and full of flavour. Seventy percent is *fränkisch trocken*. Annual production varies enormously because of the local climate, but averages 33,300 cases. Five percent is exported.
Address: Ludwigstrasse 16, W-8715 Iphofen
Tel: 09323 3033

Wisselbrunnen Rhg w

Einzellage at *Hattenheim producing good-quality, spicy Riesling wines. *Grosslage*: *Deutelsberg. Growers: Knyphausen, Lang, Reinhartshausen, Ress, Schloss Schönborn, Tillmanns.

Wolf Erben, Weingut J L Rhpf

Eighteen-hectare estate, owned by the present family for more than 80 years (the estate house, with an enclosed courtyard, was built in the Italian Renaissance style in 1840 and retains many of the original fixtures and fittings.) Holdings (90 percent Riesling) are at

*Wachenheim (including *Gerümpel and *Goldbächel), *Forst (*Ungeheuer, *Jesuitengarten, *Musenhang and *Pechstein) and *Deidesheim (*Herrgottsacker and *Leinhöhle). The wines are full of flavour. Sixty percent is *trocken*.
Address: Weinstrasse 1, W-6706 Wachenheim
Tel: 06322 8665

Wolfenweiler eG, Winzergenossenschaft Baden
Cooperative supplied by 150 hectares, planted 50 percent Gutedel, 27 percent Müller-Thurgau and 17 percent Spätburgunder. Chardonnay is planned for the future. Fifty-four percent of the production is *trocken*. Some wines are matured in *barrique* and there are two series of superior quality wines, based on reduced yields and old vines. Annual production is 125,000 cases.
Address: Kirchstrasse 2, W-7801 Schallstadt-Wolfenweiler
Tel: 07664 7013

Wolff Metternich'sches Weingut, Gräflich Baden
One of the oldest estates in the region, with 36 hectares on steep granite slopes around *Durbach and some further south at Lahr. Sole ownership of Durbacher Schloss Grohl (5·5 hectares), Schlossberg (16 hectares) and the Lahrer Herrentisch (six hectares). The whole estate is planted with 32 percent Riesling, 27 percent Spätburgunder, 12 percent Müller-Thurgau and 17 percent Ruländer. Sauvignon Blanc has been grown since 1830. Seventy-five percent of the wine is *trocken*.
Address: Grohl 4, W-7601 Durbach
Tel: 0781 42779

Wonnegau, Bereich Rhh w (r)
Covers the southern part of the Rheinhessen, the source of much good, unsophisticated, rustic wine in which the taste of the soil is sometimes present. Not a name widely known on the international market – its appearance on a label is often simply a legal requirement rather than an aid to selling.

Worms Rhh w
Cathedral city that has suffered much from war damage in its long history. The vineyards of the *Liebfrauenkirche (Church of Our

Lady) are known as the source of the original *Liebfrau(en)milch. Many events connected with wine are held in the city and its environs, including the annual, oddly named *Backfischfest* (fried-fish festival). *Grosslage*: *Liebfrauenmorgen.

Wuchtig
Describes a powerful wine, rich in extract and alcohol – perhaps a Spätburgunder from the Bereich Kaiserstuhl or a Grauburgunder *Spätlese* from the Bereich Südliche Weinstrasse.

Württemberg r w
Wine region of 9,791 hectares spreading out on either side of the river Neckar and its tributaries and including the smallest *Bereich* in Germany, the Bereich *Württembergischer Bodensee. It is a region of small vineyard holdings: more than half the growers own less than 0·25 hectares. For most, vine growing is a part-time occupation or hobby, and 88 percent of the crop is delivered to cooperative cellars for processing. More than 50 percent of the region is planted in vines bearing red grapes. Within the region, where nearly all the wine is drunk, the big demand is for the red wines made from Trollinger, Müllerrebe, Limberger, Portugieser and Spätburgunder. They are normally light in colour and tannin and often have varying amounts of residual sugar. The white wines are up to standard and are generally cheaper than the red wines. For international taste, better value for money can be found elsewhere in Germany. *Schillerwein* is a speciality of the region.

For the visitor who is interested in architecture and historic buildings, and enjoys attractive countryside, there is much to see.

Württembergischer Bodensee, Bereich Würt r w
Smallest *Bereich* in Germany, with 8·8 hectares at Kressbronn/ *Bodensee and the Ravensburger Rauenegg – one of Germany's smallest *Einzellagen*.

Württembergische Weingärtner-Zentral-Genossenschaft eG Würt
The central cellars of the cooperative movement in Württemberg supplied by 90 local cooperative cellars, mainly with must. The storage capacity is sufficient for three vintages. The list of some 200

suitable for Silvaner. From a restricted yield the wines have good body and acidity, and a scented bouquet.

Würzgarten M-S-R w
Steep *Einzellage* at ★Ürzig, 100 percent Riesling, producing some of the best wines on the river. The red sandstone, pushing in from the Eifel, adds spice (*Würze*) to the Mosel slate and flavour to the wine. *Grosslage*: ★Schwarzlay. Growers: Bischöfliche Weingüter, Christoffel, Loosen, Mönchof, Nicolay (Pauly-Bergweiler), Weins-Prüm.

The village of Ürzig at the foot of Würzgarten vineyards

Zähringer GmbH, Wilhelm, Weingut-Weinkellerei Baden
Seven-hectare estate in the Bereich ★Markgräflerland, planted 34 percent Gutedel, 30 percent Spätburgunder, 15 percent Müller-Thurgau, including interspecific crossings (*see* Rebsorte) from the Staatliches Weinbauinstitut at ★Freiburg. Ninety-seven percent of the wine is *trocken*. Annual production is 3,750 cases, with more than half being taken by restaurants.
Address: Hauptstrasse 42, W-7843 Heitersheim
Tel: 7634 925

wines covers the range of Württemberg varieties. Annual production is 2·5 million cases, mainly sold via German grocery stores and supermarkets, for which the large bottlings are ideal.
Address: Raiffeisenstrasse 2, W-7141 Möglingen
Tel: 07141 4866-0

Würzburg Franken w (r)
Fine university city and business centre, severely damaged in World War II. Many of the historic buildings have been restored. The city contains a number of old cellars belonging to top-quality estates, including those of the ★Bürgerspital, the ★Juliusspital and the Staatlicher Hofkeller (*see next entry*). The vineyards in and around the city produce Franken wines of style, grip and positive flavour. They can be superb and are expensive. *Grosslage*: Marienberg.

Würzburg Staatlicher Hofkeller Franken VDP
Estate founded in 1128, with many outstanding features but few more impressive than the magnificent vaulted cellar, filled with impeccably maintained casks. The substantial holdings cover 120 hectares at ★Würzburg (★Stein and ★Innere Leiste), ★Randersacker (including ★Teufelskeller, Pfülben), Hörstein, Grossheubach, ★Kreuzwertheim, Handthal, ★Abtswind, ★Thüngersheim, ★Hammelburg and Marktheidenfeld. Vines include Riesling, Müller-Thurgau, Silvaner, Rieslaner and many other varieties. The variations on the Franken style from so many different vines and sites are fascinating, but all the wines are true to type and 64 percent is *trocken*. One percent is *lieblich*. Approximate annual production is 70,000 cases, sold 98 percent in Germany.
Address: Residenzplatz 3, W-8700 Würzburg
Tel: 0931 30509-20

Wurzelecht
Describes an ungrafted vine, growing on its 'genuine roots'. Common in the Mosel-Saar-Ruwer where vineyards have not been rebuilt (*flurbereinigt*).

Würzer
Crossing of Gewürztraminer × Müller-Thurgau growing in 116 hectares, mainly in the Rheinhessen and the Nahe. Requires a site

Zehnthof, Weingut Franken VDP
Eleven-hectare estate in the south of Franken, planted 35 percent
Silvaner, 25 percent Müller-Thurgau, ten percent Riesling, plus
others, including the rare mutation Blauer Silvaner that produces
pale red grapes suitable only for white wine. Grüner Silvaner,
Weissburgunder and Portugieser and Domina are all *barrique*-aged
– the latter two as a blend. Annual production is 8,300 cases, 75
percent *trocken*, sold 50 percent to private customers.
Address: Kettengasse 3–5, W-8711 Sulzfeld
Tel: 09321 6536

Zell M-S-R w
There are 23 towns called Zell in the old West Germany, but little
Zell an der Mosel, stretched out along the river, is known
worldwide for its *Grosslage* ★Schwarze Katz (Black Cat). Zell has a
high proportion of Riesling in its steep vineyards and the wines are
usually described as full, elegant and fruity.

Zell, Bereich M-S-R w
Bereich that covers the vineyards downstream from Zell an der
Mosel (*see above*) to ★Koblenz, identical to the Untermosel. The
proportion of Riesling grown is high, many on their original root
stocks, and the wines are generally very true to type, firm and
positive in flavour, although the finesse of the best wines of the
★Mittelmosel is usually missing. Nearer Koblenz and the Rhein the
wine takes on some of the Mittelrhein steeliness. Most of the
exported wine comes from the Zeller ★Schwarze Katz *Grosslage*.

Zell-Weierbach Baden r w
A much-visited *Ortsteil* of Offenburg, well known in Germany for
its Spätburgunder. *Grosslage*: Fürsteneck.

Zeltingen-Rachtig M-S-R w
Important village of old wine cellars, fine patrician houses and a
long promenade by the Mosel. Its elegant wines, largely Riesling,
are usually slightly cheaper than those of its neighbours ★Wehlen
and ★Ürzig. *Grosslage*: ★Münzlay.

Zentralkellerei

Central cellars: the largest form of cooperative cellar taking in the must or wine from smaller cooperatives (*Winzergenossenschaften*), as well as grapes from its own members. Six cellars function as *Zentralkellereien*: in Baden at Breisach (*Badische Winzerkeller), in the Rheinhessen at *Gau-Bickelheim (also supplied by the Rheingau – *see next entry*), in the Mosel-Saar-Ruwer at Bernkastel-Kues (*Moselland), in the Nahe at Bad Kreuznach/Bretzenheim (*Nahe-Winzer Kellereien), in Württemberg at Möglingen (*Württembergische Weingärtner-Zentral-Genossenschaft) and in Franken at Repperndorf (Gebietswinzergenossenschaft *Franken). The wines of the first four are widely distributed abroad.

Zentralkellerei Rheinischer Winzergenossenschaft eG Rhh

Central cooperative cellar with more than 6,000 members, who have holdings in the Rheingau as well as the Rheinhessen, planted with a wide range of vine varieties. The *Zentralkellerei* has its own brand of *Liebfraumilch (called 'Little Rhine Bear'), exported all over the world. Eighty percent of the wines is *lieblich*.
Address: Wöllsteinerstrasse 16, W-6551 Gau-Bickelheim
Tel: 06701 1515

Zilliken, Weingut Forstmeister Geltz M-S-R VDP

Family estate of ten hectares that dates back to 1742; but it was the one-time Master Forester of the King of Prussia, Ferdinand Geltz (1851–1925), who built up its reputation. Today it is very active, selling its wines via brokers at the various important German wine auctions. The holdings in steep sites at *Saarburg (including *Rausch) and *Ockfen (*Bockstein) are 100 percent Riesling, some ungrafted and over 100 years old. Splendid, fruity, well-structured Saar wines – all cask-matured. Annual production is 5,000 cases; 50 percent is exported, and 25 percent is *trocken*.
Address: Heckingstrasse 20, W-5510 Saarburg
Tel: 06581 2456

Zimmermann-Graeff GmbH & Co KG M-S-R

Large firm of wine merchants established in 1886, with holdings at *Zell. Wine or grape must is bought in the main regions known on the export market.

Address: Marientaler Au, W-5583 Zell
Tel: 6542 4190

Zucker
Sugar.

Zuckerrest
See Restzucker

Zwierlein, Weingut Freiherr von Rhg Charta VDP
Estate established in 1794, planted 90 percent Riesling, ten percent
Spätburgunder, with 11 hectares of holdings at *Geisenheim
(including *Kläuserweg, *Mäuerchen and *Rothenberg) and in the
Winkeler *Jesuitengarten. The wines are made to last and are
typical of the region and the vine. Many are sold without a site
name. Spätburgunder aged in *barrique* should be available from the
1992 vintage. Annual production is 8,300 cases, 60 percent *trocken*,
ten percent exported.
Address: Schloss Kosakenberg, Bahnstrasse 1, W-6222 Geisenheim
Tel: 06722 8307

Ahr, Mittelrhein

Bonn •

• Königswinter

BEREICH
SIEBENGEBIRGE

Bad
Neuenahr-
Ahrweiler

Altenahr
•

BEREICH
**WALPORZHEIM
AHRTAL**

Ahr

Rhein

Ahr

Marienthal
Mayschoss–Altenahr
Meyer–Näkel
Nelles

Anderbach •

BEREICH
RHEINBURGENGAU

Mosel

Koblenz

Mittelrhein

Bad Hönningen
Jost
Perll, A
Perll, W
Ratzenberger
Wagner
Weiler

• Braubach

Lahn

Boppard •

Rhein

	AHR
	MITTELRHEIN

St Goar •

0.45%
0.8%

% of total
v'yd area

Bacharach •

BEREICH
BACHARACH

• Lorch

0 miles   15
0 km   25

Bingen •

Hessische Bergstrasse, Franken, Württemberg, Baden

Baden

Abril
Achkarren, Winzergenossenschaft
Auggen, Winzergenossenschaft
Badischer Winzerkeller
Bercher
Bickensohl, Winzergenossenschaft
Blankenhorn
Burkheim, Winzergenossenschaft
Dörflinger
Franckenstein
Freiburg, Staatliches Weinbauinstitut
Freiburg, Staatliches Weinbauinstitut 'Blankenhornsberg'
Gleichenstein
Göler
Heitlinger
Hoensbroech
Ihringen Winzergenossenschaft
Istein
Johner
Kappelrodeck Winzergenossenschaft
Kirchberghof
Königschauffhausen
Lahr
Laible
Lauda
Männle, Andreas
Männle, Heinrich
Markgräfler Winzergenossenschaft
Meersburg, Staatsweingut
Müller, Gebr
Nägelsförster Hof
Neveu
Oberbergen, Winzergenossenschaft
Oberrotweil
Offenburg
Salem
Salwey
Sasbachwalden, Winzergenossenschaft
Schloss Kirchberg

Schloss Ortenberg
Schloss Staufenberg
Schlumberger
'Schwarzer Adler'
Stigler
Wiesloch
Wolfenweiler
Wolff Metternich
Zähringer

BEREICH **UMSTADT**

Mainz

Darmstadt
BEREICH
STARKENBURG

Seeheim
Alsbach

Bensheim
Heppenheim

Heidelberg

BEREICH
**BADISCHE BERGSTRASSE-
KRAICHGAU**

Karlsruhe

Pforzheim

Rhein

Baden-Baden

BEREICH
ORTENAU

Durbach
Offenburg

BEREICH
BREISGAU

Neckar

BEREICH
**KAISERSTUHL-
TUNIBERG**

Breisach

Freiburg

0.35%
5.0%

9.4%

14.9%

% of total
v'yd area

BEREICH
MARKGRÄFLERLAND

Basel

Rhein

Main

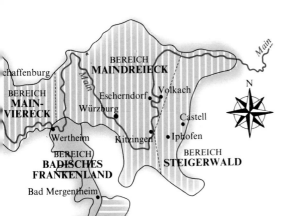

Franken

Bickel-Stumpf
Bürgerspital
Castell
Franken,
   Gebietswinzergenossenschaft
Fürst
Gebhardt
Hohenlohe Langenburg'sche
Juliusspital
Klingenberg, Weingut der Stadt
Löwenstein
Popp
Randersacker,
   Winzergenossenschaft
Ruck
Schaffer
Schloss Saaleck
Schloss Sommerhausen
Schmitt, R
Schmitt's Kinder
Schönborn
Sommerach, Winzerkeller
Thüngersheim
Wirsching
Würzburg Staatlicher Hofkeller
Zehnthof

Württemberg

Adelmann
Affaltrach
Amalienhof
Bentzel-Sturmfeder
Besigheim
Brackenheim
Burg Hornberg
Cleebronn-Güglingen-
   Frauenzimmern
Dautel
Dürrenzimmern-Stockheim
Eberstadt
Ellwanger
Flein-Talheim
Grantschen
   Weingärtnergenossenschaft
Haidle
Heilbronn-Erlenbach
Heinrich
Heuchelberg
Hofkammerkellerei Stuttgart
Hohenbeilstein
Hohenlohe Langenburg'sche
Hohenlohe-Öhringen'sche
Mundelsheim,
   Weingärtner-Genossenschaft
Neipperg
Nordheim
   Weingärtnergenossenschaft
Sonnenhof
Stapf
Weinsberg, Staatliche
   Versuchsanstalt
Württembergische
   Weingärtner

Hessische Bergstrasse

Bensheim, Weingut der Stadt
Bergstrasse, Staatsweingut
Bergsträsser Gebiets-
   Winzergenossenschaft

HESSISCHE
BERGSTRASSE

FRANKEN

WÜRTTEMBERG

BADEN

miles 0   15   30
km 0   25   50

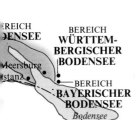

Mosel-Saar-Ruwer

Mosel-Saar-Ruwer

Beulwitz
Bischöfliche Weingüter
Christoffel
Drathen
Fischer
Friedrich-Wilhelm-Gymnasium
Fuchs
Gallais
Grans-Fassian
Haag, Fritz
Haag, Willi
Hausen-Mabilon
Heddesdorff
Heidemanns-Bergweiler
Heymann-Löwenstein
Hövel
Immich-Batterieberg
Kallfelz
Kanzemer Berg
Karlsmühle
Karp-Schreiber
Kees-Kieren
Kesselstatt
Krebs-Matheus-Lehnert

Landenberg
Lauerburg
Lenz-Dahm
Loosen
Milz
Mönchhof
Moselland
Müller, Rudolf
Müller-Scharzhof
Nell, C von
Nell, G-F von

BEREICH
BERNKAST

Piesport

Mosel Trittenheim

Eitelsbach

Trier Kasel

Konz

BEREICH
SAAR-RUWER

Wiltingen

Ayl
Saarburg

BEREICH
OBERMOSEL

12.8%

% of total
v'yd area

BEREICH
MOSELTOR

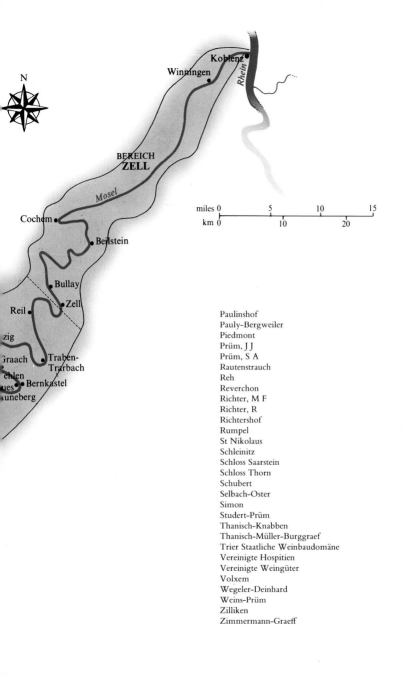

N

Koblenz

Winningen

Rhein

BEREICH
ZELL

Mosel

Cochem

Beilstein

Bullay

Reil

Zell

zig

Graach

Traben-
Trarbach

ehlen

Bernkastel

ues

uneberg

miles 0   5   10   15

km 0   10   20

Paulinshof
Pauly-Bergweiler
Piedmont
Prüm, J J
Prüm, S A
Rautenstrauch
Reh
Reverchon
Richter, M F
Richter, R
Richtershof
Rumpel
St Nikolaus
Schleinitz
Schloss Saarstein
Schloss Thorn
Schubert
Selbach-Oster
Simon
Studert-Prüm
Thanisch-Knabben
Thanisch-Müller-Burggraef
Trier Staatliche Weinbaudomäne
Vereinigte Hospitien
Vereinigte Weingüter
Volxem
Wegeler-Deinhard
Weins-Prüm
Zilliken
Zimmermann-Graeff

Nahe,
Rheinpfalz

Rheinpfalz

Bart
Bassermann-Jordan
Bergdolt
Biffar
Bonnet
Buhl
Burggarten
Bürklin-Wolf
Christmann
Deidesheim Winzerverein
Deinhard, Dr
Deutsches Weintor
Fitz-Ritter
Forster Winzerverein
Frey
Friedelsheim, Winzergenossenschaft
Giessen
Hammel
Herrenberg-Honigsäckel
Herxheim Winzergenossenschaft
Hohenberg
Kallstadt Winzergenossenschaft
Karst
Kern
Kimich
Koehler-Ruprecht
Königsbach-Neustadt
Leiningerland
Lergenmüller
Lingenfelder

Messer
Mosbacher
Mossbacher-Hof
Müller-Catoir
Neckerauer
Neustadt, Staatsweingut
Pfeffingen
Pfleger, J
Pfleger, W
Probsthof
Rebholz
Rietburg
Ruppertsberger Winzerverein 'Hoheburg'
Schäfer, K
Schuster
Siegrist
Spindler
Vier-Jahreszeiten-Kloster Limburg
Wachtenburg-Luginsland
Wegeler-Deinhard
Wilhelmshof
Wolf

Nahe

Adelseck
Anheuser, August
Anheuser, Paul
Bad Kreuznach, Staatsweingut
Bischof-Klein
Crusius
Diel
Dönnhof
Emrich-Schönleber
Finkenauer
Hehner-Kiltz
Klören
Kruger-Rumpf
Lötzbeyer
Nahe-Winzer Kellereien
Niederhausen-Schlossböckelheim
    Staatliche Weinbaudomäne
Plettenberg
Rheingrafenberg
Salm-Dalberg
Schäfer, M
Schlossmühle
Schneider, J
Schweinhardt
Tesch

Rhein

Worms

Bockenheim
uleiningen

BEREICH
**MITTELHAARDT/
DEUTSCHE
WEINSTRASSE**

N

Kallstadt
Bad Dürkheim
Wachenheim
Forst
Deidesheim
Ruppertsberg
Neustadt

Speyer

Maikammer
Edenkoben
Rhodt
Schwegenheim

Siebeldingen
Landau in
der Pfalz

BEREICH
**SÜDLICHE
WEINSTRASSE**

Bad Bergzabern

Schweigen

NAHE

RHEINPFALZ

4.8%

23.1%

% of total
v'yd area

miles 0   10
km 0   10   20

Rheingau, Rheinhessen

Rauenthal

BEREICH
JOHANNISBERG Kiedrich Wiesbade

Rhein Lorch Eltville

Hallgarten Erbach

Johannisberg Rhein

Hattenheim M

Winkel Oestrich

Assmannshausen

Geisenheim Ingelheim

Rüdesheim

Nahe Bingen

Rheinhessen

Alzey, Weingut der Stadt
Balbach
Baumann
Becker, Brüder Dr
Becker, Gernot
Braun
Buscher
Dahlem
Espenhof
Geil
Geil, Ökonomierat
Gült
Gunderloch
Guntrum
Heyl zu Herrnsheim
Koch
Liebrecht
Niersteiner Winzergenossenschaft
Ohnacker
Opel
Oppenheim, Staatsweingut
Rappenhof
St Anthony
Schales
Schmitt, H F
Schmitt'sches Weingut
Schneider, G
Schuch
Schultz-Werner
Sittmann

BEREICH
BINGEN

BEREICH
NIERSTEII

• Alzey

BEREICH
WONNEGA

miles 0   5   10
km 0   5   10   15

Saale-Unstrut, Sachsen

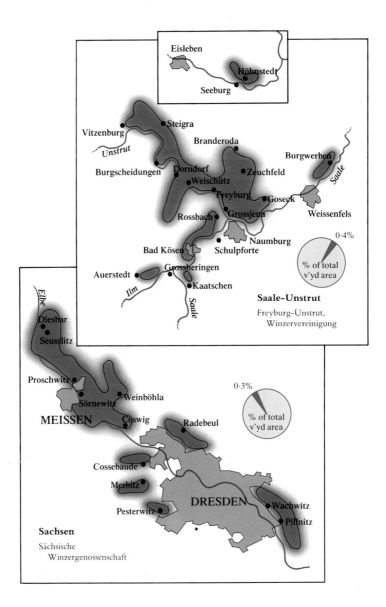

Eisleben

Höhnstedt

Seeburg

Steigra

Vitzenburg

Branderoda

Unstrut

Burgwerben

Burgscheidungen

Dorndorf

Zeuchfeld

Weischütz

Saale

Freyburg

Goseck

Rossbach

Grossjena

Weissenfels

Bad Kösen

Schulpforte

Naumburg

0·4%

Auerstedt

Grossheringen

% of total
v'yd area

Ilm

Kaatschen

Saale

Saale-Unstrut

Freyburg-Unstrut,
Winzervereinigung

Elbe

Diesbar

Seusslitz

0·3%

Proschwitz

Weinböhla

% of total
v'yd area

Sörnewitz

MEISSEN

Coswig

Radebeul

Cossebaude

Merbitz

DRESDEN

Wachwitz

Pesterwitz

Pillnitz

Sachsen

Sächsische
Winzergenossenschaft

Sonnenberg
Stallmann-Hiestand
Strub
Valckenberg
Villa Sachsen
Wehrheim
Zentralkellerei Rheinischer
   Winzergenossenschaft

Rheingau

Allendorf
Altenkirch
Aschrott
Becker, J B
Brentano
Breuer
Diefenhardt
Eltville, Staatsweingut
Erbslöh
Eser
Frankfurt, Weingut der Stadt
Geisenheim, Weingut der Forschungsanstalt
Hallgarten, Winzergenossenschaft
Hessen, Prinz von
Hupfeld
Johannishof
Jost
Kanitz
Kesseler
Knyphausen
König
Königin Victoria Berg
Krayer
Krone
Künstler
Lang
Löwenstein
Mumm
Nägler
Nikolai
Oetinger
Querbach
Ress
Riedel
Schloss Groenesteyn
Schloss Johannisberg
Schloss Reinhartshausen
Schloss Schönborn
Schloss Vollrads
Simmern
Tillmanns
Wegeler-Deinhard
Weil
Werner
Zwierlein

Main

'hheim

N

Nackenheim

stein

nheim

nheim

Guntersblum

heim

Rhein

Worms

2·9%

24·8%

% of total
v'yd area

RHEINGAU

RHEINHESSEN